Oregon Sampler:
Resorts & Recipes

*Featuring a sampling of recipes from the
resorts & people of Oregon*

Assistance League® of Corvallis

Assistance League® of Corvallis, Oregon, has been serving its community since 1969. This non-profit organization, one of 78 chapters of National Assistance League®, helps school children in the area by providing needed clothing (Operation School Bell® and Operation Toddler), dental care (Corvallis Community Dental Care Center), and by providing high school juniors and seniors experience in testing for college entrance examinations (S.A.T. Review Seminar). The group also provides teddy bears to traumatized children in conjunction with the local police department (Hug-A-Bear). Proceeds from the sale of *Oregon Sampler* will be used to help fund these philanthropic projects of Assistance League of Corvallis.

To obtain additional copies of this book, use the coupons at the back of this book or write:

Assistance League of Corvallis
534 NW Fourth St.
Corvallis, OR 97330

Suggested retail price $14.95 plus $2.05 shipping charges.

Printing by Publishers Press, Salt Lake City, Utah
Photos supplied by individual resorts
Writing by Linda Ahlers, Corvallis, Oregon
Art direction by Deb Kadas, Corvallis, Oregon

CONTENTS

OREGON'S RESORTS AND INNS:
WHERE TO FIND THEM

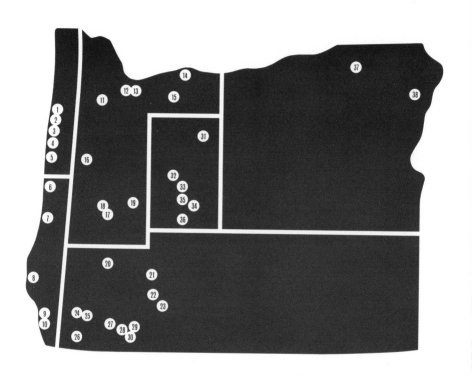

5

INTRODUCTION

Mention "Oregon" to a non-native, and often a vision is conjured up of the green forests and strikingly beautiful wilderness that greeted Lewis & Clark some 180 years ago. The forests and wilderness are still here to be sure, but so is an incredible diversity of environments that few outside of Oregon have had a chance to see:

The breathtakingly majestic Pacific Ocean with exhilarating winter storms, mild summer and fall days, storybook beachfront communities, and mile upon mile of rugged sandy beaches and protected harbors.

The lush, green Willamette Valley with exciting cities, picturesque towns, meandering rivers, and farms and orchards dotting the length of the state.

Crisp clean Central Oregon with snowcapped mountains, spectacular lava beds, tall ponderosa pine, and sparkling deep blue lakes.

Golden Eastern Oregon ripe with rolling hills of wheat, sprawling ranches, and warm desert expanses.

And lusty Southern Oregon with rushing clear rivers, snowy mountains, vast forests of native Douglas fir, and historic gold mining towns.

Recreation opportunities abound throughout our multi-faceted state: fishing, camping, skiing, river rafting, water skiing, hunting, hang-gliding, hiking, mountain climbing, biking, and of course, tennis, swimming, and golf. And, thanks to our cities and our many well-developed craft communities, shopping is indeed a form of recreation in any area of the state!

It is no surprise, then, that Oregon boasts an outstanding selection of resorts and inns that allow full enjoyment of the state's wonders. From Mobil Travel Guide Five-Star winners to small family-operated inns, you can find exactly the kind of vacation environment you'd like. Choose from a wilderness cottage . . . a college-town bed-and-breakfast . . . a big-city landmark hotel . . . a coastal hideaway . . . or a ranch-style resort.

All resorts and inns featured in this book were selected and invited to be included after recommendations from many sources. Though they are all unique establishments, they do share several common characteristics. First, they all boast restaurants or dining facilities with outstanding food, be it gourmet or down-home style. Second, they offer overnight lodging, ranging from the luxurious to the rustic. And third, they feature recreation facilities on their property or in nearby locales.

We are proud to offer recipes from the dining rooms of the 38 resorts spotlighted in this book. Other recipes within these pages are gleaned from the well-developed files of members of Assistance League of Corvallis. (Those famous rainy seasons in Oregon do give us ample opportunity to develop great recipes!) Each recipe has been tested and re-tested and has been subject to rigorous evaluation by harsh judges . . . our families!

We hope you enjoy trying our recipes and serving them to your families and friends. And, to those of you who haven't visited our great state yet, we hope to see you someday in Oregon, where you can sample our food in person!

Appetizers

APPETIZERS

MEAT
Chutney-Glazed Meatballs, 11
Grape-Glazed Meatballs, 11
Sauerkraut Balls, 12
Orange Sausage Balls, 12
Sweet-and-Sour Surprises, 13
Velvet Paté, 13
Frosted Chicken Liver Paté, 14
Frosted Paté, 15
Northwest Game Paté Filling, 18
Cashew Chicken Appetizers, 19
Oriental Chicken Wings, 19
Peanut Butter Saté, 20
Whiskey Weenies, 21
Hot Polish Sausage, 21

SEAFOOD
Hot Crab Toasties, 21
Hors d'Oeuvres Otter Crest Style, 23
Salmon Paté in Cherry Tomatoes, 24
Steamed Fresh Mussels, 25
Hot Shrimp Hors d'Oeuvres, 25
Champignon Farci, 27
Crab-Stuffed Mushrooms, 28
Deviled Crab Balls, 29
Swiss Crabwiches, 29
Crab Mousse, 30
Shrimp Tomato Mold, 30

CHEESE
Chili Con Queso, 31
Layered Mexican Dip, 31
Stuffed Mushroom Caps, 33
Cheese Squares, 34
Snappy Cheese Sticks and Olives, 35
Perpetual Cheese Dip, 36
Beer Cheese Spread, 36
Deep-Fried Cheese Balls, 36
Holiday Cheese Ball, 37
Pecan Cheese Ball, 37

MISCELLANEOUS
Herb Dip, 38
Man's Favorite Dip, 38
Artichoke Dip, 38
Egg Dip for Vegetables, 39
Chutney Cheese Spread, 39
Assistance League® Plum Chutney, 40
Pineapple Peach Chutney, 40

CHUTNEY-GLAZED MEATBALLS Yields 6 dozen

Easy to freeze and heat when you need them.

1 lb. ground pork
2¼ lbs. ground beef
1½ teaspoons salt
1½ teaspoons dry mustard
1¾ teaspoons ground
  coriander
¾ teaspoon ground allspice
3 eggs, lightly beaten
¾ cup dry bread crumbs
¾ cup thinly sliced green
  onions

● Mix ingredients together and form into small balls. Bake in jellyroll pans in a 350-degree oven for 20 to 25 minutes, or until brown. Drain and reserve.

Chutney Sauce

1 cup chutney (a spicy plum
  chutney is best)
1 cup apple jelly
1 tablespoon lemon juice

● Combine ingredients and heat until jelly melts. Pour over meatballs in chafing dish, coating the meatballs with the sauce.

GRAPE-GLAZED MEATBALLS Serves 10 to 12

3 lb. lean ground beef
salt and pepper
16 oz. grape jelly
16 oz. barbecue sauce

● Mix beef with salt and pepper. Form into small balls and bake until brown at 350 degrees. Drain.

● Combine jelly and sauce; heat through. Pour over meatballs and serve in chafing dish.

SAUERKRAUT BALLS

Yields 5 dozen

1 medium onion, minced
3 tablespoons butter
1 cup finely chopped ham
1 cup finely chopped corned
  beef
¼ teaspoon garlic salt
1 tablespoon prepared
  mustard
1 egg, beaten
3 tablespoons minced
  parsley
⅛ teaspoon pepper
2 cups sauerkraut, drained
  and finely chopped
½ cup flour
⅓ cup beef stock
2½ cups flour
2 cups milk
bread crumbs
oil

● Sauté onion in butter until
  tender. Add ham and corned beef
  and cook, stirring often, for 5
  minutes. Add next 8 ingredients;
  mix well and cook 5 to 10
  minutes, stirring often.

● Spread mixture on a jellyroll pan
  and cover with plastic wrap.
  Refrigerate overnight. Cut into
  small squares and form each into
  a small ball.

● Mix together the flour and milk.
  Dip balls in flour-milk mixture
  and roll in bread crumbs; fry in
  hot oil until brown. Drain on
  paper towels and serve hot.

ORANGE SAUSAGE BALLS

Serves 20

2 lb. pork sausage
1 can (12 oz.) frozen orange
  juice, thawed

● Form sausage into small balls
  and brown. Drain. (This can be
  done ahead.)

● To serve, heat orange juice
  concentrate and sausage balls
  until bubbly, about 15 minutes.
  Serve in a chafing dish.

SWEET-AND-SOUR SURPRISES Yields 60 appetizers

Unique combination of beef, shrimp and chicken.

½ lb. tiny meatballs, cooked
(use your favorite recipe)
½ lb. medium shrimp,
cooked and peeled
½ lb. chicken livers, cooked
and halved

● Arrange meats and shrimp
separately in chafing dish and
cover with Sweet-and-Sour
Sauce. Keep warm.

Sweet-and-Sour Sauce

2 tablespoons cornstarch
1 tablespoon sugar
1 cube chicken bouillon
1 cup pineapple juice
½ cup cider vinegar
2 tablespoons soy sauce
1 tablespoon butter

● Combine ingredients in saucepan
and place over heat. Cook, stirring, until boiling. Cover and
simmer 5 minutes.

VELVET PATÉ   Yields 5 cups

Smooth and creamy.

1 lb. chicken livers
1 Golden Delicious apple,
peeled and diced
1 stalk celery, diced
½ medium onion, diced
½ teaspoon fresh or dried
tarragon
1 cup butter
2 tablespoons brandy
3 tablespoons sherry
3 tablespoons sour cream
salt and pepper to taste

● Sauté first 5 ingredients in 2
tablespoons of butter until livers
are no longer pink. Blend in food
processor or blender until
smooth. Cool about 5 minutes.

● Cut remaining butter into ½-inch
slices and blend with liver
mixture briefly. Blend in
remaining ingredients. Pour into
oiled molds (or one bowl) and
refrigerate at least 2½ hours.
Unmold and serve with crackers.

FROSTED CHICKEN LIVER PATÉ   Serves 20

1 lb. chicken livers
½ cup chicken broth
1 teaspoon unflavored
  gelatin
1 cup butter, softened
5 tablespoons finely minced
  onion
3 tablespoons Cognac
2 teaspoons dry mustard
1 clove garlic, minced
½ teaspoon Tabasco sauce
¼ teaspoon ground nutmeg
¼ teaspoon ground cloves
1 teaspoon salt
parsley, pimiento and green
  pepper
crackers or sliced French
  bread

● Simmer livers in broth about 10 minutes or until just pink in the center; do not overcook. Drain, reserving the broth.

● Put 3 tablespoons of the reserved broth in a small saucepan; sprinkle gelatin over broth and soften a few minutes. Heat gently to dissolve.

● While the livers cool, make Cream Cheese Layer.

● To continue paté, put livers, butter, onion, Cognac, garlic and seasonings in a food processor or blender and blend until smooth. Add the dissolved gelatin. If mixture is too stiff, add additional broth.

● Pour the liver mixture over the completed cream cheese layer, which should be firm. Cover with plastic wrap and refrigerate several hours.

● To serve, invert the paté mold onto a serving dish and surround with crackers or French bread slices. Garnish with chopped parsley, pimiento and green pepper.

(continued)

14

FROSTED CHICKEN LIVER PATÉ (continued)

Cream Cheese Layer

1 teaspoon unflavored gelatin
3 tablespoons water
8 oz. cream cheese
1 can (10½ oz.) consommé, chilled
2 tablespoons Madeira

● Sprinkle gelatin over water in a small saucepan. Heat slowly until gelatin is dissolved; cool.

● Butter a round cake pan. Line it with waxed paper and butter the paper. In a food processor or blender, mix the gelatin, cream cheese, consommé and Madeira. Pour into the lined pan, cover with plastic wrap and chill until set.

FROSTED PATÉ
Yields 1½ cups

Even the youngsters will go for this.

½ lb. liverwurst
½ teaspoon grated onion
¼ cup mayonnaise
2 oz. cream cheese, softened
2 tablespoons mayonnaise
pimiento

● Mash liverwurst. Blend in onion and ¼ cup mayonnaise. Mound into desired shape. Chill.

● Blend cream cheese and remaining mayonnaise. Spread mixture over liverwurst and decorate with pimiento.

THE HEATHMAN HOTEL, Portland

In the heart of downtown Portland just steps away from museums, parks, theatres and choice shopping is a hotel that combines the finest of European elegance with the best of American convenience, The Heathman.

When The Heathman first opened in 1927, it boasted of the "most modern of appointments" and "unexcelled cuisine." Now, more than half a century later, those same descriptive phrases still ring true, thanks to a recent multimillion dollar renovation.

The early Heathman enjoyed much popularity for its location in the heart of Portland's thriving Broadway theatre district, and it became a landmark hotel to several generations of Northwest families. After many years, though, downtown Broadway and The Heathman began to show their age and lose some of their earlier allure. Luckily, some far-sighted—or maybe just sentimental—Northwesterners banded together to save The Heathman and restore it to its former grandeur.

Today's completely renovated Heathman still has its nostalgic charm firmly intact, but now it's enhanced by a fresh new vitality. And the opening of Portland's new Performing Arts Center next door has rekindled the excitement and the glitter of Portland's own

Broadway. With such close access to much of Portland's excitement, The Heathman is dubbed by some, "The resort within the city."

Throughout The Heathman, quality and personal attention are of conspicuous and utmost concern. "Small" in comparison with big chain hotels in the city, the 10-story Heathman uses its size as an asset, making guests feel comfortably at home and pampered. Red and black marble, blond travertine and brass fixtures, teak paneling, etched glass window dividers, and marbled columns add touches of elegance; original artwork throughout the hotel is impressive and diverse.

Guest rooms are decorated to convey a feeling of tasteful hominess, with furnishings of teak, brass, marble, leather-bound rattan, and original paintings and prints. Colorful English chintz bedspreads and windowshades provide just the right amount of warmth.

Daytime shoppers may enjoy taking tea by the fire in the hotel's Tea Court, an elaborate affair that hearkens to bygone days. Many patrons of the Performing Arts Center enjoy a nightcap accompanied by soft piano music in the Lobby Lounge.

The Heathman's gourmet restaurant concentrates on foodstuffs available in the Northwest, including fine seafoods, meats, produce, and dairy products. Everything served in the dining room is made in the hotel's kitchen, from ravioli, patés, terrines, soups, and sauces to gelati, sherbets, and spectacular desserts.

For additional information:
The Heathman Hotel
SW Broadway at Salmon
Portland, OR 97205
(503) 241-4100
Telex: 592023
1-800-551-0011 (Elsewhere)

(See recipe on next page)

NORTHWEST GAME PATÉ FILLING

From the Dining Room of The Heathman Hotel

1½ lbs. ground lean rabbit
1½ lbs. ground lean venison
1 lb. ground rabbit livers
1 lb. ground smoked bacon
3 garlic cloves, finely
minced
3 shallots, finely minced
1 teaspoon mixed spices,
Quatre Epices
2 tablespoons mixed herbs,
Fines Herbs
1 tablespoon juniper berries
salt and pepper to taste
5 eggs
2 oz. brandy
1½ lbs. prosciutto, thinly
sliced

● Mix all ingredients thoroughly except the prosciutto. Sauté a small amount of the mix to test for seasoning. Adjust seasoning to taste if needed.

● Line a 3-quart terrine with prosciutto, arranging the sliced meat in a decorative fashion. Fill the mold, being careful to avoid air pockets. Mound mixture toward the center so it extends ½ inch above the mold. Fold prosciutto slices over the top, neatly enclosing paté mixture. Cover with aluminum foil.

● Place terrine pan in a roasting pan that contains 1 inch of water; bake at 350 degrees. Remove from oven when paté has reached an internal temperature of 140 degrees.

● Place another pan atop paté mold and weight it with a heavy object to press the paté. Allow to cool for one hour. Remove paté from mold, wrap tightly and refrigerate. Serve with traditional condiments.

Note: If above meats are not available, feel free to substitute an equal quantity of meat of your choosing.

CASHEW CHICKEN APPETIZERS

Serves 8

Crunchy golden nuggets that will disappear fast.

¼ cup cornstarch
½ teaspoon sugar
2 egg whites, slightly beaten
1 teaspoon brandy or
  Cognac
2 whole chicken breasts,
  skinned, boned and cut
  into 1½-inch strips
1½ cups finely chopped
  cashews
vegetable oil

● In a small bowl, combine cornstarch and sugar. Stir in egg whites and brandy. Dip chicken pieces in egg white mixture, then in nuts. Fry in hot oil until golden, about 45 seconds. Drain and serve hot.

ORIENTAL CHICKEN WINGS

Serves 6 to 8

May want to double the recipe; these go fast.

10 chicken wings, jointed
  and tips discarded
⅓ cup soy sauce
3 tablespoons firmly packed
  brown sugar
1 tablespoon dry sherry
⅓ cup water
¼ teaspoon ground ginger

● Place the wing pieces in an ungreased baking dish. Combine remaining ingredients, except ginger. Pour mixture over wings and sprinkle ginger on top. Bake at 350 degrees for 1 hour, basting every 20 minutes. Serve warm.

PEANUT BUTTER SATÉ

Serves 24

2 to 3 lb. boneless pork
or chicken, cubed

- Marinate meat in Saté Marinade at least 2 hours or overnight. String marinated meat on skewers and broil over hot coals or spread meat cubes on jellyroll pan and bake in a 350-degree oven 35 to 45 minutes.

- Serve in chafing dish accompanied with chutney, chopped peanuts and shredded coconut on the side.

Saté Marinade

½ cup peanut butter
1 tablespoon ground coriander
1 teaspoon salt
½ teaspoon pepper
1 cup chopped onion
2 cloves garlic
½ cup soy sauce
¼ cup lime or lemon juice
¼ cup firmly packed brown sugar
⅓ cup vegetable oil
½ teaspoon Sambal Oelik (a hot pepper purée) or hot pepper flakes

- Combine ingredients in a blender and blend until smooth.

WHISKEY WEENIES

Serves 10

The humble hot dog in its finest form; watch the men dig in.

3 lbs. frankfurters, sliced in
  1-inch pieces
3 tablespoons brown sugar
½ cup whiskey or bourbon
1 cup catsup
¼ cup water

● Combine ingredients and bring to a simmer. Serve hot.

HOT POLISH SAUSAGE

Serves 8 to 10

Hearty appetizer that men love.

2 Polish sausage rings,
  cooked and thinly sliced
1 can (8 oz.) tomato sauce
½ cup sugar
2 tablespoons horseradish

● Combine ingredients and heat through. Serve in chafing dish.

HOT CRAB TOASTIES

Yields 32 squares

8 oz. cream cheese, softened
2 tablespoons grated onion
2 tablespoons mayonnaise
1 teaspoon Worcestershire
  sauce
2 tablespoons heavy cream
½ lb. crab
8 slices sandwich bread,
  crusts removed
butter
paprika

● Combine first 6 ingredients; set aside. Butter bread slices and cut into quarters. Spread generously with crab mixture. (Can be frozen at this point. Defrost 1½ hours before baking.) Sprinkle quarters with paprika and bake on ungreased baking sheet at 300 degrees for 25 minutes.

THE INN AT OTTER CREST, Otter Rock

High on a clifftop overlooking the ruggedly beautiful Pacific Ocean sits a romantically luxurious resort, The Inn at Otter Crest.

With all the warmth and intimacy of a secluded country inn, The Inn offers all those splendid amenities that make a stay here a welcome escape from the everyday world. Arriving guests are whisked in the resort's van to two-story, cedar-sided lodges of distinctly Northwest architecture.

The resort occupies a jutting cliffside, and lodging accommodations are staggered down the hill to allow each room a sweeping view of the ocean from a private balcony. Rooms range in size to accommodate one to eight persons; half have fireplaces, some have fully equipped kitchens, and all have refrigerators, TV, and spacious baths.

World-weary guests may indulge in a variety of activities at The Inn, including tennis, swimming in the sheltered heated pool/whirlpool, basketball, volleyball, shuffleboard, and badminton. Others may choose to play miniature golf or jog on the scenic trails in this lush forest setting.

A stroll on the secluded beach allows guests to explore tidepools, gather seashells and agates, or maybe watch a grey whale that's ventured close to shore. In the summer, a supervised children's recreation program keeps the youngsters active and happy.

Nearby are golf courses and charter fishing boats for deep sea fishing. The many charming shops, art galleries, and museums in the area also provide hours of enjoyment.

Guests can savor the bounty of the sea in The Inn's Flying Dutchman Restaurant. Fresh coastal delicacies are delivered daily and served in the chef's creative fashion, including planked Pacific salmon. The kitchen also serves a slow-roasted prime rib with Yorkshire pudding on Friday and Saturday. Salads may feature lettuce, alfalfa sprouts, sunflower seeds, and Romano cheese.

For additional information:
The Inn at Otter Crest
P.O. Box 50
Otter Rock, OR 97369
1-800-452-2101 (OR)
1-800-547-2181 (Elsewhere)

HORS D'OEUVRES OTTER CREST STYLE

From the Dining Room of The Inn at Otter Crest

Smoked Nova Scotia salmon, thinly sliced in 5-inch lengths
cream cheese softened with dry vermouth
lemon wedges
parsley sprigs

- Lay out strips of salmon. On each piece, place 1 teaspoon softened cream cheese on one corner. Roll up each piece to form a cone shape.

- Arrange rolled salmon on a cold plate. Garnish plate with lemon wedges and parsley. Serve Sauce Remoulade and cocktail breads on the side.

(continued)

Sauce Remoulade

3 cups mayonnaise
1 tablespoon Dijon mustard
1 teaspoon chopped sweet
  gherkin
1 teaspoon capers, chopped
  and squeezed dry
½ teaspoon chervil
½ teaspoon tarragon
½ teaspoon anchovy essence

● Blend ingredients together.

SALMON PATÉ IN CHERRY TOMATOES

Yields 40 appetizers

40 large cherry tomatoes
4 oz. cream cheese, softened
½ lb. smoked salmon, finely
  chopped
2 tablespoons fresh lemon
  juice
1 tablespoon finely minced
  onion
heavy cream
salt and white pepper
2 tablespoons dill weed or
  1 tablespoon capers
watercress or parsley

● Cut tops off tomatoes and scoop
  out seeds and pulp; drain. Mix
  the cream cheese, salmon, lemon
  juice and onion. Add enough
  cream to give smooth consistency. Season with salt and white
  pepper.

● With a small spoon or pastry
  bag, fill each tomato with cheese
  mixture, mounding slightly.
  Garnish with dill or capers and
  green sprig of herb.

STEAMED FRESH MUSSELS

Serves 4 to 6

Americans are learning what the French have known for years—
mussels are too good to use for fish bait.

2 to 3 dozen mussels,
scrubbed and beards
removed
1 tablespoon olive oil
3 green onions, chopped
1 clove garlic
½ teaspoon whole thyme
1 cup dry white wine
½ cup water

- Put all ingredients except
mussels in a large steaming
kettle. Bring to a boil.

- Place mussels in steamer basket
and lower into kettle with other
ingredients. Steam 10 to 12
minutes or until mussels open.
Discard any that do not open.
Serve with Dipping Sauce.

Dipping Sauce

¼ cup butter, melted
2 tablespoons chopped
parsley

- Combine ingredients and serve.

HOT SHRIMP HORS D'OEUVRES

Yields 40 appetizers

Tasty as a sandwich spread too.

3 cups shrimp meat (1½ lb.)
¼ cup chopped green onion
½ cup chopped fresh
parsley
1 cup shredded Cheddar
cheese
½ cup mayonnaise
1 cup sour cream
2 tablespoons lemon juice
1 loaf sliced cocktail rye
bread (2- to 3-inch
diameter)

- Combine all ingredients except
bread. Toast bread slices on one
side. Spread untoasted side with
a heaping spoonful of the shrimp
mixture. Place under a broiler
until bubbly and melted. Serve
immediately.

SUNRIVER RESORT, Sunriver

"A place in the sun," Sunriver is a 3300-acre resort/residential community that takes full advantage of Central Oregon's outstanding recreational opportunities.

As the largest resort in the state, Sunriver consists of more than 1,200 homes and 600 condominiums, many of which are available through the Sunriver rental program. Contemporary is the style, and all the buildings blend harmoniously with the pine-and-mountain atmosphere here.

Recreation facilities include two 18-hole golf courses, 24 miles of bike paths, 18 outdoor tennis courts, two swimming complexes, stables for horseback riding, and racquetball. A marina, game room, nature center, and arts and crafts center ensure activities to keep every age group happy.

A country mall within Sunriver houses shops, restaurants, and professional services. The resort's 4500-foot airstrip allows vacationers and homeowners easy access to this vacation wonderland.

Recreation in the nearby area includes camping, backpacking, mountain climbing, waterskiing, boating . . . just about any outdoor activity a vacationer could want. Numerous lakes and rivers provide superb fishing, while Mt. Bachelor offers excellent skiing from November right on through August. Nordic skiing is also popular at Sunriver and in the adjacent forest.

The magnificent Sunriver Lodge is a massive structure of wood and stone, with just the right combination of elegance and casualness. Several eating establishments within the Lodge serve fare from gourmet to family style, with all of them capitalizing on fresh Oregon ingredients.

For additional information:
Sunriver Resort
Sunriver, OR 97702
1-800-452-6874 (OR)
1-800-547-3922 (Elsewhere)

CHAMPIGNON FARCI (STUFFED MUSHROOMS)

Serves 6

From the Dining Room of Sunriver Resort

36 medium mushrooms
1 medium onion
2 stalks celery
¼ cup butter
1 cup white wine
1 can (6½ oz.) minced clams
1 teaspoon thyme
8 oz. red snapper, poached and finely flaked
4 oz. shrimp, cooked and finely chopped
4 oz. crab meat, shredded
½ cup finely chopped parsley
1 tablespoon lemon juice
salt and pepper to taste
1 cup thick Bechamel Sauce (see index)

● Remove stems from mushrooms; finely chop stems, onion and celery. Sauté chopped vegetables in butter until onion is transparent. Add 1 cup white wine, juice from clams and thyme. Reduce over medium heat until almost dry.

● Transfer vegetables to a bowl and add fish, shrimp, crab, parsley, lemon juice, salt, pepper and Bechamel Sauce. Combine and add enough crushed shoestring potatoes to bind; mixture should be firm enough to be formed. Set aside.

(continued)

CHAMPIGNON FARCI (continued)

shoestring potatoes
1 cup white wine
1 cup Hollandaise Sauce
   (see index)
1 cup demi-glacé

- Lightly grease a jellyroll pan and pour in 1 cup white wine. Place mushrooms in pan stem side down and cover with foil. Bake at 400 degrees for 3 to 5 minutes or until mushrooms are very lightly steamed but not done.

- Invert mushroom caps and fill with seafood mixture, mounding tops into a dome shape. Place a small amount of Hollandaise Sauce on each stuffed mushroom. Lower oven temperature to 375 degrees and bake mushrooms for 5 more minutes or until done. Serve in a pool of demi-glacé on a warmed platter or individual plates; serve 6 per person.

CRAB-STUFFED MUSHROOMS   Yields 24

24 white mushrooms
4 oz. crab, fresh, or canned and refreshed with a little lemon
2 tablespoons freshly grated Parmesan cheese
8 oz. cream cheese, softened
2½ tablespoons olive oil
2 tablespoons chopped fresh parsley
2 tablespoons fresh lemon juice
1½ teaspoons minced shallot
1½ teaspoons Cognac
1 teaspoon Dijon mustard
1 teaspoon salt
2 tablespoons freshly grated Parmesan cheese
garlic butter, chopped fresh parsley, lemon wedges

- Remove mushroom stems. Combine next 10 ingredients in a medium bowl. Beat 5 minutes.

- Fill mushroom caps, mounding the filling. Arrange on lightly buttered baking sheet and bake at 425 degrees for 10 minutes. Remove from oven and sprinkle remaining Parmesan cheese over the top.

- Preheat broiler and broil mushrooms until cheese melts and is golden brown. Garnish with garlic butter, parsley and lemon wedges.

DEVILED CRAB BALLS

Yields 24 appetizers

Microwave makes this quick and easy.

1 can (6 to 7 oz.) crab meat, drained
4 eggs, hard-boiled, peeled and chopped
⅓ cup dry bread crumbs
3 tablespoons sour cream
2 tablespoons finely chopped onion
1 teaspoon prepared horseradish
1 egg, slightly beaten
crushed cornflakes

● Combine all ingredients except cornflakes in a bowl and blend well. Form into 24 balls and roll each in crushed cornflakes.

● Place balls on paper towel on a non-metal plate. Microwave for 3 minutes on full power. Serve hot.

SWISS CRABWICHES

Yields 40 appetizers
or 5 entrée servings

¼ cup sour cream
¼ cup mayonnaise
1 teaspoon dry mustard
1 teaspoon lemon juice
¼ teaspoon garlic powder
⅛ teaspoon ground nutmeg
4 oz. bacon, fried crisp
¼ cup slivered almonds, toasted
12 oz. crab meat, fresh, or frozen and refreshed with lemon juice
¼ cup sliced green onions
2 cups shredded Swiss cheese
5 English muffins, split, toasted and lightly buttered

● Stir together sour cream, mayonnaise, mustard, lemon juice, garlic powder and nutmeg until blended. Crumble bacon and mix with almonds, crab, onions, cheese and mayonnaise mixture.

● Spoon mixture onto muffin halves and broil 6 inches from heat until golden brown. Cut into quarters for appetizers or serve two halves for each entrée serving. Serve hot.

CRAB MOUSSE

Yields 4½ cups

Oregon Dungeness crab is especially good in this dish.

1 package unflavored
 gelatin
3 tablespoons water
1 can (10¾ oz.) condensed
 cream of mushroom soup
6 oz. cream cheese
½ cup mayonnaise
½ cup sour cream
½ cup chopped parsley
½ cup chopped celery
¼ cup sliced green onions
2 tablespoons lemon juice
¼ teaspoon Tabasco sauce
¼ teaspoon dill weed
¾ cup crab meat
¾ cup cooked shrimp

● Soften gelatin in water for 5
 minutes. Heat soup in a 2-quart
 saucepan and stir in gelatin until
 dissolved. Stir in cream cheese
 until melted.

● Fold in remaining ingredients
 and pour into an oiled mold. Chill
 at least 4 hours before
 unmolding.

SHRIMP TOMATO MOLD

Serves 6

This doubles easily to serve as a luncheon entrée.

1 can (10¾ oz.) condensed
 tomato soup
1 package (3 oz.) lemon
 gelatin
8 oz. cream cheese
1 cup mayonnaise
1 cup chopped celery
1 jar (4 oz.) chopped
 pimiento
½ cup chopped green pepper
3 green onions, chopped
6 to 7 oz. cooked shrimp,
 drained
salt and pepper

● In a large saucepan, heat soup
 and gelatin over low heat until
 well blended and gelatin is
 dissolved. Remove from heat and
 add remaining ingredients,
 mixing well. Pour into oiled
 1½-quart mold and chill 6 hours
 or until set.

CHILI CON QUESO

Yields 5½ cups

A spicy cheese fondue. Could also be used as a brunch item with toasted English Muffins.

¾ lb. Monterey jack cheese,
  shredded
2 tablespoons cornstarch
½ teaspoon garlic powder
2 tablespoons vegetable oil
½ cup chopped green onions
2 medium tomatoes,
  chopped
1 can (4 oz.) diced green
  chilies
½ cup dry vermouth or
  white wine
1 teaspoon salt
8 drops Tabasco sauce

- In a bowl, toss cheese with cornstarch and garlic powder.

- Heat oil in a skillet and add green onion, tomatoes, chilies, wine, salt and Tabasco sauce. Heat to boiling, stirring gently. Reduce heat and gradually stir in cheese until melted. DO NOT BOIL.

- Serve in chafing dish over low flame. Accompany with tortilla chips.

LAYERED MEXICAN DIP

Serves 12

1 can (16 oz.) refried beans,
  seasoned to taste
2 to 3 avocados
lemon juice
½ package (1.25 oz.) taco
  seasoning mix
2 tablespoons sour cream
3 tablespoons mayonnaise
2 cups shredded Monterey
  jack or Cheddar cheese
1 bunch green onions,
  minced
2 tomatoes, chopped
1 can (4¼ oz.) chopped ripe
  olives, drained

- Mash avocados with lemon juice. Blend taco seasoning with sour cream and mayonnaise.

- Assemble components in layers, in order given, in a quiche pan or on a large platter. Chill and serve with corn chips.

TIMBERLINE LODGE, Timberline

Majestic Timberline Lodge, a huge stone "castle" on Oregon's highest mountain, is a monumental work of art as well as a monument to a unique moment in history.

Built in the 1930's as a project of the Depression's Works Progress Administration (WPA), Timberline is the epitome of ski lodges in classic European chalet style. The Lodge is the only major structure in America furnished throughout with handcrafts in wood, fabric, stone, flax and wool, wrought iron, and other like materials, most of them from nearby locales. Skilled and unskilled craftsmen created elaborate carvings, paintings, lamps, glass mosaic murals, rugs, bedspreads, furniture, etc., that make Timberline a virtual arts and crafts museum from the 30's.

A massive hexagonal stone chimney with walk-in-size fireplaces is central to the Lodge, with huge hand-hewn beams adding to the awe of the structure. Each guest room has its own original watercolor paintings of wildflowers native to the region, as well as handmade furniture. Guests may stay in a variety of accommodations, some with their own fireplaces. An outdoor heated swimming pool and jacuzzi offer year-round bathing in a spectacular setting.

Across the way from Timberline, the Wy'East Day Lodge caters to all skier-related activities, offering rental and repair services, a ski gift shop, and bar. The Wy'East kitchen serves cafeteria-style food for hearty skiers' appetites. The Day Lodge features arts and crafts work of present-day native artisans, much the same as Timberline and its 30's artwork.

Although many visit Timberline just to enjoy its beauty, most people come to take advantage of outstanding skiing on Oregon's postcard mountain, Mt. Hood. The Lodge is at the 6000-ft. level, with lifts above and below it. Summer skiing from the Palmer Chairlift offers some of the most impressive glacier skiing anywhere.

Other activities in the area include fishing for trout, steelhead, and/or salmon on nearby famed rivers: the Deschutes, the Sandy, the Hood, the Clackamas and White River. Hiking, windsurfing, and mountain biking are also popular in warmer months.

Timberline's Cascade Dining Room offers American regional cuisine with a European flair.

For additional information:
Timberline Lodge
Timberline, OR 97028
1-800-452-1335 (OR except Portland)
231-5400 (Portland)
1-800-547-1406 (WA, ID, UT, NV, N. CA)
(503) 272-3311 (Elsewhere)

STUFFED MUSHROOM CAPS   Serves 6 to 8

From the Dining Room of Timberline Lodge

2 lbs. very large
  mushrooms,
  washed and stemmed
butter
fresh bread crumbs
freshly grated Parmesan
  cheese
chopped fresh parsley for
  garnish

• Prepare Cheese Stuffing Mixture; set aside. Sauté mushroom caps in butter until soft. Allow to cool a little.

(continued)

STUFFED MUSHROOM CAPS (continued)

- Stuff caps with Cheese Stuffing Mixture. Sprinkle with a topping of half bread crumbs and half grated Parmesan cheese. Bake at 400 degrees until hot and golden brown. Garnish with fresh chopped parsley.

Cheese Stuffing Mixture

stems from 2 lb. mushrooms
butter
chablis
2 cloves garlic, minced
salt and pepper
1 lb. cream cheese, softened
1 teaspoon garlic powder
½ cup chopped parsley
1 teaspoon dill weed
½ cup butter
¼ cup sour cream

- Chop stems and sauté in butter with a little chablis and minced garlic. Season with salt and pepper. In mixing bowl combine cream cheese, garlic powder, ½ cup chopped parsley, dill weed and ½ cup butter. Drain sautéed mushroom stems and add to cheese mixture with sour cream.

CHEESE SQUARES
Serves 12-18

Must be prepared 24 hours before baking.

1 loaf unsliced sandwich
  bread
3 oz. cream cheese
¼ lb. Cheddar cheese,
  shredded
½ cup butter
2 egg whites

- Remove crusts from loaf of bread; cut loaf into 1-inch cubes. Place cubes on a cookie sheet and freeze. Melt cream cheese, shredded cheese and butter in a saucepan over low heat.

- Beat egg whites until stiff and fold into cheese mixture. Dip frozen bread cubes in the mixture and let stand, covered, in refrigerator overnight.

- To serve, bake at 400 degrees for 12 to 15 minutes or until golden brown.

Note: Can be frozen before baking.

SNAPPY CHEESE STICKS AND OLIVES

Yields 4 dozen sticks and 2½ dozen olives

Tasty cold; a nice salad accompaniment.

ingredients for a 2-crust pie
4 oz. sharp Cheddar cheese,
  shredded
¼ teaspoon dry mustard
2 teaspoons paprika
30 small stuffed green
  olives

● Combine ingredients for pie crust with cheese, mustard and paprika. Form into a ball. Divide dough in half. Using first half, wrap about 1 teaspoon dough around each olive. Bake on ungreased baking sheet at 425 degrees for 10 to 12 minutes or until golden brown.

● Roll second half of dough on floured surface to 12x8-inch rectangle. With pastry wheel or knife, cut into ½x4-inch sticks and bake on ungreased baking sheets at 425 degrees for 8 to 10 minutes.

PERPETUAL CHEESE DIP

Yields 3 cups

A "create-as-you-go" dip or spread.

16 oz. cream cheese,
  softened
3 oz. Oregon blue cheese,
  softened
5 tablespoons olive oil
6 tablespoons brandy
1 tablespoon dry mustard

● Mix ingredients together well
and store in refrigerator in a
small, covered crock. Add more
ingredients and mix well with
additional brandy as it is used
over time.

BEER CHEESE SPREAD

Yields 5 cups

1 lb. sharp Cheddar cheese,
  shredded
1 lb. mild cheese, shredded
3 oz. tomato paste
1 teaspoon garlic salt
3 tablespoons Worcester-
  shire sauce
1½ cups beer

● Combine ingredients and mix
well to make a smooth spread-
able mixture. Serve with
crackers, or spread on bread and
grill to make small sandwiches.

Note: Can be refrigerated 2 to 3 weeks in a covered crock.

DEEP-FRIED CHEESE BALLS

Serves 8 to 10

1½ cups shredded American
  cheese
¼ teaspoon salt
dash Tabasco sauce
⅓ teaspoon dry mustard
1 tablespoon flour
3 egg whites, stiffly beaten
finely crushed cracker
  crumbs
vegetable oil

● Mix cheese, salt, Tabasco,
mustard and flour. Add egg
whites and shape into small
balls. Roll in cracker crumbs and
fry in hot oil until golden brown.
Drain and serve.

HOLIDAY CHEESE BALL

Yields 3 cups

Colorful and festive.

8 oz. cream cheese, softened
3 cups shredded sharp
Cheddar cheese
2 tablespoons chopped
pimiento
2 tablespoons chopped green
pepper
2 tablespoons finely
chopped green onion
2 teaspoons Worcestershire
sauce
1 teaspoon lemon juice
⅛ teaspoon salt
finely chopped nuts

● Blend cream cheese until light
and fluffy. Mix in rest of
ingredients and shape into a ball.
Roll in finely chopped nuts. Wrap
in plastic wrap and chill at least
4 hours or overnight.

PECAN CHEESE BALL

Serves 8 to 10

A zesty combination of flavors.

16 oz. cream cheese,
softened
1 can (8½ oz.) crushed
pineapple, drained
1 cup chopped pecans
¼ cup chopped green pepper
2 tablespoons chopped onion
1 tablespoon seasoned salt
chopped pecans

● Combine ingredients and form
into a ball or log. Roll in
additional chopped pecans and
chill. Serve with crackers.

HERB DIP

Yields 1¾ cups

Good with both crackers and fresh vegetables.

1 cup mayonnaise
1 cup cottage cheese
1 clove garlic, minced
¼ cup minced chives
2 tablespoons chopped
   parsley
2 tablespoons chervil
1 tablespoon dill weed
1 tablespoon dried basil
dash Worcestershire sauce
dash Tabasco sauce
1 head red cabbage

● Combine all ingredients except cabbage in food processor or blender. Blend until smooth. Chill. Hollow out the head of cabbage and fill with dip just before serving.

MAN'S FAVORITE DIP

Yields 2 cups

Quick and easy; especially good with crunchy vegetables.

1 cup mayonnaise
½ cup cottage cheese
⅓ cup minced onion
½ teaspoon garlic salt
¼ teaspoon pepper
⅛ teaspoon Tabasco sauce
¼ teaspoon caraway seed
¼ teaspoon celery seed
¾ teaspoon dry mustard
3 teaspoons Worcestershire
   sauce
½ teaspoon chili sauce

● Combine all ingredients and chill 1 hour before serving.

ARTICHOKE DIP

Yields 4 cups

1 cup mayonnaise
8 oz. artichoke hearts
   (not marinated)
1 cup freshly grated
   Parmesan cheese
1 can (7 oz.) diced green
   chilies

● Process artichoke hearts in food processor or blender; add remaining ingredients and blend. Pour into chafing dish and heat. Serve with corn chips or crackers.

EGG DIP FOR VEGETABLES

Yields 2 cups

8 oz. cream cheese
½ cup mayonnaise
½ cup chopped parsley
1 hard-boiled egg white,
  chopped
2 tablespoons chopped onion
2 cloves garlic, minced
1 tablespoon anchovy paste
  (optional)
dash salt and pepper
1 hard-boiled egg yolk,
  finely grated

● Beat cream cheese until softened and add mayonnaise. Mix until smooth. Add remaining ingredients except egg yolk. Sprinkle grated egg yolk over top and serve with raw vegetables.

CHUTNEY CHEESE SPREAD

Yields 3½ cups

16 oz. cream cheese,
  softened
3 tablespoons golden
  raisins, chopped
3 tablespoons sour cream
3 tablespoons curry powder
¾ cup chopped peanuts
¼ cup crumbled crisp-fried
  bacon
½ cup chopped green onion
1 cup Assistance League
  Plum Chutney* or a
  mango chutney
toasted coconut

● Mix all ingredients together well and pack into a mold or form into a ball. Sprinkle with toasted coconut and serve with assorted crackers.

*See recipe on next page.

39

ASSISTANCE LEAGUE PLUM CHUTNEY

Yields 9 cups

3½ lbs. Italian prune-plums, halved
1 cup brown sugar
1 cup sugar
¾ cup cider vinegar
1 cup seedless white raisins
⅓ cup chopped onion
1 clove garlic, minced
2 teaspoons mustard seed
3 tablespoons chopped crystallized ginger
2 teaspoons salt
¾ teaspoon cayenne pepper

● Bring sugars and vinegar to a boil in a large saucepan. When sugars have dissolved, add remaining ingredients and bring to a boil again.

● Reduce heat and simmer 45 to 50 minutes, or until thick. Ladle into clean jars, seal and process 5 minutes in a hot water bath.

Note: Excellent used as appetizer—on a cracker with cream cheese, on a cracker with cheese and salami, mixed with sour cream as a dip, mixed with mayonnaise as a sauce for cold shrimp, served with egg rolls.

PINEAPPLE PEACH CHUTNEY

Yields 10 cups

1 lemon, thinly sliced, quartered and seeded
5 cups peeled and coarsely chopped fruit (pineapple, apple and peaches in any proportion)
2 cloves garlic, chopped
2¼ cups brown sugar
1 cup seedless raisins
¾ cup chopped crystallized ginger
2 teaspoons salt
1 teaspoon cayenne pepper
2 cups cider vinegar

● Combine all ingredients and cook over medium-high heat, uncovered, until mixture is thick. Stir to prevent scorching.

● Ladle into sterilized jars and seal. Process 5 minutes in a hot water bath.

Note: Excellent served with lamb, turkey, wild game, curries, or as a glaze on baked ham, chicken or pork.

Soups

SOUPS

MEAT
Hearty 3x3 Soup, 43
Chicken Soup with Corn, 44
Mulligatawny, 44
Mexican Meatball Soup, 45
Tamale Soup, 45

SEAFOOD
Salmon Chowder, 47
Oregon Bouillabaisse, 48
Clam Chowder, 49
Christmas Eve Chowder, 50

CHEESE
Velvet Cheese Soup, 50
Beer Cheese Soup, 51

VEGETABLE
Snappy Soup, 51
Sopa Verde de Flote, 53
Creamed Fresh Asparagus Soup, 56
Cold Cucumber Soup, 56
Cream of Broccoli Soup, 57
Cream of Zucchini Soup, 57
Lentil Soup, 59
Corn Chowder, 60
Fresh Potato Soup with Swiss, 60

HEARTY 3x3 SOUP

Yields 4 to 5 quarts

Good with zinfandel. Start the day before you plan to serve it.

¾ cup dried white pea beans
¾ cup dried pinto beans
¾ cup dried black or red beans
2 slices bacon, minced
2 carrots, finely chopped
1 medium onion, minced
1 clove garlic, minced
1 German or Polish sausage ring, cut into ¼-inch slices
2 quarts stock from ham hocks, or chicken or beef stock
1 lb. knockwurst, cut into ¼-inch slices, or hot dogs
1 slice ham, cut into ½-inch cubes
1 bay leaf
½ teaspoon dried thyme
1 tablespoon chopped parsley

• Soak beans separately overnight in 3 cups cold water each. Drain and cook separately in fresh water until tender (30 to 45 minutes).

• Fry bacon until soft and add chopped vegetables and sausage. Continue to cook on medium heat until onions are soft. Bring stock to a low boil in an 8-quart soup pot.

• Drain beans and add to stock. For a thick soup, mash about ⅓ of white beans before adding to stock. Drain liquid from sausage and vegetables and add them to hot stock and beans.

• Add knockwurst, ham, bay leaf and herbs. If stock is from ham hocks, their meat may be added at this time. Simmer for at least 2 hours, preferably longer, and salt to taste. Garnish with parsley.

Note: Can be frozen.

CHICKEN SOUP WITH CORN (SOPA DE POLLO CON MAIZ)

Serves 4

Crisp tortillas add crunch to this soup.

4 cups canned corn kernels
¼ cup butter
2 cloves garlic, chopped
2 cups chicken broth
1 cup milk
½ teaspoon dried oregano
salt and pepper to taste
2 tablespoons canned
  chopped green chilies
1 whole chicken breast,
  cooked and diced
1 cup diced fresh tomato
1 cup cubed Monterey jack
  cheese
2 tablespoons minced fresh
  parsley
corn tortillas, cut into
  squares, fried crisp and
  drained

- Sauté corn and garlic briefly in butter until tender. Puree mixture in a blender or food processor.

- In a 3-quart saucepan, combine corn mixture, broth, milk, spices and chicken. Heat until completely warmed. (Soup may be held or frozen at this point.)

- To finish soup, heat but do not boil. Place some tomato and cheese in bottoms of four bowls. Add soup and stir gently.

- Top with parsley and some crisp tortilla squares. (If tortilla squares are not crisp, warm in oven for a few minutes.)

MULLIGATAWNY

Serves 6 to 8

An exotic spicy soup.

1 onion, sliced
½ cup sliced carrots
½ cup sliced celery
1 green pepper, chopped
¼ cup butter
¼ cup flour
1 teaspoon curry powder
4 whole cloves
2 tablespoons chopped
  parsley
1 cup diced cooked chicken
1 can (16 oz.) tomatoes with
  juice
1 quart chicken stock
salt and pepper

- Sauté onion, carrots, celery and green pepper in butter. Blend in flour and cook several minutes.

- Add curry, cloves, parsley, chicken, tomatoes and chicken stock. Season with salt and pepper and simmer for 1 hour. Remove cloves before serving.

MEXICAN MEATBALL SOUP

Serves 12

Best if made one day ahead.

1 can (16 oz.) tomato sauce
1 can (46 oz.) tomato juice or
  clamato juice
1 can (16 oz.) stewed
  tomatoes
1 package (1.25 oz.) taco
  seasoning
1 tablespoon sugar
1½ lb. lean ground beef or
  sausage
½ cup instant rice
1 egg
½ teaspoon dried oregano
½ cup red wine
2 carrots, peeled and sliced
  (optional)

● In a large saucepan, combine
  tomato sauce, juice, stewed
  tomatoes, ½ the taco seasoning
  and sugar. Bring to a boil, then
  simmer.

● Make meatballs by combining
  ground meat and remaining taco
  seasoning, rice, egg and oregano.
  Form into small balls and drop
  into hot soup. Add wine and
  carrot slices and simmer for 1
  hour. Chill and remove any
  congealed grease. Reheat and
  serve.

TAMALE SOUP

Serves 4

3 large potatoes, peeled and
  cubed
2 cups corn
2 cans (16 oz. each) chili
  beans or chili with beans
1 teaspoon cumin (optional)
1 quart beef stock
1 can tamales, unwrapped
  and cut into ¾-inch pieces
salt and pepper to taste
shredded cheese

● Boil potato cubes 12 to 15
  minutes or until tender; drain.
  In a large saucepan or crock pot,
  combine potatoes, corn, chili
  beans, cumin and stock. Bring to
  a boil, then simmer 15 minutes.

● Add tamale pieces and stir
  gently until heated through.
  Adjust seasonings and serve,
  garnished with shredded cheese.
  Freezes well.

Note: If using a crock pot, cook all but corn and tamales at low
temperature for 2 hours. Add the corn and cook 30 minutes, then
add tamales.

THE INN AT FACE ROCK, Bandon

A stunning ocean view of world-famous Bandon-by-the-Sea beach is a highlight of a stay at The Inn at Face Rock.

Private beach access for guests allows them to wander on the beach to explore tidepools teeming with sea life or just watch a picture-perfect sunset. Up the beach a series of massive rocks along the shoreline calls to mind the folklore that gave Face Rock its name: One rock resembles the upturned face of a beautiful Indian maiden, said to have been turned to stone as she waded too far into the surf.

The Inn's golf course was designed to appeal to all levels of golfers. As such, it manages to intrigue the accomplished golfer and hold the interest of the average one.

Artistic interior design, comfortable furnishings, and a crackling fire in the fireplace give each guest suite a charming warmth that welcomes every visitor. Queen-size beds, kitchenettes, private ocean-view decks, and two baths per suite assure comfort and convenience for all.

Dining in the Inn's restaurant is a visual as well as a culinary delight. The dining room is an open, airy greenhouse design with curved windows capturing the sunlight and a sweeping view of the Pacific Ocean. Fresh seafood and meat entrées, fresh-baked breads, and an extensive wine list enhance guests' dining pleasure.

For additional information:
The Inn at Face Rock
3225 Beach Loop Road
Bandon, OR 97411
(503) 347-9441

SALMON CHOWDER
Yields 2½ quarts

From the Dining Room of The Inn at Face Rock

1 lb. fresh salmon
4 cups water
3 stalks celery, chopped
1 medium onion, chopped
5 to 6 potatoes, peeled and
 diced
¼ cup butter
½ cup flour (more if needed)
1 quart half and half
salt and pepper to taste
minced parsley

● Place salmon, water, celery, and onion in a 3-quart saucepan. Bring to a boil, reduce heat and simmer until salmon flakes. Remove salmon and reserve stock.

● Add potatoes to fish stock; cook over medium heat until tender. Melt butter in a small saucepan; add enough flour to form a thick roux. Mix into fish stock and stir until thickened.

● Break salmon into small pieces, discarding all skin and bones. Return salmon to thickened stock. Scald half and half and stir into thickened stock. Salt and pepper to taste. Serve garnished with minced parsley.

OREGON BOUILLABAISSE
Serves 8

An Oregon version of a classic.

¼ cup olive oil
1 cup butter
2 medium onions, chopped
1 leek, sliced, white part
  only
2 green peppers, diced
4 cloves garlic, minced
3 cans (16 oz. each) tomatoes
1 can (6 oz.) tomato paste
2 cans (8 oz. each) tomato
  sauce
1 bay leaf
½ teaspoon dried oregano
½ teaspoon dried whole
  thyme
½ teaspoon dried basil
6 whole peppercorns
½ teaspoon ground cayenne
  pepper
2 cups dry white wine
1 cup canned clam juice
salt to taste
24 live butter clams in the
  shell, or use whole shelled
  canned clams
3 to 4 fresh Dungeness
  crabs (cooked) or
  1 lb. crab meat
1 lb. medium shrimp, peeled
  and deveined
¼ lb. scallops
2 lb. firm-fleshed fish, cut
  into 2-inch pieces

● In a large soup pot, sauté onions, leek, green peppers, and garlic in oil and butter until soft. Add tomatoes, tomato paste and sauce, and seasonings and simmer over low heat for 15 minutes. Add wine and clam broth and cook 10 minutes.

● Clean crab; crack legs but leave intact with meat inside. Shell body meat and reserve. Scrub clams well and discard any which are not tightly closed.

● To the soup pot, add scallops, fish, then clams on top. Simmer until clams open, about 20 minutes.

● Add shrimp, crab body meat and the cracked but unshelled legs. Cook 10 minutes more or until all seafoods are heated through. Remove bay leaf and peppercorns and serve.

CLAM CHOWDER

Serves 6

An Oregon staple.

3 slices bacon, diced
1 medium onion, chopped
1 stalk celery, chopped fine
¼ cup finely diced green
  pepper
2 large baking potatoes,
  peeled, diced and reserved
  in salted water
2 cans (6 to 7 oz. each)
  chopped clams, liquid
  reserved
1 can (12 oz.) clam juice
1 tablespoon flour
1 teaspoon salt
½ teaspoon freshly ground
  pepper
1½ quarts half and half
1 teaspoon filé powder
½ teaspoon dried whole
  thyme
dash ground cayenne pepper
6 pats butter

● Cook bacon in a large saucepan
until clear. Add onion, celery and
green pepper; sauté until
vegetables are soft. Add cubed
potatoes, drained well.

● Mix together clam juice, flour
and salt and stir into vegetables.
Simmer until potatoes are tender.
Add clams.

● Stir in cream and seasonings and
heat until just hot, not boiling.
Add more salt if needed. Serve
with a pat of butter in each bowl.

CHRISTMAS EVE CHOWDER

Serves 10

A delicious soup when you have little time to cook but still want something impressive.

1 can (10¾ oz.) condensed tomato soup
1 can (11¼ oz.) condensed green pea soup
1 can (10¾ oz.) condensed cream of chicken soup
2 cans (12 oz. each) evaporated milk
1 quart water
1 package (10 oz.) frozen chopped spinach, thawed and drained
¾ lb. cooked crab meat
¾ lb. cooked shrimp
¾ lb. cooked lobster, in small pieces
1 teaspoon seafood seasoning
½ cup dry sherry

● Combine all ingredients and heat gently to serving temperature.

VELVET CHEESE SOUP

Serves 8

An elegant first-course selection.

¼ lb. butter
½ cup finely chopped carrots
½ cup chopped onion
½ cup chopped celery
½ cup flour
4 cups chicken broth
2 cups milk
3 cups shredded Cheddar cheese
½ teaspoon Dijon mustard
1 teaspoon Worcestershire sauce
6 slices bacon, fried crisp and crumbled

● In a large saucepan, sauté vegetables in butter until soft but not brown, about 15 minutes. Add flour and cook 2 minutes, stirring constantly, until well blended. Slowly add 3 cups of broth and whisk until mixture comes to a boil.

● Purée mixture, in batches, and return it to a clean saucepan. Stir in remaining 1 cup broth and milk. Add cheese, Worcestershire and mustard. Simmer over low heat until soup is hot and cheese is melted. Garnish each serving with crumbled bacon.

BEER CHEESE SOUP

Serves 8

Beer adds a delicious tang to this Oregon favorite. If possible, use famous Tillamook Cheddar, the sharper the better.

1 cup butter
1 cup finely chopped celery
1 cup finely chopped carrots
1 cup finely diced onion
¾ cup flour
1 teaspoon prepared
  mustard
8 cups chicken stock
2 cups shredded Cheddar
  cheese
11 oz. beer, preferably flat
3 tablespoons freshly grated
  Parmesan cheese
chopped parsley

● Cook vegetables in butter until tender but not brown. Remove vegetables and purée. Reserve the butter. Make a roux of reserved butter, flour and mustard. Add chicken stock and cook 5 minutes to thicken, stirring constantly.

● Add beer and stir to combine. Mix in puréed vegetables and cheese and simmer 20 minutes, stirring occasionally until cheese is melted. Top each serving with a little grated Parmesan and chopped parsley.

SNAPPY SOUP

Serves 2

1 can (10½ oz.) beef
  consommé
¾ cup tomato juice
1 5-inch celery stick
½ teaspoon Worcestershire
  sauce
½ teaspoon grated lemon
  rind
¼ teaspoon sugar
1 bay leaf
lemon slices

● Combine all ingredients except lemon in a saucepan and bring to a boil. Reduce heat and simmer 2 minutes. Remove celery and bay leaf. Serve garnished with lemon slices.

THE WINCHESTER INN, Ashland

Site of the first hospital in Southern Oregon, the century-old Winchester Inn is a picture of Victorian charm, to the delight of its many guests.

Handsomely renovated with attention to authenticity, The Winchester Inn is located in Ashland's historic district and has six guest rooms, all designed for sophisticated country living. All rooms are air-conditioned and have private baths. Complimentary gourmet breakfasts are served overlooking the Inn's tiered gardens.

The Winchester Inn is located just two blocks from Ashland's nationally acclaimed Shakespearean Festival, so guests are able to walk to the highly enjoyable plays. Main street shopping is within a block. Other activities in the nearby area include river rafting, snow skiing, boating, and fishing.

The Inn's critically acclaimed international menus make lunch, dinner, and Sunday brunch a gourmet's delight. The elegant restaurant features fine French china, linen, and a charming view of the gardens, lighted at night. During summer months, guests may dine on the patio.

For additional information:
The Winchester Inn
35 South Second Street
Ashland, OR 97520
(503) 488-1113

SOPA VERDE DE FLOTE

Serves 6

From the Dining Room of The Winchester Inn

½ cup butter
1 medium onion, diced
4 to 5 cloves garlic, minced
3 cups tomatillos (Mexican
  green tomatoes)
1 lb. fresh corn kernels
10 romaine leaves, shredded
4 jalapeno peppers, minced
1 bunch cilantro, minced
3 quarts chicken stock
salt to taste
6 corn tortillas
oil
4 pasilla or ancho chilies

● In a large soup pot, sauté onion
and garlic in butter for 5
minutes. Crush tomatillos and
add with lettuce and corn to the
pot. Cook 10 minutes or until
lettuce is wilted.

● Add jalapenos and cook 1
minute. Add cilantro and stock;
simmer 20 minutes. Meanwhile,
cut tortillas into small squares
and deep-fry until crisp; reserve.

● In a heavy sauté pan, heat oil
until hot; toast pasilla chilies for
3 minutes, rolling them around
occasionally. Remove chilies and
let cool. When they are brittle,
crush them coarsely; reserve.

● Purée soup, leaving some chunks.
Season with salt and garnish
with tortilla squares and toasted
chilies.

PARADISE RANCH INN, Grants Pass

Nestled in the north end of the Rogue River valley is a picturebook ranch that offers elegant country living, fine dining, abundant recreation, and breathtaking scenery—Paradise Ranch Inn.

The sprawling 300-acre ranch is set amidst lush pastures and stately trees and is surrounded by clean white fences that give the establishment an air of refinement. Within the last few years the ranch has changed from an action-packed, horse-oriented dude ranch to a fashionable country retreat.

Many efforts have been made to attract wildlife to this naturally beautiful setting. Four ponds are stocked with rainbow trout, bass and catfish; the largest pond has two small islands with nesting boxes for ducks, and two stately muted white swans glide serenely over the water. Colorful wood ducks are year-round residents, and migratory fowl often rest up on the ranch during their journeys.

The ranch grounds are lighted with floodlights at night, lending a fairytale quality to the surroundings. Landscaping includes a variety of native plants such as huckleberries and hazelnuts, which appeal to the wild animals and birds.

Activities on the ranch include pedal boats and row boats for enjoying the pond life at close viewpoint. Lighted tennis courts, a heated swimming pool, and a spa ensure plenty of action for guests.

A recreation/social room is complete with high beamed ceilings, a fireplace, a piano, and comfortable overstuffed chairs. The game room features shuffleboard, ping pong, pool tables, and cozy window seats perfect for enjoying a good book.

Accommodations include 15 rooms tastefully furnished and sporting 4-poster beds, tiled bathrooms, and beamed ceilings. Personalized service gives a homey feeling to the ranch and allows guests to feel nicely pampered.

Other activities in the area include fishing on the Rogue and Umpqua Rivers, whitewater rafting, attending the Oregon Shakespearean Festival, and skiing on Mt. Ashland. Crater Lake National Park and the Oregon Caves National Monument are also nearby.

Food is a major reason for Paradise Ranch Inn's popularity, with guests enjoying meals in a small and elegant dining room which looks out on a pond and surrounding pastures and hills. The menu changes monthly to take advantage of fresh, in-season foods, with the chef regularly creating such gourmet entrées as Veal Scallopini Neopolitan, Stuffed Scampi Broil, and Breast of Chicken a la Washington.

For additional information:
Paradise Ranch Inn
7000 Monument Drive
Grants Pass, OR 97526
(503) 479-4333

(See recipe on next page)

CREAMED FRESH ASPARAGUS SOUP Serves 8

From the Dining Room of Paradise Ranch Inn

1 quart whole milk
3 tablespoons drawn butter
3 tablespoons flour
1 tablespoon drawn butter
1 medium onion, diced small
2 stalks celery, diced small
1 carrot, diced small
½ teaspoon white pepper
½ teaspoon ground savory
1 quart chicken stock
1 lb. fresh asparagus, tough
   parts removed, sliced
   diagonally into 1-inch
   pieces
½ cup water
¼ cup cornstarch

- In a double boiler, scald the milk. Combine 3 tablespoons drawn butter and flour to make a roux. Stir into hot milk with a wire whisk. Simmer 1 hour, whisking often, until cream sauce is shiny.

- While soup simmers, sauté vegetables in 1 tablespoon drawn butter with the seasonings. Cook until vegetables are transparent. Add chicken stock and simmer 30 minutes. Cook asparagus in stock until tender, approximately 30 more minutes.

- In a small bowl, mix cornstarch and water. Slowly pour into simmering soup mixture, stirring constantly. Continue stirring another 5 minutes.

- Add the cream sauce; stir well with a wooden spoon. Correct seasonings. Thin with a little stock, if necessary.

COLD CUCUMBER SOUP   Serves 4 to 6

A wonderful introduction to a salmon dinner.

1 medium cucumber, peeled
2 cups chicken broth
1 scallion
1 tablespoon chopped
   parsley
1 tablespoon dill weed
1 teaspoon salt
¼ green pepper (optional)
1 cup sour cream
chopped chives or parsley

- Purée all ingredients in a blender or food processor. Chill. Serve garnished with chopped chives or parsley.

CREAM OF BROCCOLI SOUP

Serves 4 to 6

1½ cups chicken broth
½ cup chopped onion
2 cups chopped fresh
  broccoli
½ teaspoon dried thyme
1 small bay leaf
dash garlic powder
2 tablespoons butter
2 tablespoons flour
½ teaspoon salt
white pepper to taste
1 cup milk
sour cream

● Combine first 6 ingredients in a saucepan. Bring to a boil, reduce heat, cover and simmer 10 minutes or until broccoli is tender. Remove bay leaf and purée vegetables in blender until smooth. Return purée to broth and reserve.

● In another saucepan, melt butter and add flour, salt and pepper. Cook a few minutes then add milk, stirring constantly to make a thick sauce. Combine with the vegetable-broth mixture and heat through. Serve hot or cold garnished with a spoonful of sour cream on top.

CREAM OF ZUCCHINI SOUP

Serves 4

Try crumbled crisp bacon on top for an added treat.

1 medium onion, chopped
½ cup butter
1½ lbs. zucchini, shredded
  or diced
2 cups chicken stock
½ teaspoon grated nutmeg
1 teaspoon dried basil
1 teaspoon salt
freshly ground pepper
1½ cups heavy cream
chopped chives

● Sauté onion in butter until very soft. Add zucchini and stock. Simmer 15 minutes or until zucchini is soft. Purée mixture and return it to the saucepan. Add seasonings and cream. Serve hot or cold garnished with chopped chives.

OREGON CAVES CHATEAU, Oregon Caves

Oregon Caves Chateau is a splendid combination of modern convenience and rustic architecture, a deliberately quaint structure of cedar shakes and logs built some 50 years ago.

The Chateau rises six stories, but its size goes almost unnoticed since its simple style blends so well with the surrounding virgin Douglas fir forest and moss-covered marble ledges. Guests enjoy the casualness of the rambling structure as well as the many historical pictures and artifacts on display. The Chateau has 22 guest rooms on three floors throughout the building, including some suites.

The limestone caves next door to the Chateau (the "Marble Halls of Oregon") attract visitors from every state to view the unusual formations created by a stream that runs through the caves. Established in 1909, the national monument is located in the Siskiyou Mountains; guided tours are scheduled throughout the day in summer and on a limited schedule during the winter.

The Chateau's dining room features hearty homestyle cooking served by friendly college students who work summers at the monument. A section of the cave stream meanders through the dining room, adding rustic charm. The nearby coffee shop is reminiscent of yesteryear's corner soda fountain shop, with furnishings and service much the same as 50 years ago.

For additional information:
Oregon Caves Co.
P.O. Box 128
Cave Junction, OR 97523
(503) 592-3400

LENTIL SOUP
Serves 4 to 6

From the Dining Room of Oregon Caves Chateau

1 small onion, diced
2 cloves garlic, crushed
2 tablespoons butter
1½ cups lentils
4 cups water
2 cups tomato juice
1 teaspoon salt
pinch dill seed
1 bay leaf

● Sauté garlic and onion in butter; add lentils and water. Cook over low heat for 30 to 40 minutes. Add remaining ingredients and cook 30 to 40 minutes more or until lentils are soft. Remove bay leaf before serving.

Note: Best made the day before and reheated.

CORN CHOWDER

Serves 6 to 8

A mild, south-of-the-border taste.

4 to 6 slices bacon
1 large onion, chopped
1 large potato, peeled and
diced
1 cup water
2 cans (16 oz. each) cream-
style corn
⅓ cup diced green chilies
1 jar (2 oz.) sliced pimiento,
drained
2 cups light cream or milk
½ teaspoon garlic salt
pepper to taste

● In a 4-quart saucepan, cook bacon until crisp over medium heat. Remove bacon and reserve, leaving 2 tablespoons drippings in pan. Add onion and cook until limp.

● Stir in potato and water. Bring to a boil and then simmer, covered, for 15 minutes or until potato is tender. Stir in corn and remaining ingredients. Heat, uncovered, just until steaming. Serve garnished with crumbled bacon.

FRESH POTATO SOUP WITH SWISS

Serves 6 to 8

6 slices lean bacon, coarsely
chopped
1 medium onion, coarsely
chopped
3 cups white cabbage,
chopped
1 leek, white part only,
sliced
1 lb. baking potatoes,
coarsely chopped
2½ cups chicken stock
salt and pepper
1 cup shredded Swiss cheese
1 cup half and half
1 tablespoon finely chopped
fresh dill (or dill weed)

● In a 3-quart saucepan, sauté bacon over medium heat until almost crisp. Add onion, cabbage and leek and sauté for about 5 minutes, stirring occasionally. Add potatoes, chicken stock, salt and pepper and bring to a boil. Reduce heat, cover and simmer for 40 minutes.

● Purée in batches in a blender and strain soup back into saucepan. Keep warm over low heat. Add cheese a little at a time and stir until soup is smooth. Do not boil.

● Just before serving, adjust seasonings and stir in the half and half. Sprinkle each serving with dill.

Salads

SALADS

TOSSED

Insalata Verde Mosto, 63
La Plaza Salad, 65
Italian Riviera Salad, 66
Spinach Salad, 66
Spinach Salad with Chutney
  Dressing, 67
Warm Spinach Salad with Smoked
  Duck, 69
Layered Spinach Salad, 70
High-Powered Salad, 71

PASTA AND RICE

Somen Salad, 72
Crunchy Cabbage Salad, 73
Chicken Pasta Salad, 74
Oriental Chicken Pasta Salad, 74
Broccoli Pasta Salad, 75
Creamy Mandarin Rice Salad, 75
Brown Rice Salad, 76
Maifun Salad, 76

VEGETABLE

Sauerkraut Salad, 77
Oriental Cabbage Slaw, 77
Marinated Veggie Salad, 78
Marinated Vegetable Salad, 79
Festive Salad Bowl, 80
Broccoli Salad with Eggs, 80
Fresh Broccoli Salad, 81
Broccoli Salad, 81
Artichokes Vinaigrette, 82
Herb-Marinated Tomatoes, 82
Marinated Cold Asparagus, 83
Marinated Mushrooms, 83

MOLDED

Orange Juice Salad, 84
Frozen Strawberry Salad, 84
Tomato Aspic with Shrimp, 85
Seafood Surprise Salad, 85
Reception Salad, 86
Cheese Surprise Salad, 86

MISCELLANEOUS

Crunchy Shrimp Salad, 87
Salad Niçoise, 89
Marinated Potato Salad, 90
Marinated Shrimp and Artichoke
  Hearts, 91
Quick Spinach Salad, 92
Tabbouli Salad, 92

DRESSINGS

Blue Cheese Dressing, 93
Oregon Blue Cheese Dressing, 93
Sunshine French Dressing, 94
French Dressing, 94
Tomato French Dressing, 94
Special Pasta Salad Dressing, 95
Orange Dressing, 95
Low-Calorie Tomato Dressing, 96
Mayonnaise, 96
Fruit Salad Dressing, 96

INSALATA VERDE MOSTO

Serves 12

NOT a boring salad . . . everyone will love this.

2 heads romaine
2 heads Bibb lettuce
2 bunches spinach, stemmed
2 cucumbers, sliced
½ cup pine nuts or chopped
  walnuts
⅔ cup seasoned croutons
4 tomatoes, quartered
2 cups sliced mushrooms
¾ cup garbanzo beans,
  drained
2 jars (6½ oz. each)
  marinated artichoke
  hearts
grated Parmesan cheese
freshly ground pepper

● Wash and trim greens; tear into
bite-size pieces. Place in large
salad bowl with cucumbers, nuts,
croutons, tomatoes, mushrooms
and beans.

● Toss with Anchovy Dressing and
garnish each serving with two
marinated artichoke hearts,
Parmesan and pepper.

Anchovy Dressing

4 cloves garlic, minced
12 anchovy fillets
¾ cup vegetable oil
¾ cup olive oil
½ cup red wine vinegar
¼ cup fresh lemon juice
½ teaspoon salt
freshly ground pepper to
  taste
2 teaspoons minced oregano
2 teaspoons minced sweet
  basil
2 teaspoons prepared
  horseradish
2 tablespoons Worcester-
  shire sauce
2½ cups grated Romano
  cheese

● In a wooden bowl, mash garlic
and anchovy thoroughly. Add
oils, vinegar and lemon juice,
stirring briskly until well
blended.

● Add seasonings and then slowly
add half the cheese, stirring to
blend well. Gradually add
remaining cheese, stirring
constantly until blended.

THE INN AT SPANISH HEAD, Lincoln City

Breathtakingly different, The Inn at Spanish Head is a spectacular resort that rises 10 stories up the side of a rugged cliff above the Pacific Ocean.

With an unparalleled view of the ocean from each of 146 rooms, Spanish Head guests can relax and let the ever-changing mood of the ocean entertain them. The warm Spanish decor is both elegant and inviting. Most rooms and condominium-style suites include fully equipped kitchens.

Guests can step right onto the long sandy beach from the first floor of the Inn to enjoy a stroll beside the pounding surf or a try at surfing or building sand castles. An outdoor heated swimming pool, saunas, and a recreation room provide additional activities.

Just minutes away from Spanish Head are numerous arts and crafts galleries, live summer theatre, and shaded Coast Range hiking trails. The Inn will also make arrangements for a day of deep sea fishing, tennis, or golf.

Diners in the Inn's La Plaza Restaurant enjoy a sweeping ocean view from the tenth floor location. Fresh seafood and gourmet entrées are featured daily, while fine music from the lounge contributes to the romantic setting.

For additional information:
The Inn at Spanish Head
4009 South Highway 101
Lincoln City, OR 97367
1-800-452-8127 (OR)
1-800-547-5235 (WA, ID, NV, UT, N. CA)
(503) 996-2161 (Elsewhere)

LA PLAZA SALAD
Serves 4

From the Dining Room of The Inn at Spanish Head

1 bunch spinach, torn into
  small pieces
½ head romaine, torn into
  small pieces
1 tomato, cut into eight
  wedges
¼ cucumber, thinly sliced
4 medium mushrooms,
  thinly sliced
4 slices bacon, cooked and
  crumbled
1 large egg, hard-boiled and
  coarsely grated
4 lemon slices

● Mix spinach and romaine in a
  stainless bowl; toss lightly with
  La Plaza Dressing. Divide into
  four portions using tomato and
  cucumber as garnish on all four
  sides of each salad. Sprinkle egg,
  bacon and mushrooms over
  salads. Add a slice of lemon for
  garnish.

La Plaza Dressing

1 tablespoon prepared
  horseradish
½ cup mayonnaise
1 teaspoon lemon juice
2 drops Tabasco sauce
3 drops Worcestershire
  sauce

● Combine all ingredients; refrigerate at least 1 hour.

ITALIAN RIVIERA SALAD

Serves 6

Hearty and tangy.

1 head crisp lettuce, torn
1 head romaine, torn
3 eggs, hard-boiled and
  diced
1 cup julienned prosciutto
  or hard salami
1 cup croutons, sautéed in
  garlic oil

● Wash and dry lettuces. Toss together with rest of ingredients and Dressing.

Herb Dressing

¾ teaspoon salt
⅛ teaspoon oregano
½ teaspoon dill weed
¼ teaspoon celery seed
¼ cup tarragon vinegar
¾ cup olive oil

● Combine ingredients well.

SPINACH SALAD

Serves 8

Save precious last-minute time by making dressing ahead.

1 lb. fresh spinach, stemmed
1 cup fresh bean sprouts
4 oz. sliced water chestnuts,
  drained
1 cup fresh mushrooms,
  sliced
½ lb. bacon, cooked and
  crumbled
⅓ cup toasted sesame seeds

● Pour boiling water over bean sprouts. Let stand 5 minutes, drain and chill. Combine with other ingredients; chill until serving time. Toss with Spicy Dressing just before serving.

Spicy Dressing

¼ cup soy sauce
½ cup vegetable oil
2 tablespoons lemon juice
1½ tablespoons minced
  onion
½ teaspoon sugar
½ teaspoon pepper

● Combine ingredients and let flavors blend 2 to 3 hours or overnight.

SPINACH SALAD WITH CHUTNEY DRESSING

Serves 4 to 6

Be prepared for requests for your recipe when you serve this.

1 lb. fresh spinach, washed, trimmed and dried
12 fresh mushrooms, sliced
1 can (8 oz.) sliced water chestnuts
6 slices bacon, cooked crisp and crumbled
1 cup fresh bean sprouts
1 cup shredded Gruyère cheese

- Toss all ingredients with Chutney Dressing and serve at once.

Chutney Dressing

¼ cup wine vinegar
1 tablespoon sugar
3 tablespoons Assistance League chutney* or Major Grey's
1 clove garlic, minced
1 teaspoon dry mustard
½ cup vegetable oil

- Combine first 5 ingredients in a blender and whirl until smooth. With machine running, add oil slowly until dressing is thick and smooth.

- Let dressing stand at room temperature 1 hour before serving. Refrigerate if longer storage is needed.

*See index.

67

COLUMBIA GORGE HOTEL, Hood River

Columbia Gorge Hotel, an elegant tourist resort on the scenic Columbia River highway, enjoys fame for its setting as well as its 1920's splendor.

Guests can stroll the beautiful parklike grounds and revel in the breathtaking beauty of the roaring Columbia River below . . . or they may choose to sit and enjoy the peacefulness of a romantic stone bridge and a still pond. Privacy and relaxation are assured in this carefully planned haven.

The Hotel was constructed in 1921, the dream of Oregon's "lumber king," Simon Benson. With all the glitter and extravagance of a Hollywood set, Columbia Gorge Hotel was an instant success not only with Oregonians but also with notables from around the world who considered the Hotel the ideal getaway.

The Hotel has been completely restored in recent years and features rooms with spectacular views, many with their own fireplaces. Comfortable furniture, including canopy beds and plush wingback chairs, gives each guest the feeling that he's as welcome as the many celebrities who have visited there.

A short side trip from this impressive Hotel may take visitors to Multnomah Falls, second highest falls in the United States and certainly one of the most picturesque anywhere in its sylvan glade setting. Also nearby is Bonneville Dam, with a self-guided hatchery tour explaining the phases of salmon raising, a pond where children (and adults!) can throw vending machine food to the fish, and fish ladders showing the eternal struggle of salmon to reach their spawning beds.

Many Hotel guests plan their visits to coincide with spring blossom time, when thousands of acres throughout the area display white-tinted orchards of pear and apple trees. The more adventuresome may choose to indulge in wind surfing on the Columbia atop one-man sailboards.

The Hotel's massive dining room with its elegant fixtures draws visitors from near and far. Gourmet foods and friendly hospitality ensure a pleasant dining experience for all.

For additional information:
Columbia Gorge Hotel
4000 West Cliff Dr.
Hood River, OR 97031
(503) 386-5566

WARM SPINACH SALAD WITH SMOKED DUCK™

Serves 2

From the Dining Room of the Columbia Gorge Hotel

5 bunches spinach, washed
  and stemmed
1 breast of smoked duck,
  cut in strips
4 tablespoons crisp bacon
  bits
2 tablespoons Cognac
1 egg, hard-boiled and
  chopped

● Heat bacon bits and smoked duck in a saucepan. Add Spinach Salad Dressing and simmer a few minutes. Remove bacon bits and duck and reserve. Pour dressing over prepared spinach and toss.

● Heat reserved bacon and duck again; flame with 2 tablespoons Cognac and smother on spinach to wilt. Sprinkle chopped egg on top. Toss and serve.

(continued)

WARM SPINACH SALAD WITH
SMOKED DUCK (continued)

Spinach Salad Dressing

1 tablespoon dry mustard
2 tablespoons Worcester-
　shire sauce
⅛ cup sugar
1 cup olive oil
½ cup red wine vinegar

● Combine ingredients well.

LAYERED SPINACH SALAD   Serves 6

Finally—a salad that *likes* to sit overnight!

1 large bunch fresh spinach
8 slices bacon, cooked,
　drained and crumbled
1 cup fresh bean sprouts
1 cup chopped celery
3 green onions, finely
　chopped
1 package (10 oz.) frozen
　small peas, thawed
1 cup shredded Cheddar
　cheese
1 cup sour cream
1 cup mayonnaise
2 teaspoons powdered sugar
1 can (8 oz.) sliced water
　chestnuts

● Wash, dry and stem spinach.
Tear into bite-sized pieces. Layer
in order spinach, bacon, bean
sprouts, celery, green onion, peas
and cheese in a 9x13-inch dish.

● Mix together sour cream, mayonnaise and sugar; frost salad and
top with water chestnuts.
Refrigerate all day or overnight
before serving.

HIGH-POWERED SALAD

Serves 4 to 6

A crunchy, healthy way to get lots of vegetables in one dish.

2 to 3 quarts assorted salad greens, including some dark green and red leaves
1 pint alfalfa sprouts
1 cup creamed cottage cheese
1 tomato, diced
½ cucumber, sliced, or 4 Jerusalem artichokes, diced
½ cup sunflower seeds or other seeds of choice
½ cup chopped nuts (walnuts, almonds or cashews)
2 small carrots, grated
½ beet, grated
½ to 1 cup diced Cheddar cheese
salt and pepper and herbs of choice to taste
2 to 3 hard-boiled eggs, sliced

● Toss together all ingredients except sliced eggs. Garnish each serving with sliced eggs and serve.

Note: This salad needs no other dressing.

SOMEN SALAD

Serves 6 to 8

1 lb. Somen noodles
1 head romaine lettuce,
  chopped
½ head bok choy, finely
  chopped
1 cucumber, finely chopped
1 cup thinly sliced cooked
  ham or chicken
2 eggs, beaten
1 fish cake, thinly sliced
  (optional—available at
  specialty food stores)
3 green onions, chopped

Sesame Dressing

3 tablespoons toasted
  sesame seeds
3 tablespoons sugar
½ teaspoon salt
¾ cup vegetable oil
¼ cup rice wine vinegar
3 tablespoons soy sauce

● Fry eggs in pan to make 4 thin
  cakes. Slice in strips and reserve.

● Boil noodles 4 minutes; rinse and
  let stand in cold water until
  ready to use, then drain and chop
  slightly. Place noodles in large
  bowl and add greens, cucumber
  and Dressing.

● Serve in bowl, or divide onto 6 to
  8 serving plates, and top with
  meat, eggs, fish cake and onions.

● Combine ingredients well.

CRUNCHY CABBAGE SALAD

Serves 8

Ingredients sound strange, but wait till you taste this crowd-pleaser!

½ head cabbage, finely chopped
2 teaspoons toasted sesame seeds
½ cup toasted slivered almonds
4 green onions, chopped
1 package (3.1 oz.) Ramen noodles, chicken flavor

- Toss together first 4 ingredients. Crunch the dry noodles and add to the cabbage mixture (reserve seasoning packet for Dressing). Just before serving, add Dressing and toss ingredients well.

Ramen Dressing

2 teaspoons sugar
1 tablespoon vinegar
½ cup vegetable oil
1 teaspoon salt
¼ teaspoon pepper
1 packet Ramen chicken seasoning (included in noodle package)

- Combine all ingredients and mix well.

CHICKEN PASTA SALAD

Serves 6 to 8

This flavorful salad holds well on a buffet table or at a picnic.

6 oz. pasta twists or shell
  macaroni
salted boiling water
¼ cup sesame seeds,
  toasted
½ cup vegetable oil
1 teaspoon sesame oil
⅓ cup light soy sauce
⅓ cup rice wine vinegar or
  white wine vinegar
3 tablespoons sugar
¼ teaspoon pepper
½ teaspoon ground ginger
3 cups shredded, cooked
  chicken breast
¼ cup chopped parsley
⅓ cup sliced green onion
6 cups torn spinach

● Cook pasta in boiling water until just done. Rinse under cold water and drain well. Set aside.

● Combine sesame seeds, oils, soy sauce, vinegar, sugar, pepper and ginger in a small bowl. Pour over pasta in a large serving bowl. Add chicken and parsley.

● Chill for at least 1 hour to blend flavors. Add green onion and spinach and toss before serving.

ORIENTAL CHICKEN PASTA SALAD

Serves 4

Make at least 3 hours ahead to develop flavors.

4 oz. pasta twists, uncooked
2 cups fresh pea pods,
  trimmed, blanched and
  cooled
2 cups cubed cooked chicken
½ cup sliced green onions
½ cup sliced water
  chestnuts
½ cup mayonnaise
2 teaspoons soy sauce
¼ teaspoon pepper
⅛ teaspoon ground ginger
1 teaspoon sake or sherry
lettuce leaves
¼ cup slivered almonds,
  toasted

● Cook pasta in salted water until just tender. Drain and rinse with cold water. In a large bowl, combine pasta, pea pods, chicken, green onions and water chestnuts.

● In a small bowl, combine mayonnaise, soy sauce, pepper and ginger. Add sake or sherry and mix well. Pour over pasta and toss to mix. Cover and refrigerate for at least 3 hours.

● Line a bowl or individual serving plates with lettuce leaves and spoon salad over them. Garnish with toasted almonds.

BROCCOLI PASTA SALAD

Serves 8 to 10

A unique salad that gets rave reviews.

1 lb. fresh broccoli, cut in
  ½-inch pieces
4 green onions, sliced
½ lb. Monterey jack cheese,
  shredded
½ lb. Cheddar cheese,
  shredded
¼ cup sesame seeds, toasted
1 lb. fresh spaghetti, cooked
  al dente and drained
½ lb. fresh mushrooms,
  sliced

- Steam broccoli until tender yet crisp. Rinse with cold water and drain.

- Combine with remaining ingredients. Add Dressing and toss to coat well. Serve at room temperature.

Rice Vinegar Dressing

¾ cup vegetable oil
1 tablespoon Schilling
  Vegetable Supreme
  seasoning
¾ cup rice wine vinegar

- Combine ingredients and shake well.

CREAMY MANDARIN RICE SALAD

Serves 6

3 cups cooked and cooled
  rice
16 oz. Mandarin oranges,
  drained
1½ cups sliced celery
½ cup diced green pepper
¾ cup sour cream
1 tablespoon lemon juice
1 teaspoon seasoned salt
½ teaspoon pepper
sliced almonds
6 lettuce leaves

- Blend first 8 ingredients thoroughly and chill. Serve on lettuce leaves and garnish with sliced almonds.

BROWN RICE SALAD

Serves 8 to 10

Piquant! Crunchy! Delicious!

2 cups cooked short-grain
brown rice
1 jar (2 oz.) pimiento
1 can (8 oz.) water
chestnuts, finely chopped
1 green pepper, finely
chopped
1 lb. mushrooms, finely
chopped
½ cup finely chopped chives
½ cup chopped parsley

● Mix all ingredients together.
Add Spicy Mustard Dressing.
Toss lightly and serve slightly
chilled.

Spicy Mustard Dressing

½ cup vegetable oil
3 tablespoons wine vinegar
2 tablespoons spicy brown
mustard
1 tablespoon soy sauce

● Mix ingredients together well.

MAIFUN SALAD

Serves 8

A very unusual salad with lots of crunchies.

oil for deep frying
2½ oz. Maifun rice sticks
4 oz. mushrooms, sliced
2 cups cooked, sliced veal or
chicken breast
1 head iceberg lettuce,
shredded
3 to 4 green onions, sliced
½ cup toasted almonds
1 can (4 oz.) water chestnuts,
chopped

● Puff the rice sticks in hot oil
(400 degrees); do not brown.
Drain on paper towels. Just
before serving, combine all
ingredients and dressing and toss
to mix.

Maifun Dressing

¼ cup rice vinegar
¼ cup vegetable oil
1 tablespoon cider vinegar
2 tablespoons sugar
¼ teaspoon pepper
½ teaspoon salt

● Combine ingredients, shake well
and chill until needed.

76

SAUERKRAUT SALAD

Serves 6

Perk up your winter menus with this lively salad.

1 can (2½ lb.) sauerkraut, squeezed dry and chopped
1 cup finely chopped celery
1 cup finely chopped green pepper
1 large onion, finely chopped
1¼ cups sugar, or less to taste
chopped pimiento (optional)

● Mix all ingredients together and refrigerate for 1 hour or more.

ORIENTAL CABBAGE SLAW

Serves 8

An easy last-minute salad.

1 medium cabbage, shredded
½ cup chopped green onions
1 can (8 oz.) sliced water chestnuts, drained
1 can (8 oz.) sliced bamboo shoots, drained
2 tablespoons chopped pimiento

● Combine vegetables in large bowl; toss with Dressing.

Soy Dressing

¾ cup mayonnaise
2 tablespoons soy sauce
2 teaspoons sugar
½ teaspoon salt (optional)

● Combine ingredients well.

MARINATED VEGGIE SALAD

Serves 16

Try this with barbecued meats!

1 head cauliflower, broken
  into florets
1 bunch broccoli, broken
  into florets
1 lb. fresh mushrooms,
  whole or sliced
1 can (8 oz.) pitted ripe
  olives, drained
1 can (8 oz.) pitted green
  olives, drained
1 can (16 oz.) green beans,
  drained
2 medium tomatoes,
  chopped, or 1 pint cherry
  tomatoes
2 cans (8 oz. each) artichoke
  hearts, drained
1 medium cucumber, thickly
  sliced

● Marinate all ingredients 8 to 10 hours in Dressing. Stir every few hours.

Dill Seed Dressing

1 cup vinegar
1 tablespoon dill seed
1 teaspoon garlic salt
1 teaspoon salt
1 tablespoon sugar
1 teaspoon pepper
1½ cups vegetable oil

● Combine ingredients well.

MARINATED VEGETABLE SALAD   Serves 16

Handy to keep waiting in refrigerator up to 2 weeks.

1 large cauliflower
4 stalks celery
4 large carrots
½ lb. fresh green beans
2 green peppers
1½ bunches green onions
1 can (8 oz.) pitted ripe
  olives, drained
1 can (16 oz.) garbanzo
  beans, drained

• Separate cauliflower into small florets; cut celery, carrots and green beans diagonally into 1-inch pieces; cut green pepper into 1-inch pieces. Place all into 6-quart saucepan.

• Pour Dressing over vegetables. Cover and simmer for 5 minutes. Cut green onions into 1-inch diagonal pieces and add with olives and garbanzo beans to other vegetables; simmer 3 minutes. Chill in liquid overnight.

Wine Vinegar Dressing

1½ cups red wine vinegar
1½ cups water
½ cup vegetable oil
2 tablespoons sugar
4 cloves garlic, minced
2 teaspoons dried oregano
1 teaspoon dried basil
½ cup chopped parsley
2 teaspoons salt
¼ teaspoon pepper

• Combine ingredients and store until needed.

FESTIVE SALAD BOWL

Serves 6 to 8

Red, green and white colors look festively Italian.

1 lb. raw green beans
1 can (8 oz.) water
  chestnuts, drained and
  sliced
½ lb. fresh mushrooms,
  sliced
1 can (8 oz.) pitted ripe
  olives
16 cherry tomatoes, halved
2 jars (6 oz. each) marinated
  artichoke hearts (reserve
  marinade)

● Trim beans and boil until just tender; drain, plunge into cold water and drain again. Place in large salad bowl or large brandy snifter. Add remaining ingredients and Dressing. Cover and chill before serving.

Lemon-Herb Dressing

reserved artichoke marinade
½ teaspoon dried basil or
  1 tablespoon chopped
  fresh
¼ teaspoon oregano
¼ teaspoon grated lemon
  peel
2 teaspoons lemon juice
½ teaspoon garlic salt
pepper to taste

● Combine ingredients and pour over prepared vegetables.

BROCCOLI SALAD WITH EGGS

Serves 8 to 10

Contains enough protein to serve as luncheon entrée.

2 large bunches fresh
  broccoli
1 cup green olives with
  pimiento, sliced
2 small green onions,
  chopped
4 hard-boiled eggs, peeled
  and chopped
½ cup prepared Italian
  dressing
1 cup mayonnaise

● Wash broccoli and break off florets. Chop tender pieces of the stem; discard tough parts. Combine all ingredients and refrigerate overnight. Serve chilled.

FRESH BROCCOLI SALAD

Serves 8

A sweet-and-sour salad with a creamy dressing.

2 large bunches fresh broccoli
10 slices bacon, cooked and crumbled
⅔ cup raisins
½ cup chopped onion
1 cup mayonnaise
¼ cup sugar
2 tablespoons cider vinegar, or to taste

● Peel tough stems and chop broccoli into small pieces. Combine with bacon, raisins and onion.

● In a small bowl, mix remaining ingredients. Pour over broccoli mixture, toss and chill at least 2 hours. Toss before serving.

BROCCOLI SALAD

Serves 4

Simple to toss together for a potluck dinner.

1 bunch broccoli, cut in bite-size pieces
1 bunch green onions, sliced
1 cup cubed Monterey jack cheese
1 small tomato, chopped
toasted sunflower seeds (optional)

● Mix raw vegetables and cheese together. Marinate in Dressing for up to 3 hours. Add seeds and serve.

Rice Wine Vinegar Dressing

¼ cup rice wine vinegar
½ cup vegetable oil
Schilling Salad Supreme mix, to taste

● Combine ingredients well.

ARTICHOKES VINAIGRETTE

Serves 4

1 package (9 oz.) frozen
  artichokes or 2 cups
  trimmed and halved fresh
  artichoke hearts
6 tablespoons olive oil
2 tablespoons red wine
  vinegar
3 tablespoons minced sweet
  pickle
1 tablespoon sweet pickle
  liquid
2 tablespoons minced
  parsley
2 tablespoons minced
  pimiento

● Cook artichoke hearts in boiling
  salted water until tender. Drain
  and place in medium bowl. Add
  remaining ingredients and mix
  gently. Cover and chill 4 hours or
  overnight.

● Lift artichoke hearts from
  marinade and arrange on
  individual serving plates. Spoon
  chopped ingredients from
  marinade over artichokes and
  serve.

HERB-MARINATED TOMATOES

Serves 8

A pretty garnish for a dinner plate.

8 medium firm, ripe
  tomatoes
1 cup French dressing
1 teaspoon basil
½ teaspoon tarragon
salad greens
tiny pickled onions
1 tablespoon minced parsley

● Place tomatoes in boiling water
  for 1 minute; cool and peel.
  Hollow out and place in a
  shallow dish (use insides for
  another dish).

● Combine French dressing with
  basil and tarragon; pour over
  tomatoes. Cover and chill at least
  2 hours.

● Fill tomatoes with pickled
  onions. Top with parsley and
  serve on bed of salad greens.

MARINATED COLD ASPARAGUS · Serves 4

1 lb. fresh asparagus

● Cut asparagus diagonally into 2½-inch slices. Blanch in boiling water for 2 minutes only. Rinse in cold water immediately.

Oyster Sauce Dressing

½ teaspoon sugar
1 to 2 teaspoons soy sauce
1 tablespoon oyster sauce
few drops sesame oil
salt and pepper to taste

● Mix ingredients well and toss with blanched asparagus. Chill slightly before serving.

MARINATED MUSHROOMS · Serves 12

Equally suitable for side dish or appetizer.

1 cup butter, melted
3 lb. firm, whole mushrooms
1 cup vegetable oil
½ cup orange juice
½ cup cream sherry
1 teaspoon garlic powder
1 teaspoon rum extract

● In a large skillet, sauté mushrooms in ½ cup butter until tender yet crisp. Combine remaining ingredients and remaining melted butter in large bowl. Add sautéed mushrooms and pan juices. Marinate several hours at room temperature before serving.

ORANGE JUICE SALAD

Serves 6

1 package (3 oz.) orange
  gelatin
1 cup hot water
1 can (6 oz.) frozen orange
  juice
1 can (8 oz.) crushed
  pineapple, drained
2 cups diced banana
1 cup heavy cream
½ cup sugar
1 teaspoon vanilla

● Pour hot water over gelatin to
  dissolve; add frozen orange juice
  and fruits.

● Whip the cream and sweeten
  with sugar and vanilla; fold into
  gelatin mixture and pour into
  mold. Chill until set. Unmold and
  serve.

FROZEN STRAWBERRY SALAD

Serves 12

Luscious pink salad to dress up your table.

16 oz. frozen strawberries,
  thawed and drained
1 cup liquid from berries
  (add water if necessary)
1 package (3 oz.) strawberry
  gelatin
8 oz. cream cheese
½ cup mayonnaise
¼ cup chopped walnuts
2 cups miniature
  marshmallows
1 pint heavy cream, whipped

● Bring berry liquid to a boil; add
  gelatin and stir to dissolve. Cool
  for 10 minutes. Beat cream
  cheese, mayonnaise and gelatin
  together.

● Fold in nuts, berries, marshmallows and whipped cream.
  Pour into individual molds or
  5x9-inch loaf pan. Freeze.
  Unmold to serve. Loaf can be
  sliced.

TOMATO ASPIC WITH SHRIMP

Serves 10

1 envelope unflavored
  gelatin
2 tablespoons cold water
4 cups tomato juice, heated
2 packages (3 oz. each)
  lemon gelatin
4 tablespoons sugar
4 tablespoons vinegar or
  lemon juice
½ teaspoon ground cloves
2 tablespoons chopped onion
2 tablespoons chopped
  celery
½ cup chopped green olives
½ cup chopped nuts
3 to 4 oz. cooked shrimp

● Soften gelatin in cold water; add
  to hot tomato juice and add
  lemon gelatin. Stir until
  dissolved.

● Add sugar; stir until dissolved
  and add remaining ingredients.
  Pour into mold; chill until set.
  Unmold and serve.

SEAFOOD SURPRISE SALAD

Serves 8

2 packages (3 oz. each)
  lemon gelatin
2 cups boiling water
2 tablespoons lemon juice
1 cup heavy cream, whipped
1 cup chopped celery
1 cup sliced stuffed green
  olives
5 eggs, hard-boiled and
  cubed

● Dissolve gelatin in boiling water;
  add lemon juice and let partially
  set in refrigerator. Whip mixture
  and fold in whipped cream,
  celery, olives and eggs. Pour into
  mold and chill until set. Unmold
  on bed of lettuce and serve with
  Sauce.

Seafood Cheese Sauce

8 oz. cream cheese, softened
1 cup chili sauce
½ cup catsup
1 cup mayonnaise
½ cup diced sweet pickle
½ lb. fresh crab meat or
  cooked shrimp or
  combination

● Blend cheese with chili sauce.
  Add catsup and mayonnaise.
  Blend until smooth. Add
  remaining ingredients.

RECEPTION SALAD

Serves 6 to 8

A creamy chicken luncheon entrée impressive in a mold.

1 envelope unflavored
  gelatin
¼ cup cold water
½ teaspoon salt
1 cup mayonnaise
1 cup heavy cream, whipped
1½ cups diced cooked
  chicken
¾ cup chopped blanched
  almonds
¾ cup fruit (grapes, orange
  sections or canned
  pineapple tidbits)
ripe olives, green pepper
  and grapes

● Soften gelatin in cold water;
  place pan over boiling water and
  stir until dissolved. Cool.
  Combine with salt, mayonnaise
  and whipped cream.

● Fold in chicken, almonds, and
  fruit and spoon into 6-cup mold.
  Chill until set. Unmold and
  garnish with olives, green pepper
  and grapes.

CHEESE SURPRISE SALAD

Serves 6

A creamy version of tomato aspic.

1 can (10¾ oz.) condensed
  tomato soup
6 oz. cream cheese
2 envelopes unflavored
  gelatin
½ cup cold water
1 cup mayonnaise
½ cup each finely chopped
  celery, green pepper, onion

● Bring soup to boiling point and
  stir in cream cheese until smooth.
  Soften gelatin in cold water and
  add to soup mixture. Cool.

● Add remaining ingredients and
  pour into 1½-quart mold. Chill
  until set. Unmold to serve.

CRUNCHY SHRIMP SALAD

Serves 4 to 6

½ lb. small shrimp, cooked
  and cooled or 2 cans
  (4 oz. each) small shrimp,
  drained
1 cup bean sprouts
1 can (4 oz.) sliced water
  chestnuts, drained
¼ cup chopped green onions
¼ cup sliced celery
5 oz. chow mein noodles
4 to 6 lettuce leaves

● Combine all but the noodles and
  lettuce in a medium bowl. Chill
  until serving time. Add Ginger
  Dressing and noodles and serve
  on lettuce leaves.

Ginger Dressing

¾ cup mayonnaise
1 tablespoon lemon juice
1 tablespoon soy sauce
¼ teaspoon ground ginger
  or grated fresh ginger

● Combine ingredients and chill
  until serving time.

THE WESTIN BENSON, Portland

An historic landmark in the heart of Oregon's largest city, the Westin Benson exemplifies the special old-world tradition of excellence in both its service and accommodations.

Built in 1913 in French Baroque style with a mansard roof, the Westin Benson features Circassian walnut columns and paneling imported from Imperial Russia, Italian marble staircase and flooring, a classical coffered ceiling, and elegant cut-glass chandeliers from Austria—all in the impressive lobby.

The 350 guest accommodations are tastefully decorated and are available in a variety of rooms, suites, and penthouse rooms. A barber shop, beauty shop, and gift shop are also available for guests.

The city of Portland offers a myriad of activities and entertainments for all. Among them are Old Town, a nearby historic area with more than 120 specialty shops and restaurants; Saturday Market, an outdoor market featuring hand-crafted items; Washington Park, a 145-acre wooded parcel for picnicking, bicycling, jogging, and tennis; and the Pittock Mansion, a 1913 hilltop estate open to tour by visitors.

Dining at the Westin Benson is always a special occasion. The award-winning London Grill features continental cuisine and one of the most extensive wine lists in the city, plus a Sunday Brunch that's a Portland tradition. World-famous Trader Vic's offers fresh seafood and barbecued meats from an authentic Chinese oven.

For additional information:
The Westin Benson
SW Broadway at Oak
Portland, OR 97205
1-800-228-3000 (Reservations)
(503) 228-9611

SALAD NIÇOISE   Serves 6

From the Dining Room of The Westin Benson Hotel

2 cups cold cooked green
  beans, cut in half
2 cups cut green and red
  peppers
1 cup sliced onions
10 oz. small cocktail shrimp
1 can (12 oz.) tuna fish in
  chunks (reserve 3 oz. for
  garnish)
½ cup pitted black olives
½ cup pitted green olives
6 to 12 anchovy fillets
2 cloves garlic, minced
⅓ cup chopped parsley
1 can (12 pieces) artichoke
  hearts, cut in half
1½ cups French dressing
  (a vinaigrette, not sweet)
freshly ground black pepper
herbs (sweet basil, tarragon,
  etc.)
3 tomatoes, quartered
3 eggs, hard-cooked and
  quartered

● Toss all ingredients except tomatoes and hard-cooked eggs in a large bowl with French dressing and seasonings.

● Decorate salad with tomatoes, interspersed with hard-cooked eggs and chunks of reserved tuna. For a beautiful presentation, use a few leaves of butter lettuce and radicchio on the plate.

MARINATED POTATO SALAD   Serves 6

A tasty new version of everyone's favorite.

**8 to 10 small new red
  potatoes
chopped pimiento**

- Cook unpeeled potatoes in salted water until tender. Drain and chill in cold water a few minutes. Drain again, peel and slice into medium bowl.

- Toss with Creamy Egg Dressing, cover and chill until serving time. Garnish with pimiento.

Creamy Egg Dressing

**1 egg, hard-boiled
½ cup mayonnaise
1 tablespoon fresh lemon
  juice
¼ cup half & half
½ cup minced green onion
½ cup minced sweet pickle
⅓ cup minced green or
  sweet red pepper
1 tablespoon minced parsley
1 teaspoon salt
½ teaspoon dill weed
¼ teaspoon marjoram
½ teaspoon summer savory
¼ teaspoon pepper**

- In medium bowl, mash egg and stir in mayonnaise and lemon juice. Add half & half, mix well and add rest of ingredients.

MARINATED SHRIMP AND ARTICHOKE HEARTS

Serves 8

A pretty luncheon salad or a popular appetizer.

3 lbs. large shrimp, cooked, drained and peeled
2 cans (14 oz. each) artichoke hearts, drained and halved
1 small onion, sliced into thin rings
1 can (8 oz.) water chestnuts, drained and sliced

- In a 4-quart container, place all ingredients and the Marinade. Cover and refrigerate 8 to 10 hours, stirring occasionally to coat with marinade.

Marinade

1 cup vegetable oil
½ cup white vinegar
⅓ cup white wine
1 tablespoon snipped parsley
1 teaspoon sugar
½ teaspoon salt
½ teaspoon paprika
¼ teaspoon whole black peppercorns
1 clove garlic, minced

- Combine all ingredients in a jar and shake well to blend.

QUICK SPINACH SALAD

Serves 8

2 packages (10 oz. each)
frozen chopped spinach,
thawed
½ cup chopped celery
½ cup chopped onion
1 cup shredded sharp
Cheddar cheese
2 eggs, hard-boiled and
chopped

● Squeeze all liquid from thawed
spinach; mix with remaining
ingredients. Toss with Horseradish Dressing and serve.

Horseradish Dressing

1 to 2 tablespoons prepared
horseradish, or more to
taste
½ teaspoon salt
2 teaspoons vinegar
1¼ cups mayonnaise

● Combine ingredients.

TABBOULI SALAD

Serves 4 to 6

1 cup bulgur wheat,
uncooked
2 cups boiling water
½ cup vegetable oil
⅛ cup fresh lemon juice
½ teaspoon salt
freshly ground pepper
3 tablespoons chopped fresh
mint or 2 teaspoons dried
½ cup chopped parsley
1 bunch green onions,
chopped (including tops)
2 medium tomatoes, diced

● Pour boiling water over bulgur
wheat in medium bowl. Let stand
for 1 hour or until wheat is
puffed and soft. Drain well in
colander, pressing wheat with the
back of a spoon.

● Combine with remaining
ingredients. Blend and chill at
least 1 hour to bring out flavors.
Serve on lettuce leaves.

BLUE CHEESE DRESSING

Yields 1 pint

Horseradish and beer give an extra zing.

2 cups mayonnaise
2 oz. Oregon blue cheese or
  other blue-veined cheese
1 teaspoon prepared
  horseradish
½ teaspoon minced garlic
¼ cup beer

- Combine ingredients and refrigerate until needed.

OREGON BLUE CHEESE DRESSING

Yields 2½ cups

Oregon blue cheese is widely known. Be sure to try this dressing with a fruit salad.

1 cup sour cream
1 cup mayonnaise
1 teaspoon cider vinegar
1 clove garlic, finely minced
⅛ teaspoon dry mustard
⅛ teaspoon freshly ground
  black pepper
¼ cup olive oil
6 oz. Oregon blue cheese,
  crumbled, or other blue-
  veined cheese

- Mix all ingredients and chill until served. If dressing seems too thick, add a little milk.

SUNSHINE FRENCH DRESSING

Yields 1 pint

Wonderful with citrus fruits, avocados and apples.

⅓ cup vinegar
⅓ cup sugar
⅓ cup catsup
1 cup vegetable oil
1 tablespoon Worcestershire
  sauce
1 clove garlic, chopped
1 small onion, chopped
salt and pepper to taste

● Combine all ingredients in a
  blender and process until smooth.

FRENCH DRESSING

Yields 1 quart

A nice combination of sweet and tart.

2 cups vegetable oil
1 cup cider vinegar or juice
  of 2 lemons
1 cup sugar
½ cup chili sauce
1 teaspoon salt
1 teaspoon pepper
1 small onion, finely
  chopped

● Mix ingredients well by hand or
  electric mixer; do not use
  blender. Serve with greens and/or
  fruit.

TOMATO FRENCH DRESSING

Yields 3 cups

A last-minute dressing with on-hand ingredients; wonderful on spinach salads.

1 can (10¾ oz.) condensed
  tomato soup
⅔ cup vinegar
⅔ cup vegetable oil
2 tablespoons minced onion
2 tablespoons sugar
2 teaspoons dry mustard
1 teaspoon salt
¼ teaspoon pepper

● Combine all ingredients in a
  quart jar and shake well.

SPECIAL PASTA SALAD DRESSING

Yields 1 cup

½ cup olive oil
¼ cup fresh lemon juice
1 teaspoon salt
¼ teaspoon freshly ground
  pepper
⅛ teaspoon crushed red
  pepper
2 cloves garlic, crushed
2 tablespoons snipped
  chives
1 tablespoon snipped fresh
  basil or 1 teaspoon dried
½ teaspoon dill weed

● Combine all ingredients in a jar
  with a tight lid and shake well.
  Refrigerate until ready to use.

ORANGE DRESSING

Yields 1 pint

Especially good over spinach and romaine; make 24 hours ahead.

½ cup catsup
½ cup vegetable oil
2 tablespoons brown sugar
2 tablespoons vinegar
1½ tablespoons prepared
  mustard
1½ teaspoons Worcester-
  shire sauce
½ teaspoon salt
1 clove garlic, minced
½ medium orange,
  unpeeled, cut into thin
  slices, then quartered

● Combine all ingredients except
  orange slices in a quart jar.
  Cover and shake well. Add
  orange slices and chill overnight.

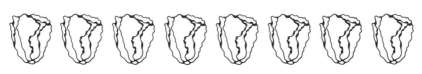

LOW-CALORIE TOMATO DRESSING

Yields 3 cups

A French-style dressing without the calories.

1 quart tomato juice
½ cup vinegar
2 envelopes unflavored
    gelatin
1 tablespoon dry onion
½ teaspoon ground
    cinnamon
4 to 5 whole cloves
sugar substitute equal to
    2 teaspoons sugar
¼ teaspoon pepper
salt to taste

● Combine all ingredients in a saucepan. Bring to a boil, then simmer until reduced to 2½ to 3 cups. Dressing will continue to thicken as it cools. Discard cloves before serving.

MAYONNAISE

Yields 2 cups

1 egg
2 cups vegetable oil
½ cup fresh lemon juice
1 teaspoon sugar
1 teaspoon salt
1 teaspoon dry mustard
paprika for color

● Beat egg until very stiff.

● With mixer running, add oil a few drops at a time at first, then in a small stream (follow directions exactly). When mixture is thick, stir in remaining ingredients.

Note: Add 1 teaspoon curry powder for a nice appetizer dip or salad dressing.

FRUIT SALAD DRESSING

Yields 1½ cups

Good with citrus fruits and avocados.

1 teaspoon dry mustard
1 teaspoon paprika
1 teaspoon salt
1 teaspoon celery seed
1 tablespoon onion juice, or
    finely grated onion
½ cup sugar
¼ cup vinegar
1 cup vegetable oil

● Combine first 6 ingredients in a mixer bowl and add vinegar. Gradually add oil, beating well.

Eggs & Cheese

EGGS AND CHEESE

BRUNCH EGGS

Serves 6

A moist scrambled egg dish loved by young and old alike.

4 slices bacon, diced
2 tablespoons butter
2½ oz. dried beef, sliced or
shredded
¼ lb. fresh mushrooms,
sliced
¼ cup flour
2 cups milk
¼ teaspoon pepper
8 eggs
½ teaspoon salt
½ cup evaporated milk
2 tablespoons butter
¾ cup shredded Cheddar
cheese

● Sauté bacon until crisp; drain off fat. Add 2 tablespoons butter, dried beef and mushrooms to the bacon and cook until mushrooms are done. Add flour, stirring constantly, and cook 2 minutes.

● Add 2 cups milk and pepper and cook until thick and smooth, stirring constantly. Mix the eggs with salt and evaporated milk. Soft-scramble in 2 tablespoons butter.

● Put a small amount of sauce in a buttered 9x9-inch baking dish. Layer eggs, remaining sauce and the cheese. Bake uncovered at 275 degrees for 1 hour.

Note: Can be assembled up to two days ahead. Cover and refrigerate until ready to bake.

MADISON INN, Corvallis

Across the street from a quiet park and next door to the town's picturesque Arts Center stands Madison Inn in Corvallis.

Built in 1897, the beautiful Queen Ann home is within walking distance of Oregon State University and the downtown shopping area. Having once served as a fraternity house, the spacious Madison Inn now has five bedrooms for guests. Its spectacular woodwork and architectural detail have helped place the Inn on the National Historic Register.

Jogging, biking, tennis, and golf are popular activities within Corvallis, as is a summertime tour of the fragrant rose gardens in the nearby park. Many events at the university are also open to the public.

A family-run operation, the Madison Inn is full of early American atmosphere and genuine hospitality. As a bed-and-breakfast establishment, it features delicious full breakfasts of home-baked breads and special egg dishes.

For additional information:
Madison Inn
660 SW Madison
Corvallis, OR 97333
(503) 757-1274

SWISS EGG RAMEKINS

Serves 4

From the Dining Room of the Madison Inn

2 tablespoons butter
2 large onions, chopped
4 hard-boiled eggs,
   quartered lengthwise
1½ cups shredded Swiss
   cheese

- In a wide frying pan, melt butter over medium heat. Add onions and cook slowly, stirring often, until limp and golden (about 30 minutes). Onions should not show signs of browning during first 15 minutes; if they do, reduce heat.

- Divide onions evenly among four 10-ounce custard cups or ramekins. Place 4 egg quarters, yolk side up, in each dish. Equally distribute cheese and then White Sauce over eggs. Bake uncovered at 350 degrees for about 30 minutes or until bubbly.

White Sauce

1 tablespoon butter
1 tablespoon flour
1 cup milk
½ teaspoon Dijon mustard
½ teaspoon salt
⅛ teaspoon white pepper
2 teaspoons chopped parsley

- Melt butter in a 1-quart saucepan over medium heat. Stir in flour and cook until bubbly. Gradually stir in milk and cook, stirring constantly, until thick and smooth. Stir in mustard, salt, pepper and parsley.

Note: Can be made ahead and held in refrigerator overnight.

SWISS BAKED EGGS

Serves 6

An easy way to serve eggs to a crowd.

1 cup shredded Swiss cheese
6 eggs
¾ cup heavy cream
1 tablespoon sherry
salt and pepper to taste

● Lightly butter a 7x11-inch baking dish; sprinkle half the shredded cheese over bottom. Break eggs gently into pan without crowding them.

● Mix together cream and sherry and pour over eggs. Sprinkle remaining cheese over top and season with salt and pepper. Bake at 325 degrees for 15 to 20 minutes.

Note: Can be prepared in muffin tins for individual servings.

EGGS BUCKINGHAM

Serves 4

Fit for a king and queen!

4 eggs
salt and pepper to taste
1 tablespoon butter
2 English muffins, split and toasted
½ cup shredded cheese
4 slices tomato, ⅜-inch thick

● Prepare Beef Sauce and set aside.

● Beat eggs; season with salt and pepper. Melt butter in a skillet and add eggs. Cook until softly set.

● Place prepared muffin halves on a cookie sheet and top with Beef Sauce, eggs, tomato slices and cheese. Bake at 350 degrees for approximately 5 minutes.

Beef Sauce

2 tablespoons butter
4 teaspoons flour
¾ cup milk
3 oz. thin sliced beef, cut into pieces

● Melt butter and make a roux by adding flour. Cook a few minutes and add milk, stirring constantly. When sauce is smooth and thickened, add beef.

EASY CHEESY EGGS

Serves 4

An easy brunch dish. Can be made the day before and reheated.

1 cup finely shredded onion
⅓ cup butter
¼ cup flour
2 cups milk
1 egg yolk
¼ teaspoon salt
¼ teaspoon cayenne pepper
4 to 6 hard-boiled eggs,
   peeled and sliced
2 tablespoons grated
   Parmesan cheese
1 tablespoon paprika

● Sauté onions in butter until transparent. Stir in flour and cook over low heat for 3 to 5 minutes.

● Mix egg yolk and milk. Add to onion mixture slowly, stirring constantly. Add salt and pepper and cook slowly over low heat until sauce thickens, about 8 minutes.

● Remove from heat and add egg slices (reserve a few slices for garnish). Mix gently and spoon into a buttered casserole or individual au gratin dishes.

● Sprinkle with Parmesan and paprika. Place in a 350-degree oven for 3 to 6 minutes to heat through. Garnish with reserved egg slices.

CHANTICLEER INN, Ashland

Guests feel pampered the minute they walk in the door at Chanticleer Inn: complimentary beverages, fresh flowers in rooms, imported soaps and lotions for the bath, and copies of all the season's plays from the nearby Ashland Shakespearean Festival await them.

Chanticleer was built as a family home in the 1920's bungalow style, but it has been magically transformed into a French country inn. The snug and cozy seven-room guest house is located in a quiet residential neighborhood, a short walk from the Shakespearean Theatre, Lithia Park, and the shops and restaurants of Ashland's plaza.

Guest rooms are furnished with antiques and fluffy comforters with matching wallpapers; all have private baths. Some rooms overlook the Bear Creek valley and Cascade foothills, while others open onto a peaceful brick patio.

Guests are welcome to curl up in the living room with a good book or magazine. The open hearth fireplace is especially inviting on a nippy winter's evening.

Activities within the area include Shakespearean plays from February through October, skiing at nearby Mt. Ashland, and white water rafting and fishing on the Rogue River. Cross country skiing enthusiasts enjoy Chanticleer's proximity to the spectacular beauty of Crater Lake.

Breakfast at Chanticleer is a gourmet treat, with cheese baked eggs, croissants, fresh tropical fruits, and dark roast coffee just some of the offerings. Breakfast is served in the Inn's sunny dining room, or guests may opt to have breakfast in bed.

For additional information:
Chanticleer Inn
120 Gresham
Ashland, OR 97520
(503) 482-1919

CHEESE BAKED EGGS   Serves 1

From the Dining Room of Chanticleer Inn

1 teaspoon butter, melted
1 tablespoon cream
1 large egg
Havarti cheese, shredded
salt and pepper

● Butter a 3½ oz. ramekin; add cream. Gently crack a farm-fresh egg into ramekin. Season with salt and pepper. Sprinkle shredded cheese over top. Bake at 425 degrees for 8 to 10 minutes.

CAMPUS COTTAGE, Eugene

A homey alternative for overnight lodging in Eugene is Campus Cottage, a bed-and-breakfast inn just blocks from the University of Oregon campus.

The Cottage's two guest rooms are charmingly furnished with antiques, comforters, and fresh flowers, and each has a private bath. Guests are invited to relax and curl up in the living room in front of a warm fire to read, visit, or work on the current jigsaw puzzle. Warmer days and evenings may find guests relaxing outside on the deck overlooking the garden.

The Cottage provides bicycles for guests who want to pedal their way around town or campus. Other activities in the area include jogging (in "the jogging capital of the world"), enjoying cultural events at the city's Hult Center, attending university happenings, or just soaking up the atmosphere in this highly livable city.

The Cottage boasts good down-home cooking with breakfasts of fresh fruits and juices, pastries, special egg dishes, and "lots of good hot coffee or tea." Guests may eat with others in the living room or may request breakfast served in their rooms.

For additional information:
Campus Cottage
1136 E. 19th Ave.
Eugene, OR 97403
(503) 342-5346

COTTAGE BAKED EGGS
Serves 8

From the Dining Room of Campus Cottage

10 eggs
½ cup flour
1 teaspoon baking powder
1¾ cups cottage cheese
12 oz. cheese, shredded
    (select one that
    complements the other
    ingredients)
chopped vegetables and/or
    cooked meats (i.e., raw
    mushrooms, green onions,
    ham, sausage, bacon)
¼ cup butter

● Beat eggs; add flour and baking powder and beat again. Stir in cottage cheese and cheese. Add vegetables and/or meats of your choice.

● Melt butter in a 2-quart baking dish. Pour in egg mixture and bake at 350 to 375 degrees for 30 minutes or until slightly browned and puffy. Serve immediately.

Note: This can be made in 8 individual baking dishes. Bake 20 minutes.

SPINACH-CHEESE CUSTARD

Serves 8

¼ cup margarine
1 large onion, chopped
½ lb. fresh mushrooms, sliced
1 package (10 oz.) frozen chopped spinach, thawed and squeezed dry
1 cup small curd cottage cheese
1 cup plain yogurt
8 eggs
½ teaspoon salt
½ teaspoon pepper
½ teaspoon freshly grated nutmeg
1 cup shredded provolone cheese
1 cup shredded Cheddar cheese

● Sauté onion and mushrooms in margarine until limp and nearly dry; spread in a layer over bottom of a buttered 7x11-inch baking pan.

● Stir together spinach, cottage cheese and yogurt. Beat eggs with salt, pepper and nutmeg. Add to spinach mixture and spread over vegetable mixture in pan.

● Bake at 325 degrees for 30 minutes. Sprinkle with cheese and continue baking for 15 minutes or until custard is set in the center. Let stand 10 minutes before serving.

CHILI EGGS

Serves 4 to 6

Similar to a quiche, with a bit of spice.

5 eggs, slightly beaten
¼ cup sour cream
½ cup shredded Monterey jack cheese
½ cup shredded Cheddar cheese
3 tablespoons green chili salsa
1 stalk celery, sliced diagonally
5 fresh mushrooms, sliced
salt and pepper

● Grease a 9x9-inch casserole. Blend eggs with sour cream. Reserve a little of each cheese for garnish and add remainder to eggs.

● Stir in remaining ingredients and pour mixture into casserole. Top with reserved cheeses. Bake at 375 degrees for 30 minutes or until knife inserted in center comes out clean.

NO-CRUST QUICHE FOR A CROWD   Serves 24

Perfect potluck fare.

1 lb. thick-sliced bacon,
  diced
4 cups chopped onion
16 eggs
2 teaspoons salt
1 teaspoon pepper
½ teaspoon nutmeg
6 cups milk
2 lbs. Gruyère or Swiss
  cheese, diced

- Sauté bacon until partially cooked. Add chopped onion and cook until tender but not brown; pour off fat.

- Combine eggs, salt, pepper and nutmeg in a medium bowl and beat well. Add milk and blend.

- Spread bacon-onion mixture over bottom of two 9x13-inch baking pans. Cover each evenly with diced cheese. Divide egg mixture between two pans. Bake at 375 degrees for 35 to 45 minutes or until knife inserted in center comes out clean.

BAKED SHRIMP FONDUE   Serves 4 to 6

Flavorful brunch dish to prepare in advance.

1 lb. cooked shrimp meat
1 tablespoon lemon juice
6 slices bread, cubed
½ lb. sharp Cheddar cheese,
  cubed
¼ cup butter, melted
3 eggs, beaten
1 teaspoon dry mustard
½ teaspoon seasoned salt
1 teaspoon Worcestershire
  sauce
2 cups milk

- Sprinkle lemon juice over shrimp. Alternate layers of shrimp, bread cubes and cheese cubes in a buttered 2-quart casserole. Pour melted butter over top.

- In a small bowl, combine eggs, salt, mustard and Worcestershire sauce with milk; blend well. Pour over bread mixture; cover and refrigerate overnight. Bake at 350 degrees for 1 hour. Let rest 5 minutes before serving.

CHEESE SOUFFLÉ ROLL

Serves 6 to 8

¼ cup butter
½ cup flour
2 cups milk
½ teaspoon salt
4 eggs, separated
1 cup shredded Swiss cheese

- Grease a 10x15-inch jelly roll pan and line with waxed paper or foil. Grease and flour paper slightly.

- In a saucepan, melt butter; add flour, then milk. Stir until thickened. Remove from heat; add egg yolks gradually, beating well. Stir in cheese.

- Beat egg whites until soft peaks form. Fold whites into cheese sauce. Pour into prepared pan and bake at 325 degrees for 30 minutes.

- Unmold onto waxed paper or a cloth towel. Remove paper or foil from soufflé. Spread with filling of your choice and roll. Cut soufflé into thick slices and serve.

Chicken and Spinach Filling

2 tablespoons butter
½ cup chopped onion
¼ lb. mushrooms, sliced
1 package (10 oz.) frozen spinach, thawed and drained
2 to 3 cups cooked chicken, chopped
3 oz. cream cheese
1 cup sour cream
2 teaspoons Dijon mustard
salt to taste
dash ground nutmeg
½ cup chopped water chestnuts or celery (optional)

- Sauté onion and mushrooms in butter. Add cream cheese and sour cream and cook until smooth. Add remaining ingredients and stir to blend. Heat through and reserve ½ cup for garnish.

- Fill roll and slice; top each slice with some reserved filling.

(continued)

110

CHEESE SOUFFLÉ ROLL (continued)

Ham and Broccoli Filling

● Prepare as Chicken and Spinach Filling, omitting mushrooms and substituting broccoli for spinach and 1¼ cups chopped cooked ham for chicken.

Broccoli and Cheese Filling

3 tablespoons butter
3 tablespoons flour
1½ cups milk
¼ teaspoon dry mustard
½ cup shredded Swiss cheese
1 lb. fresh broccoli
½ cup shredded Swiss cheese for garnish

● Make a sauce with the butter, flour, milk, mustard and ½ cup cheese. Cut broccoli into 3-inch lengths, discarding tough bottom pieces; then chop into ½-inch pieces. Cook in boiling salted water until tender; drain.

● Spread broccoli over soufflé roll, top with remaining ½ cup cheese and ½ cup of the sauce. Roll soufflé. Slice and serve with the rest of the sauce on the side.

111

THE JOHNSON HOUSE, Florence

Situated in the Old Town section of Florence, the authentically restored Johnson House evokes a picture of life on the Oregon coast nearly 100 years ago.

The handsome two-story building is a fine example of domestic Italianate architecture and is furnished with attractive rugs, antiques, old linens, and glassware. Each guest room in this comfortable bed-and-breakfast establishment has a feather bed, an easy chair or two, a washbasin, and appealing reading material. Authentic 19th-century lithographs and photographs enhance the decor of each room.

The location of The Johnson House makes it particularly appealing to history buffs or anyone interested in the pleasant small towns of days past. In recent years, Old Town Florence has experienced a renaissance of architectural restoration, and picturesque small shops and businesses now thrive there.

Florence lies at the heart of an unusually diverse mix of natural beauty. The town is at the northern end of the Oregon Dunes National Recreation Area, which is bound by the Pacific Ocean on the west and forests on the east. The sand dunes are some of the most spectacular anywhere, and tourists come from around the country to enjoy them.

Numerous lakes and streams in the area provide excellent fishing and boating. The sizable Siuslaw River produces trout, perch, herring, shad and sea-run trout in season, with salmon and steelhead plentiful in the fall. Crabbing, clamming, and salmon fishing in the ocean are other favorite activities. The Siuslaw area is a birdwatcher's paradise, providing a natural habitat for 276 bird species.

Guests at The Johnson House reap the benefits of the hosts' careful attention to detail and concern for everyone's comfort. Hearty breakfasts include fruit, bread, eggs, ham, cheese, coffee or tea, and the specialty of the house.

For additional information:
The Johnson House
216 Maple St.
Florence, OR 97439
(503) 997-8000

CHEESE SOUFFLÉ
Serves 4 to 6

From the Dining Room of The Johnson House

2 cups milk
6 large eggs
3 tablespoons butter
4 tablespoons flour
salt and freshly ground
    pepper
⅛ teaspoon freshly grated
    nutmeg
pinch cayenne pepper
2 teaspoons cornstarch
1 tablespoon water
¼ cup finely grated
    Parmesan cheese
¾ cup coarsely shredded
    Swiss or Gruyère cheese

● Heat milk just to the boiling point; reserve. Separate eggs; put whites in clean mixing bowl and set aside.

● Melt butter in a medium saucepan. Add flour, stirring with a whisk. Add the hot milk, whisking constantly. Add salt, pepper, nutmeg and cayenne and cook for about 5 minutes, stirring constantly.

(continued)

CHEESE SOUFFLÉ (continued)

- Blend cornstarch with water and add to the white sauce; stir well. Remove sauce from heat and add egg yolks, stirring rapidly. Pour mixture into a large mixing bowl. Add Parmesan cheese and stir to blend.

- Beat egg whites until stiff. Add half to the sauce and fold in with a whisk. Add shredded cheese. Fold in remaining whites until completely incorporated.

- Pour mixture into buttered 5-cup soufflé dish. Bake in 375-degree oven for 20 minutes or until as firm as desired. Serve immediately.

Note: At The Johnson House, this soufflé is accompanied by thick slices of ham, assorted fresh fruit and freshly baked muffins or coffee cake.

CHILI RELLENO SOUFFLÉ   Serves 6 to 8

1 lb. Cheddar cheese, shredded
1 lb. Monterey jack cheese, shredded
8 oz. whole green chilies
1 can (12 oz.) evaporated (not condensed) milk, chilled
½ cup flour
3 eggs
7 oz. green chili salsa

- Mix cheeses and put half on bottom of a greased 9x13-inch baking pan. Arrange chilies over top of cheese to cover completely. Top with remaining cheese.

- Whip evaporated milk until thick. Add flour and eggs and beat until blended. Pour milk mixture over the cheese.

- Bake at 350 degrees for 25 minutes. Spread salsa over casserole and bake 5 minutes more.

114

BACHELOR'S EASY CHEESE SOUFFLÉ

Serves 4

Marvelous do-ahead dish.

4 slices white bread
soft butter
mild mustard
½ lb. sharp Cheddar cheese,
  shredded
4 eggs
2 cups milk

● Spread bread with butter, then mustard. Cut each slice into five or six fingers and arrange half in the bottom of an 8-inch square baking dish. Cover with half the shredded cheese. Repeat layers.

● Beat eggs and milk together and pour over bread. Cover and refrigerate 4 hours or overnight. Bake, uncovered, at 350 degrees for 1 hour, until puffy and browned.

ONION PIE

Serves 6

Use sweet summer onions, such as the Northwest Walla Walla Sweets.

9-inch pie shell, partially
  baked
6 medium onions, cut in
  thin slices
3 tablespoons margarine
2 large eggs
½ cup sour cream
½ teaspoon salt
⅛ teaspoon pepper
⅓ cup crumbled, cooked
  thick bacon
½ cup shredded Swiss
  cheese

● In a large skillet, cook onions in margarine over very low heat for about 30 minutes or until transparent but not browned. Add a little water to prevent browning if necessary.

● In a small bowl, beat eggs; add sour cream and seasonings. Sprinkle bacon into pie shell; top with cooked onions.

● Pour egg mixture over all and top with shredded cheese. Bake at 350 degrees for 30 minutes. Serve at room temperature.

115

TUNA-SPROUT QUICHE

Serves 6

3 tablespoons margarine
2 large onions, chopped
½ cup finely chopped celery
1½ cups fresh bean sprouts
1 teaspoon dried basil
2 cups shredded sharp
 Cheddar cheese
1 can (7 oz.) tuna, drained
4 eggs
½ cup milk
2 tablespoons flour
½ teaspoon salt
pepper to taste

● Sauté onion and celery in margarine over medium heat until soft. Remove from heat and stir in bean sprouts and basil. Stir in cheese and gently add tuna. Place in a greased 9-inch pie pan.

● Beat eggs, milk, flour, salt and pepper together and pour into pie pan. Bake at 350 degrees for 45 minutes, or until custard is firm in the center. Let stand 10 minutes before serving.

SAUSAGE AND EGG CASSEROLE

Serves 8

8 slices bread
1 lb. bulk sausage
2 cups shredded sharp
 Cheddar cheese
½ cup chopped green onions
4 eggs
1½ cups milk
1 teaspoon dry mustard
2 teaspoons Worcestershire
 sauce
½ teaspoon poultry
 seasoning
1 can (10¾ oz.) condensed
 cream of mushroom soup
½ cup milk

● Grease a 9x13-inch baking pan. Cube bread and arrange in pan. Brown sausage and drain; spread over bread cubes. Top with shredded cheese and green onions.

● Beat eggs with 1½ cups milk; mix in the mustard, Worcestershire and poultry seasoning. Pour over bread mixture and refrigerate overnight.

● Just before baking, mix the soup and ½ cup milk; pour over casserole. Bake at 350 degrees for 1½ hours.

Entrées

ENTRÉES

BEEF

Broiled Beef Tenderloin with
Mushroom Sauce, 119
Flank Steak Roll-Ups, 120
Barbecued Beef Brisket, 121
Paprika Beef Roll, 122
Piquant Broiled Steak, 123
Fillet of Beef Mozzarella, 124
Beef Parmesan, 125
Green Pepper Steak, 126
Sweet-and-Sour Beef, 126
Beef Marsala, 127
Sweet-and-Sour Beef, 129
Sweet-and-Sour Meatballs, 130
Hamburger Quiche, 130
Stuffed Pasta Shells, 131
Flying M Beef Roll, 133
Chili Con Carne, 134

PORK AND HAM

Barbecued Mandarin Pork, 135
Pork Turnovers, 136
Stir-Fry Pork, 137
Diamond Lake Special Pizza, 139
Noodles Alfredo, 140
Pasta with Fresh Asparagus, 141

LAMB

Dijonnaise-Glazed Roast Leg of
Lamb, 141
Sherry-Glazed Roast Leg of Lamb, 142
Butterflied Leg of Lamb, 142
Lamb Shish Kebabs, 143
Barbecued Lamb, 143
Seasoned Lamb in Phyllo, 146
Kheema, 147

CHICKEN

Hawaiian Chicken, 148
Chicken Breasts with Orange
Sauce, 149
Autumn Fruited Chicken, 150
Herbed Chicken, 150
Party-Perfect Chicken, 151
Chicken au Gratin, 152
Chicken with Peaches, 152
Sesame Chicken, 153
Chicken Breasts in Mushroom Chive
Sauce, 154
Stuffed Chicken Legs, 154
Chicken Sauterne, 155
Oven Chicken Linguine, 156

GAME

Wild Duck in Wine, 157
Tipsy Roast Wild Duck or Goose, 157
Wild Duck, 158
Wild Ducks and Green Pepper
Sauce, 158
Fruit-Stuffed Wild Duck, 159
Baked Pheasant, 160
Fricasseed Fowl, 160

FISH

Red Snapper au Gratin, 161
Snapper Parmigiana, 161
Ling Cod Florentine with Hollandaise
Sauce, 163
Baked Salmon with Caper Sauce, 165
Baked Whole Salmon, 166
Salmon Steaks with Mousseline
Sauce, 167
Depoe Bay Salmon, 168
Salmon Loaf, 168
Stuffed Fillet of Sole, 169
Fillet of Sole "Marguery," 171
Sole Caledonia, 172
Florentine Sole, 173
Halibut Royale, 173
Halibut with Shrimp Sauce, 174

SHELLFISH

Shrimp Etouffé, 175
Shrimp au Gratin, 176
Crab and Shrimp Casserole, 176
Mo's Seafood Cioppino, 177
Baked Seafood Salad, 178
Seafood Lasagne, 178
Scallops in Wine, 179
Shrimp and Scallops Gruyère, 179
Crab Fettuccine, 180
Clams in Shells, 180
Steamed Clams Oriental, 181
Clam Fritters, 181
Oven-Baked Oysters, 182
Yaquina Bay Baked Oysters, 182

BROILED BEEF TENDERLOIN WITH MUSHROOM SAUCE

Serves 8

A real beef-lover's dish.

1 whole beef tenderloin, 5 to 6 lbs.

- Preheat oven and broiler pan to 550 degrees. Have meat at room temperature. Broil meat 2 inches from heat source for 8 minutes on one side, 7 minutes on the other side.

- Place meat in a roaster pan, pour Mushroom Sauce over and bake, uncovered, at 350 degrees for 10 minutes. Place meat on a heated serving platter. Pour sauce from pan over it and serve.

Mushroom Sauce

6 tablespoons butter
1 large clove garlic, slivered
½ lb. fresh mushrooms, sliced
2 medium onions, sliced
¼ lb. hamburger
2 tablespoons chili sauce
1 tablespoon Escoffier Sauce Diable
pinch marjoram
pinch thyme
pinch hickory smoked salt
4 drops Tabasco sauce
2 dashes Worcestershire sauce
⅔ cup dry red wine
¼ cup condensed beef broth
salt and pepper to taste
½ teaspoon flour

- Melt butter in large skillet; add garlic, mushrooms and onions and sauté for 5 minutes. Add hamburger and remaining ingredients; stir and let simmer until ready to add to beef.

FLANK STEAK ROLL-UPS

Serves 4

1 flank steak
garlic salt
parsley, chopped
chives, chopped
6 strips bacon

● Pound and score flank steak. Sprinkle with garlic salt and generous amounts of parsley and chives.

● Cook strips of bacon until almost done, then lay them crosswise on flank steak and roll it up like a jellyroll, starting with the narrow end.

● Cut roll in 1-inch slices. Secure ends with toothpicks. Broil on each side and serve with Beárnaise Sauce, if desired.

Beárnaise Sauce

¼ cup white wine vinegar
¼ cup dry white wine
1 tablespoon minced shallots
1 tablespoon minced fresh tarragon or ½ tablespoon dried
⅛ teaspoon pepper
dash salt
3 egg yolks
½ cup melted clarified butter
2 tablespoons minced fresh tarragon or parsley

● Boil vinegar, wine, shallots, tarragon, salt and pepper over medium heat until liquid is reduced to 2 tablespoons; cool and strain. Over hot water in a double boiler, beat egg yolks and strained vinegar mixture until thickened.

● Add clarified butter by droplets, beating constantly. Continue cooking until sauce reaches desired thickness. Add 2 tablespoons minced tarragon or parsley to the finished sauce.

BARBECUED BEEF BRISKET

"Barbecued" in the oven for year-round pleasure.

6 lbs. lean brisket of beef
garlic salt, onion salt, celery
  salt
3 oz. liquid smoke
salt and pepper
Worcestershire sauce
6 oz. barbecue sauce
2 tablespoons flour
½ cup water
¼ teaspoon Tabasco sauce

- Sprinkle brisket generously on all sides with garlic, onion and celery salts. Pour liquid smoke over roast and cover completely with foil. Refrigerate overnight.

- When ready to bake brisket, sprinkle all sides with salt and pepper to taste and a little Worcestershire sauce. Cover with foil, including sides of pan to seal, and bake at 275 degrees for 5 hours. Do not uncover.

- After 5 hours, add barbecue sauce and bake 1 more hour, covered with the foil. Remove meat from sauce and let stand at least 1 hour before cutting.

- Skim and discard fat from the sauce; whisk in flour, water and Tabasco sauce. Cook to thicken sauce and serve over sliced meat.

Note: Good with hot German potato salad, green beans, rye bread. Also excellent for sandwiches.

PAPRIKA BEEF ROLL

Serves 6

This takes practice but is worth the effort.

3 lbs. round steak
salt, pepper and paprika
¼ to ½ lb. mushrooms,
  sliced
2 onions, sliced
1 jar (2 oz.) sliced pimiento
bread crumbs
½ cup butter or bacon
  drippings, melted
1 tablespoon boiling water
1 egg
1 jar (4 oz.) stuffed green
  olives
¼ cup butter
6 whole mushrooms
3 small whole onions
1 cup red wine

● Pound steaks until quite thin;
  rub in salt, pepper and paprika to
  taste.

● Form one large steak by arranging steaks in a single layer, overlapping edges and pressing to
  seal. Spread with sliced mushrooms, sliced onions and
  pimiento. Cover with bread
  crumbs.

● Beat together ½ cup butter,
  water and egg and dribble
  mixture over bread crumbs.
  Arrange olives in a row on long
  side of overlapped meat. Roll
  meat around olives and tie firmly
  in several places.

● Flour outside of the roll. Brown
  in butter or bacon drippings in a
  heavy roaster pan. Sprinkle with
  salt, pepper and paprika to taste.
  Add red wine, whole mushrooms
  and onions. Roast, uncovered, at
  350 degrees for 2 hours. Can be
  served hot or cold.

PIQUANT BROILED STEAK

Serves 4 to 6

Easy, but very impressive.

1 large porterhouse steak,
  1½-inch thick
olive oil
fresh ginger, minced
hickory flavored salt
garlic powder
½ teaspoon freshly ground
  pepper
4 tablespoons butter,
  softened
1 teaspoon dry mustard
2 teaspoons Worcestershire
  sauce
½ teaspoon paprika

● Rub olive oil into both sides of steak. Let stand at room temperature for at least 1 hour. Just before broiling, sprinkle one side with fresh ginger.

● Broil, seasoned side to the heat, for 6 minutes. Sprinkle with smoked salt, pepper and garlic powder. Turn and sprinkle uncooked side with same seasonings and broil 4 minutes.

● Make a paste of butter, dry mustard, Worcestershire sauce and paprika. Remove meat to a hot platter. Spread half the butter paste over each side of hot steak and serve.

FILLET OF BEEF MOZZARELLA

Serves 12

An Italian variation of the well-known German favorite. Excellent!

12 (4 oz. each) fillets of beef
¾ teaspoon salt
freshly ground pepper
3 cloves garlic, minced
24 thin slices prosciutto
12 thin slices mozzarella
    cheese
6 tablespoons thin slices
    truffle or mushrooms
3 teaspoons chopped fresh
    parsley
3 tablespoons grated
    Romano cheese
9 eggs, well-beaten
¾ cup milk
2¼ cups fine bread crumbs
9 tablespoons clarified
    butter
6 tablespoons olive oil
juice of 3 lemons
¾ cup dry white wine
¾ cup chicken broth
watercress or curly endive
    sprigs

- Preheat oven to 375 degrees. Heat a large serving platter and keep it warm. Horizontally slice each fillet butterfly-style and leave one edge intact, so fillet is not completely cut through. Season with salt, pepper and garlic.

- In the center of each fillet place 2 slices prosciutto, 1 slice mozzarella and several slices of truffle or mushrooms. Close halves of each fillet like a sandwich. Press meat together around edges to seal.

- Beat parsley and grated cheese into eggs. Dip fillets into milk, then into bread crumbs and finally into egg mixture. Heat butter and oil in sauté pan until bubbling hot. Add fillets and cook over low heat until browned, turning once.

- Drain off cooking fat. Add lemon juice, wine and chicken broth to pan and place in preheated oven for approximately 10 minutes (less time is required for rare, longer for well done).

- To serve, place meat on heated platter, pour pan juices over and garnish with sprigs of watercress or endive.

BEEF PARMESAN

Serves 6

Like Italian? You'll love this!

1½ lbs. round steak
1 egg, beaten
⅓ cup freshly grated
 Parmesan cheese
⅓ cup dry bread crumbs
⅓ cup vegetable oil
1 medium onion, finely
 chopped
½ teaspoon salt
¼ teaspoon pepper
⅓ cup sugar
1 can (6 oz.) tomato paste
2 cups hot water
½ lb. mozzarella or
 Monterey jack cheese,
 shredded

● Flatten meat to ½-inch thickness; cut into 6 to 8 pieces. Beat egg with a fork. Mix together Parmesan cheese and bread crumbs.

● Dip meat first into egg and then in crumb mixture. Brown in skillet with ⅓ cup hot oil; place meat in 9x13-inch baking dish.

● In remaining oil, sauté onion. Add salt, pepper, sugar, tomato paste and water; boil 5 minutes.

● Pour half the sauce over meat. Cover with cheese and then with remaining sauce. Bake at 300 degrees for 1½ hours.

GREEN PEPPER STEAK
Serves 4

1½ lbs. top round or sirloin steak (1-inch thick)
¼ cup vegetable oil
1 cup water
1 medium onion, sliced ¼-inch thick
2 medium green peppers, sliced ¼-inch thick
½ teaspoon garlic salt
¼ teaspoon ground ginger
1 tablespoon cornstarch
2 to 3 tablespoons sugar
2 to 3 tablespoons soy sauce
2 medium tomatoes, wedged

● Trim fat from meat; cut into strips 2x¼-inch. Heat oil and brown meat.

● Stir in water, onion, garlic salt and ginger. Bring to a boil, reduce heat, cover and simmer 12 to 14 minutes for round or 5 to 8 minutes for sirloin. Add green pepper during last few minutes of cooking.

● Blend cornstarch, sugar and soy sauce and stir into meat mixture. Cook until thickened and sauce is clear. Add tomatoes just to heat. Serve over rice.

SWEET-AND-SOUR BEEF
Serves 4 to 6

Especially delicious with poppy seed noodles.

2 lb. boneless rump or chuck beef, cut in 1-inch cubes
⅓ cup flour
1 teaspoon salt
¼ teaspoon pepper
2 tablespoons oil
½ cup catsup
¼ cup red wine vinegar
¼ cup firmly packed brown sugar
1 teaspoon salt
1 tablespoon Worcestershire sauce
1 cup water
1 large onion, chopped
4 large carrots, cut into 2-inch lengths

● Dredge beef cubes in mixture of flour, salt and pepper. Brown in hot oil in Dutch oven. Combine remaining ingredients, except carrots, and pour over meat.

● Cover pan and simmer for 1½ hours. Add carrots and cook one more hour. Serve over rice or noodles.

BEEF MARSALA

Serves 6

Wonderfully hearty dish for a cold winter's evening.

1½ lb. top-round beef steak
1 egg
3 tablespoons milk
¼ cup grated Parmesan
   cheese
1¼ cups dried bread crumbs
1 teaspoon salt
⅛ teaspoon pepper
¾ cup butter or margarine
1 clove garlic, sliced
¾ cup water
2 teaspoons flour
½ cup Marsala wine
¼ cup parsley, minced
1 cube beef-flavored bouillon

● Pound beef to ⅛-inch thickness. Cut into 4x2-inch pieces. Beat egg and milk together.

● On waxed paper, combine cheese, bread crumbs, salt and pepper. Dip meat in egg, then coat with crumb mixture.

● In a 12-inch skillet over medium heat, melt 2 tablespoons butter. Add garlic and ⅓ of the meat; cook until lightly browned. Remove meat to a platter and keep warm. Repeat with remaining meat, using ½ cup butter in all.

● Discard garlic and melt remaining butter in skillet; add water and flour (mixed together), Marsala, parsley and bouillon cube. Cook, stirring until thickened; pour over meat to serve.

WALLOWA LAKE LODGE, Joseph

High in Oregon's Wallowa Mountains is a well-kept secret spot that many Oregonians escape to each summer: Wallowa Lake Lodge.

Here, in the Eagle Cap Wilderness, more than 50 mountain lakes, scores of alpine waterfalls and rushing streams, and great snow-peaks contribute to the rugged grandeur of the area. Fishing in the lakes is generally good to excellent, with an abundance of eastern brook trout and golden, lake, and rainbow trout. Interesting geological formations can be found on a number of peaks, and a riotous display of wildflowers covers the meadows and hillsides during the summer months.

Wallowa Lake Lodge is a large woodframe clapboard building constructed in 1923 and now housing a dining room, a lounge with a bar, a gift shop, a massive stone fireplace, and 31 guest rooms—15 private rooms with bath and eight two-room connecting suites. Approximately half the rooms view the majestic Wallowas, while the other half view the cool blue expanse of Wallowa Lake. Surrounding the Lodge and lake are eight cabins equipped with kitchens, fireplaces, and baths.

Rustic serenity is the magic attraction of this high-mountain retreat. Guests can enjoy fishing, water skiing, and swimming in the lake. Pack trips and hikes into the surrounding area are available for the energetic. And, for the young or just young-at-heart, there are activities such as biking, miniature golf, go karts, and roller skating.

Dining in the Lodge offers gourmet-style meals in portions large enough to satisfy hungry appetites. Dress is casual to accommodate outdoor-oriented wardrobes.

For additional information:
Wallowa Lake Lodge
Rt. 1, Box 320
Joseph, OR 97846
(503) 432-9821

SWEET-AND-SOUR BEEF

Serves 12

From the Dining Room of Wallowa Lake Lodge

5 lbs. lean beef, cubed
½ cup flour
2 teaspoons salt
1 teaspoon pepper
2 medium onions, chopped

● Dredge meat in mixture of flour, salt and pepper. Place meat in a large baking pan; sprinkle with chopped onion.

● Pour Sweet-and-Sour Sauce over all and bake at 350 degrees for 2 hours or until tender. Add water as needed during cooking to prevent burning. Serve with rice or noodles.

Sweet-and-Sour Sauce

1½ cups catsup
¾ cup sugar
¼ cup vinegar
1½ cups water
¼ cup Worcestershire sauce
½ cup soy sauce

● Combine ingredients, stirring to dissolve sugar.

Note: For maximum flavor, prepare the day before and reheat.

SWEET-AND-SOUR MEATBALLS

Serves 6

A very unusual sauce makes these special.

2 lbs. ground beef
2 eggs, beaten
½ cup water
1 envelope (1 oz.) onion soup
  mix

● Mix all ingredients together, form into balls and brown quickly in hot oil. Pour half of Sauce into bottom of 13x9-inch baking pan. Add browned meatballs; top with rest of Sauce.

● Cover with foil and bake at 325 degrees for 20 minutes. Uncover and bake for 15 to 20 minutes more or until sauce is thick and glazed. Serve over rice.

Sauerkraut Sauce

1 can (16 oz.) sauerkraut,
  drained and chopped
1 can (8 oz.) whole
  cranberry sauce
¾ cup water
¾ cup chili sauce
⅓ cup firmly packed brown
  sugar

● Mix all ingredients well.

HAMBURGER QUICHE

Serves 6 to 8

A good entrée from inexpensive ingredients.

1 (8- or 9-inch) unbaked pie
  shell
¾ lb. lean ground beef
½ cup mayonnaise
½ cup milk
2 eggs
1 tablespoon cornstarch
1½ cups shredded Cheddar
  and/or Swiss cheese
½ cup chopped onion
dash pepper

● Brown meat over medium heat; drain off fat. Pat dry with paper towel. Blend next 4 ingredients with whisk until smooth.

● Stir in meat, shredded cheese, onion and pepper. Turn into pastry shell. Bake at 350 degrees for 35 minutes, or until golden brown and knife inserted in center comes out clean.

Note: For 10-inch pie, make 1½ recipe. Excellent frozen and reheated.

STUFFED PASTA SHELLS

Serves 4 to 6

Can prepare ahead and refrigerate till ready to bake.

25 jumbo pasta shells
(2-inch shells for stuffing)
¾ lb. lean ground beef
¼ cup minced onion
⅓ cup bread crumbs
⅓ cup grated Parmesan
cheese
3 eggs, beaten
¾ package (10 oz.) frozen
chopped spinach, thawed
and drained
1 teaspoon salt
¼ teaspoon pepper
16 oz. spaghetti sauce
1 can (8 oz.) tomato sauce
6 oz. mozzarella cheese,
shredded

● Parboil pasta for 9 minutes;
drain. Brown beef and onion;
drain fat and mix with bread
crumbs, Parmesan cheese, eggs,
spinach, salt and pepper. Stuff
into shells.

● Mix spaghetti sauce and tomato
sauce; pour one cup into a
shallow baking dish. Arrange
stuffed shells over sauce. Pour
remaining sauce over all; top
with cheese.

● Cover and bake at 350 degrees
for 30 to 45 minutes or until hot
and bubbly; uncover the last 5
minutes.

FLYING M RANCH, Yamhill

Tucked away in the rolling foothills of the Coast Range is a rustic dude ranch that began some 110 years ago as a hotel for stage-coach-weary passengers: Flying M Ranch.

Visitors fly in and land on the Ranch's turf airstrip or arrive by more conventional means, the automobile. Ahead of them is a vacation that features quiet country living amid a spectacular wooded setting . . . and lots of horse-oriented activities.

The Flying M is located at the edge of a meadow where the North Yamhill River and Hanna Creek join. At the heart of the ranch is a beautiful spacious lodge constructed of golden Douglas fir logs, a sparkling new structure just recently built to replace the original lodge which burned down in 1983. Nighttime finds the lodge alive with the music of a country-western band.

With horses an integral part of ranch life, guests can enjoy one-hour and overnight trail rides and rides to the beach on the old stage road. Trails meander along the river and up to Trask Mountain. Overnight trips feature hearty wrangler-style breakfasts, satisfying sack lunches, and nightly homestyle feasts . . . with grilled-to-perfection steaks and a seafood barbecue on the beach ride.

Guest accommodations on the Ranch include campsites, cabins and "motel rooms." Cabins sleep eight and contain kitchens and sleeping lofts. Motel rooms are built like an old-fashioned bunkhouse, with queen-size beds and private bath in each.

Other activities on the Ranch include camping, picnicking, and tennis. Swimming in the city-block-long pond is a fun sport for the whole family.

Food at the Flying M dining room tends to be hearty, homestyle, and delicious. Homemade biscuits and gravy at the Sunday breakfast are a special treat.

For additional information:
Flying M Ranch
23029 NW Flying M Rd.
Yamhill, OR 97148
(503) 662-3222

FLYING M BEEF ROLL

Serves 10 to 14

From the Dining Room of the Flying M Ranch

5 lbs. lean ground beef
3 eggs
1 tablespoon salt
1 teaspoon pepper
1 teaspoon sweet basil
1 teaspoon oregano
2 teaspoons freshly chopped
   parsley
½ cup finely chopped onion
½ cup diced green pepper
1 clove garlic, minced
¼ cup catsup
1 cup dry bread crumbs
¾ lb. trimmed ham, sliced
¾ lb. Swiss cheese, sliced

● Mix all ingredients thoroughly except ham and cheese; shape into a rectangle about ¼-inch thick. Lay slices of ham and cheese over surface, leaving a narrow border.

● Roll meat tightly from long side; place in a baking pan. Bake at 350 degrees for 1 hour. Serve with Spanish Sauce.

(continued)

FLYING M BEEF ROLL (continued)

Spanish Sauce

vegetable oil
½ medium onion, chopped
2 stalks celery, chopped
½ green pepper, chopped
½ clove garlic, minced
2 cups chopped tomatoes
1 cup beef stock
½ bay leaf
pinch of thyme
1 teaspoon sugar
cornstarch

● Sauté onion, celery, green pepper and garlic in a small amount of oil. When vegetables are tender, add tomatoes, stock, bay leaf, thyme and sugar. Simmer 30 minutes. Mix cornstarch with a little water; stir enough into sauce to thicken it.

CHILI CON CARNE   Serves 4 to 6

Make the day before to allow flavors to meld.

3½ lb. top round, cut into
    ½-inch cubes
5 tablespoons vegetable oil
2 cups coarsely chopped
    onion
4 cloves garlic, minced
2 tablespoons chili powder
1½ teaspoons oregano
2 teaspoons ground cumin
1 teaspoon crushed dried
    red pepper, or more to
    taste
2 cups beef broth
1 can (28 oz.) whole
    tomatoes
1 can (6 oz.) tomato paste
1 tablespoon salt
1 teaspoon sugar
1 to 2 tablespoons yellow
    cornmeal, if needed

● Heat 3 tablespoons oil in a large heavy pan. Add meat and sear it until all pieces are browned.

● Remove meat; add remaining oil and sauté onion and garlic. Stir in chili powder, oregano, cumin and red pepper. Add broth, tomatoes and their juice, tomato paste, salt and sugar and blend well.

● Add meat to the sauce, cover and simmer 1 hour. Uncover and simmer for 40 to 50 minutes, or until meat is tender.

● Cool, cover and refrigerate overnight. To serve, heat slowly; if necessary, thicken with cornmeal. Serve with rice.

BARBECUED MANDARIN PORK

12 thick pork chops,
  trimmed of all fat and
  boned
1 cup apple juice
½ cup soy sauce
½ cup honey
2 cloves garlic, crushed
½ teaspoon powdered
  ginger
1 tablespoon dry mustard
dash Worcestershire sauce
½ cup dark rum

- Combine all ingredients except pork chops; marinate pork in mixture overnight in refrigerator. Drain and reserve marinade.

- Grill chops over medium hot coals until done, basting frequently with Apple Basting Sauce. Arrange meat on a heated platter and pour remaining sauce over to serve.

Apple Basting Sauce

reserved marinade
1 cup apple jelly
¼ cup soy sauce
2 tablespoons fresh lemon
  juice

- Bring all ingredients except lemon juice to a boil in a small saucepan and reduce by about ⅓. Add lemon juice.

PORK TURNOVERS

Serves 4 to 6

Similar to Cornish pasties but easier. Good for tailgate parties and picnics.

1 tablespoon vegetable oil
½ lb. lean ground pork
1 medium onion, chopped
1 clove garlic, minced
2 teaspoons chili powder
1 teaspoon curry powder
salt and pepper to taste
1 green pepper, chopped
1 green apple, chopped
¼ lb. Monterey jack cheese, shredded

- Sauté pork and onion in oil; drain off any fat. Add garlic and seasonings; stir to mix. Add remaining ingredients and set aside.

- Divide Pastry in half and roll each into a 9-inch circle on a baking sheet. Spoon half the filling over each and fold circle in half. Crimp edges to seal. (Can be refrigerated at this point.)

- Bake at 425 degrees for 20 minutes. Serve hot or at room temperature.

Pastry

2 cups flour
⅔ cup shortening
½ teaspoon salt
3 to 4 tablespoons cold water

- Cut shortening into flour and add salt. Add water, a little at a time, to form dough.

Note: Ground beef may be substituted for the pork. Add 1 beef bouillon cube to the meat mixture.

STIR-FRY PORK

Serves 6

6 pork loin chops
2 tablespoons soy sauce
1 teaspoon sesame oil
¼ teaspoon pepper
1 tablespoon cornstarch
¾ cup plus 1 tablespoon
  vegetable oil
10 oz. snow pea pods, fresh
  or frozen
¼ cup water
1 16-oz. can apricot halves,
  drained, with ¼ cup syrup
  reserved
1 teaspoon cornstarch
1 cup cashews

● Trim fat from pork, cube and pound to thin strips. Mix together soy sauce, sesame oil, pepper and 1 tablespoon cornstarch. Add meat and let marinate 15 minutes.

● Heat a wok or electric frypan to high and add ¾ cup oil. Brown meat, cooking it in oil for about 3 to 4 minutes; remove and drain meat. Discard oil and wipe out wok.

● Heat 1 tablespoon oil in wok; add snow peas and cook 30 seconds. Add water; cover and steam for 30 seconds. Add meat and apricots, cook another 30 seconds.

● Dissolve 1 teaspoon cornstarch in reserved ¼ cup apricot syrup and add to meat; cook until thick and clear. Serve over hot rice, garnished with cashews.

DIAMOND LAKE RESORT, Diamond Lake

High in the heart of the Cascade Mountains, Diamond Lake Resort sits nestled on the shores of crystal clear Diamond Lake.

The lake and the surrounding Umpqua National Forest offer multiple activities to keep vacationers happy throughout the year. In summer and fall, guests can enjoy fishing for rainbow trout, swimming, camping, sailboarding, hiking, horseback riding, and hunting. The Resort's marina rents fishing boats, canoes, and sailboards; fishing and hunting guides are also available. Twice a day a charter boat offers trout fishing trips, and in the evening there's a scenic boat tour around the lake.

Winter's cold weather brings downhill skiing on Mt. Bailey (intermediate and advanced), snowmobiling, cross country skiing, and just sitting by a crackling fire in the Lodge. The Resort has more than 200 miles of groomed snowmobile trails and offers several snowmobile tours.

Lodging at Diamond Lake Resort includes spacious cabins or motel sleeping units. Cabins, some with fireplaces, are available in the woods or on the lake.

Guests can choose from three restaurants at Diamond Lake Resort: the Lodge Cafe, the Diamond Room Lounge, or the South Shore Pizza Parlor. During winter, guests can ride the Pizza Express sleigh ride to the pizza parlor. All three restaurants offer excellent eating fare to satisfy every kind of taste.

For additional information:
Diamond Lake Resort
Diamond Lake, OR 97731
(503) 793-3333

DIAMOND LAKE SPECIAL PIZZA

Yields 3 large pizzas

From the Dining Room of Diamond Lake Resort

4 cups flour
1 teaspoon salt
2 tablespoons sugar
¼ cup dry milk
4 tablespoons shortening
4 tablespoons yeast
2¼ cups water
shredded American cheese
shredded mozzarella cheese

● Mix flour, salt, sugar, dry milk and shortening together for 5 minutes. Combine yeast and water; add to dry mixture and blend well. Let rise twice.

● Roll dough to ¼-inch thickness; shape to fit three pizza pans. Spread Pizza Sauce over dough; cover with a mixture of cheeses. Arrange Toppings of choice over cheese. Bake at 425 degrees for 20 to 25 minutes.

(continued)

DIAMOND LAKE SPECIAL PIZZA (continued)

Pizza Sauce

1 onion, finely chopped
½ cup finely chopped celery
¼ cup vegetable oil
3 cans (8 oz. each) tomato
  sauce
3 cans (6 oz. each) tomato
  paste
1 can (16 oz.) whole
  tomatoes crushed
1 teaspoon oregano
½ teaspoon basil
¼ cup parsley flakes
½ teaspoon garlic
½ teaspoon pepper
½ teaspoon salt
½ teaspoon sugar

• Sauté onion and celery in oil in large pan; add remaining ingredients. Bring to a boil, then simmer for 1 hour. Adjust seasonings to taste.

Pizza Toppings

3 cups cooked sausage
3 cups sliced pepperoni
1 cup chopped onions
2 cups sliced mushrooms
2 cups sliced black olives
2 cups chopped green
  pepper

• Add or delete toppings to suit your taste.

NOODLES ALFREDO   Serves 4

Be sure to use *freshly* grated Parmesan for best flavor.

1 lb. egg noodles
¼ lb. ham, cut in ⅛x3-inch
  strips
¼ lb. cooked turkey or
  chicken breast, cut in ⅛x3-
  inch strips
4 tablespoons butter
4 egg yolks
1 cup heavy cream
4 oz. Parmesan cheese,
  freshly grated
salt and pepper to taste

• Warm serving bowl and plates. Cook noodles in salted boiling water until tender (about 5 minutes); drain. Melt butter in a skillet and brown ham and turkey lightly. Add drained noodles and heat through.

• Blend cream and egg yolks; toss with noodles until liquid is absorbed. Season with Parmesan, salt and pepper and serve.

PASTA WITH FRESH ASPARAGUS   Serves 4 to 6

Delightful way to welcome spring.

¼ cup butter
½ cup chopped onion
½ cup chicken broth
½ to 1 lb. fresh asparagus,
  chopped or thinly sliced
1½ cups chopped cooked
  ham
1 tablespoon flour
2 tablespoons butter,
  melted
¾ cup heavy cream
salt and white pepper
½ lb. spaghetti or fettucini
¼ cup grated Parmesan
  cheese

● Heat butter; add onion and
sauté until soft. Add broth and
boil slowly until slightly reduced.
Add asparagus and simmer until
tender yet crisp.

● Add ham and then flour mixed
with melted butter. Blend well
and add cream; cook until
thickened. Season with salt and
pepper to taste.

● Cook pasta in salted boiling
water until done; drain and place
in warmed bowl. Pour sauce over
and toss to blend. Sprinkle with
grated cheese.

Note: The amount of ham above is for an entrée-size serving. For a
pasta course, decrease the amount to ¼ cup ham.

DIJONNAISE-GLAZED ROAST   Serves 6
LEG OF LAMB

1 (6 to 8 lb.) leg of lamb
1 clove garlic, slivered
½ cup Dijon mustard
½ teaspoon ground ginger
1 tablespoon vegetable oil
2 tablespoons soy sauce
1 teaspoon fresh or dried
  rosemary or thyme
sliced onions, green peppers
  and carrots

● Insert garlic slivers in gashes cut
deep in leg of lamb. Mix mustard
and ginger and beat in oil by
droplets to make a mayonnaise-
like sauce. Add soy sauce and
herbs and paint lamb with sauce.
Marinate for 3 to 4 hours.

● Place lamb on a bed of sliced
vegetables in a large baking pan.
Roast at 350 degrees for 1½
hours for a pinkish roast or for
2½ hours for well-done.

SHERRY-GLAZED ROAST LEG OF LAMB

Serves 6 to 8

1 (5 to 6 lb.) leg of lamb
1 clove garlic, slivered
3 to 4 sprigs fresh mint or
  1 teaspoon dried
½ teaspoon powdered
  thyme
salt and pepper
1 medium onion, cut in
  eighths
⅓ cup sherry
⅓ cup mint or currant jelly

● Make gashes in roast near the bone and insert slivers of garlic. Mix thyme, mint, salt and pepper; rub into roast.

● Place roast on bed of onions in a roasting pan. Bake at 325 degrees for 35 minutes per pound for rare or 40 minutes per pound for well-done.

● Mix together sherry and jelly. About ½ hour before roast is done, cover it with sherry-jelly mixture. This gives the roast a beautiful glaze and flavors the drippings for gravy.

BUTTERFLIED LEG OF LAMB

Serves 6 to 8

1 whole leg of lamb,
  butterflied
2 tablespoons Dijon
  mustard
½ teaspoon salt
¼ teaspoon pepper
4 tablespoons brown sugar
2 tablespoons soy sauce
2 tablespoons vegetable oil
1 clove garlic, crushed
⅓ cup lemon juice

● Combine all ingredients except lamb. Brush lamb with sauce mixture and roast at 450 degrees for 35 minutes or barbecue over medium hot coals. Baste with sauce frequently.

● Allow lamb to rest 5 minutes before slicing across the grain. The meat should be served rare to medium.

LAMB SHISH KEBABS

Serves 8 to 12

Three days of marinating makes this extra flavorful and tender.

1 (6 lb.) leg of lamb
3 to 4 cloves garlic, crushed
1½ teaspoons salt
1 bay leaf
½ teaspoon each pepper, ground cloves, ground allspice, ground ginger
1 cup sour cream
small boiling onions, peeled
green pepper, chunked
cherry tomatoes
large mushrooms

● Cut meat into 2-inch cubes. Combine seasonings and sour cream; marinate meat cubes in mixture for 3 days, refrigerated.

● Thread meat cubes and prepared vegetables alternately on skewers. Broil over hot coals until meat is brown and vegetables are cooked (meat should still be slightly pink inside).

BARBECUED LAMB

Serves 10 to 12

Can be skewered and cooked over hot coals or roasted whole in the oven.

10 lb. boneless lamb from the leg, cut into uniform-sized chunks or left whole
2 onions, chopped
3 cups dry red wine
1 clove garlic, chopped
6 tablespoons Worcestershire sauce
1 cup fresh lemon juice
salt and pepper to taste

● Thoroughly combine all ingredients except lamb; pour over lamb and marinate for 48 hours to meld flavors. To barbecue, thread lamb on skewers and cook over hot coals until browned to desired doneness.

● To roast, bake at 375 degrees to desired doneness. Use a meat thermometer to check internal temperature.

143

STEAMBOAT INN, Idleyld Park

A food-fancier's find where the summer fishing just happens to be spectacular too is Steamboat Inn, 38 miles east of Roseburg.

Perched among a forest of towering Douglas firs, this cozy country inn is right on the banks of the magnificent North Umpqua, a summer steelheading river known around the world for its challenging fishing. Steamboat is in the middle of a 31-mile stretch designated fly fishing only, so the fishermen who head here are serious indeed.

The average summer steelhead caught in this area is eight pounds, but an occasional lucky angler will reel in fish up to 15 pounds. So dedicated are these fishermen that most of them choose to just chortle in delight over their catch and then release it to provide sport for another day. Famous avid fishermen who have frequented this river include Zane Grey, Jack Hemingway, Herman Melville, and Dick Hugo.

Steamboat Inn is a friendly, unpretentious wood-and-rock structure that houses the dining room and a well-stocked fly shop. Guests—who come from around the world—gather here to swap fish stories and learn about each other's varied interests.

144

Eight pine-paneled cabins for guests are located below the Inn, successfully hidden in the trees and even closer to the river. A common veranda allows guests to sit outside and enjoy the forest sights and sounds.

Other activities within the nearby area include floating and swimming on nearby Canton and Steamboat Creeks and hiking on nature trails in a "botanist's wonderland." Steamboat can also arrange for fishing guides or for float trips on the lower Umpqua.

Outstanding though the fishing may be in these parts, not all visitors come here for that; many are lured by Steamboat's reputation for outstanding gourmet food, rated again and again as some of Oregon's best. Each summer evening (and winter weekend), the Fisherman's Dinner is proudly presented to guests, who sit at a 20-foot-long table. Fare varies each night and might include such entrées as Chicken Breasts with Prosciutto and Fontina, Tournedos Medoc, or Pork Tenderloin with Sour Cream Sauce.

For additonal information:
Steamboat Inn
Steamboat, OR 97447
(503) 496-3495
(503) 498-2411

(See recipe on next page)

SEASONED LAMB IN PHYLLO

Serves 3 to 6

From the Dining Room of Steamboat Inn

1 lb. ground lamb
1 egg
4 green onions, minced
½ cup minced parsley
1 large clove garlic, minced
1 teaspoon ground cumin
½ teaspoon freshly ground
  pepper
salt to taste
¼ cup butter
1 oz. pine nuts
8 to 10 small mushroom
  caps, quartered
1 large carrot, cut in 1-inch
  julienne strips and cooked
  until tender
1 package (10 oz.) frozen
  chopped spinach, thawed
  and squeezed dry
2 oz. feta cheese
⅛ teaspoon freshly grated
  nutmeg
salt and freshly ground
  pepper
2 egg whites, lightly beaten
6 sheets phyllo dough
¼ cup melted butter

● Combine lamb, egg, green onion, parsley, garlic, cumin, pepper and salt. Divide and shape into 3x4x½-inch thick patties.

● Sauté in a hot skillet just long enough to sear both sides. Drain and reserve. Melt 1 tablespoon butter in a skillet and toast pine nuts lightly. Remove from pan and set aside.

● Melt remaining 3 tablespoons butter and sauté mushrooms. Add pine nuts and remaining ingredients except phyllo and ¼ cup melted butter.

● Place one sheet phyllo dough on work surface. Brush with melted butter and top with a second sheet.

● Working lengthwise with dough, place a lamb pattie ¼ of the way down from the top edge, top with ⅓ of the spinach mixture. Fold top edge of pastry over filling; brush with butter. Fold sides inward and roll up, brushing final fold with butter.

● Repeat with remaining patties. Place on an ungreased baking sheet, brushing tops with butter. Bake at 400 degrees for 20 minutes. Remove, cut diagonally and serve.

KHEEMA
(CURRIED GROUND LAMB)

A spicy and unusual treatment of lamb.

1 lb. ground lamb (or beef)
3 large onions
3 tablespoons peanut oil
1 tablespoon chopped fresh
   ginger
1 clove garlic, minced
1 teaspoon salt
1 tablespoon curry powder
¼ teaspoon ground
   cinnamon
½ teaspoon ground turmeric
½ teaspoon ground
   coriander
½ teaspoon ground cumin
¼ teaspoon crushed hot red
   pepper flakes (optional)
freshly ground pepper to
   taste
2 tablespoons plain yogurt
4 cups chopped peeled
   tomatoes
cooked rice
3 tablespoons finely
   chopped fresh coriander,
   if available, or substitute
   parsley

● Peel onions, cut and slice lengthwise into paper-thin slivers. Heat
oil and add 1 cup of onions. Fry
10 to 15 minutes, until richly
browned and somewhat crisp.
Transfer to bowl lined with paper
towels and reserve for later.

● Add remaining onions, ginger,
garlic and salt to the oil and cook
over medium heat, stirring
constantly, for 7 to 8 minutes or
until onions are soft and golden
brown. Add meat and continue
cooking, stirring, until there is no
trace of pink in the meat.

● Mix together curry powder,
cinnamon, turmeric, coriander,
cumin, red pepper and pepper;
add to meat and cook 3 to 4
minutes to bring out the flavors.

● Add yogurt and tomatoes and
bring to a boil, stirring
constantly. Reduce heat, cover
and simmer 10 minutes. Serve
over rice, topped with chopped
fresh coriander or parsley and the
reserved fried onions.

HAWAIIAN CHICKEN
Serves 8

Exotic and easy to assemble.

4 large chicken breasts,
  boned, skinned and halved
dash salt
1 tablespoon sesame seeds

● Flatten chicken breasts between sheets of waxed paper. Sprinkle lightly with salt. Top each piece with some of Pork and Veal Stuffing. Roll up and place seam side down in a greased baking dish.

● Spread Honey Butter Sauce over the breasts. Bake at 325 degrees for 35 to 45 minutes, basting with the juices, until chicken is fully cooked and tender. Sprinkle with sesame seeds. Turn oven up to 450 degrees and bake 10 minutes or until well browned. Watch carefully to prevent burning.

Pork and Veal Stuffing

¼ cup light cream
1 cup fresh bread crumbs
2 tablespoons butter
⅓ cup finely chopped onion
1 can (5 oz.) water
  chestnuts, drained and
  finely chopped
1 teaspoon ground ginger
¼ lb. ground veal
½ lb. ground pork
1 egg
1 tablespoon soy sauce
⅛ teaspoon cayenne pepper

● Pour cream over bread crumbs and let soak. Sauté onion and water chestnuts in butter. Add bread crumbs and remaining ingredients, mixing well.

Honey Butter Sauce

4 tablespoons butter,
  softened
2 tablespoons honey
2 tablespoons soy sauce

● Cream butter and honey together. Slowly beat in soy sauce.

Note: If there is extra stuffing, form it into small balls and bake with the chicken.

CHICKEN BREASTS WITH ORANGE SAUCE

Serves 6

3 whole chicken breasts,
  split
½ teaspoon salt
1 medium onion, sliced
¼ cup chopped green
  pepper
1 cup sliced mushrooms
paprika
orange slices

● Place chicken breasts skin side up on a broiler rack and broil 10 minutes or until brown. Do not turn. Place browned chicken in a shallow baking pan or casserole. Sprinkle with salt and top with the onion, green pepper and mushrooms.

● Pour Orange Sauce over and bake at 375 degrees for 45 minutes or until tender. Baste several times during cooking. Serve garnished with paprika and orange slices.

Orange Sauce

1 cup orange juice
¼ cup dry sherry
½ cup water
1 tablespoon firmly packed
  brown sugar
1 teaspoon salt
¼ teaspoon pepper
1 teaspoon grated fresh
  orange rind
1 tablespoon flour
2 teaspoons chopped parsley

● Combine all sauce ingredients and simmer until slightly thickened.

AUTUMN FRUITED CHICKEN

Serves 6

12 pieces chicken
½ cup flour
½ teaspoon salt
dash pepper
½ cup vegetable oil
1 tablespoon brandy
3 cloves garlic, minced
1 medium onion, minced
2 cups sliced fresh
  mushrooms
1½ cups apple wine
2 each fresh pears and
  apples, peeled and quartered, rinsed in lemon
  water
2 teaspoons cornstarch
¼ cup water
cooked noodles or rice

● Dust chicken pieces in flour, salt and pepper and brown in half the oil; pour brandy over and flame. Set aside.

● Sauté the garlic and onion in remaining oil in a separate skillet. Place chicken, onion mixture, mushrooms and wine in a baking dish. Add pears and apples.

● Bake, covered, at 350 degrees for 30 minutes or until chicken is done. Remove chicken and fruit to a heated platter and thicken sauce with cornstarch which has been mixed with water. Serve over noodles or rice.

HERBED CHICKEN

Serves 6

3 chicken breasts, boned,
  skinned and halved
½ cup butter
salt and pepper
6 slices mozzarella cheese
flour
fresh bread crumbs
1 egg, beaten
2 tablespoons chopped
  parsley
¼ teaspoon rubbed sage
¼ teaspoon ground
  rosemary
¼ teaspoon dried thyme
½ cup dry white wine

● Flatten chicken pieces between sheets of waxed paper; spread with half the butter. Season with salt and pepper. Place one slice of cheese on each piece and roll up, tucking in edges. Coat each lightly with flour; dip into beaten egg and roll in bread crumbs.

● Arrange pieces in shallow baking dish. Melt the remaining butter and add the parsley, sage, rosemary and thyme. Bake chicken at 350 degrees for 30 minutes, basting with the seasoned butter. Pour wine over chicken and bake 20 minutes more. Baste several times with pan liquid during baking time.

PARTY-PERFECT CHICKEN

Serves 8

2 fryers, quartered, or
  4 whole chicken breasts,
  halved
6 tablespoons flour
1½ teaspoons salt
1 tablespoon ground ginger
6 tablespoons butter

- Prepare Curry Glaze.

- Shake chicken in flour, salt and ginger mixture. Melt butter in large baking pan and roll floured chicken in butter. Place skin side up in pan. Do not overlap pieces. Bake at 400 degrees for 20 minutes.

- Spoon half of Curry Glaze over meat and bake 20 minutes more. Spoon on remaining glaze and bake a final 20 minutes or until chicken is tender and slightly browned.

Curry Glaze

½ cup chopped onion
6 slices bacon, uncooked and
  diced
2 tablespoons flour
1 to 3 teaspoons curry
  powder
1 tablespoon sugar
1 can (10½ oz.) condensed
  beef broth
2 tablespoons coconut,
  shredded
2 tablespoons applesauce
2 tablespoons catsup
2 tablespoons lemon juice

- Combine glaze ingredients and simmer 15 minutes.

CHICKEN AU GRATIN

Serves 8 to 12

A wonderfully rich dish for special occasions.

8 whole chicken breasts,
split, boned and skinned
1½ lb. Jarlsberg cheese, cut
into 1x3-inch fingers
2 eggs, beaten
2 tablespoons milk
2 cups dry bread crumbs
1 cup freshly grated
Parmesan cheese
1 tablespoon chopped
parsley
pepper to taste
½ cup vegetable oil
2 pints heavy cream
¼ cup dry vermouth
½ lb. Jarlsberg cheese,
shredded
3 tablespoons chopped
parsley

● Pound the chicken breasts flat
and roll a finger of cheese inside
each. Secure with a toothpick.

● Combine the beaten eggs and
milk. Mix together bread crumbs,
Parmesan, 1 tablespoon chopped
parsley and pepper. Dip the
chicken pieces first in egg
mixture, then in crumb mixture
to coat completely. Brown
chicken in hot oil and place in
greased 9x13-inch baking dish.

● In a saucepan, heat the cream, 3
tablespoons chopped parsley,
vermouth and half the shredded
Jarlsberg. Pour this over the
chicken and top with the rest of
the shredded cheese. Bake at 350
degrees for 30 to 35 minutes.

CHICKEN WITH PEACHES

Serves 4 to 6

1 (3 lb.) chicken, cut into
serving pieces
½ cup flour
2 teaspoons salt
¼ teaspoon pepper
½ teaspoon paprika
½ cup shortening
1 cup orange juice
2 tablespoons firmly packed
brown sugar
2 tablespoons vinegar
1 teaspoon grated nutmeg
1 teaspoon dried basil
12 small potatoes
1 can (13 oz.) cling peach
halves, drained
parsley

● Lightly coat chicken with mixture of flour, salt, pepper and
paprika; sauté in shortening
until golden on all sides. Combine
orange juice, sugar, vinegar and
seasonings. Pour over chicken.

● Place potatoes between chicken
pieces and cook, covered, over
medium heat until tender, about
25 minutes. (Or bake at 350
degrees for 1 hour.) Add peaches,
heat 5 minutes and serve,
garnished with parsley.

SESAME CHICKEN

Serves 4 to 6

An easy dish the whole family will love.

3 to 4 chicken breasts
3 tablespoons vegetable oil
¼ cup sesame seeds
½ cup soy sauce
¼ cup firmly packed brown
  sugar
1 teaspoon ground ginger
½ teaspoon pepper
4 cloves garlic, minced
4 green onions, thinly sliced

● Skin and bone chicken breasts; cut into 1-inch chunks.

● In a large skillet, cook sesame seeds in oil over medium-low heat, stirring occasionally, until seeds are golden, about 2 minutes. Cool. Stir in soy sauce, sugar, ginger, pepper, garlic and half the green onions. Mix in chicken. Cover and chill 1 to 4 hours.

● Arrange meat in a single layer in a baking pan; pour marinade over meat. Broil 6 inches from heat until golden, about 10 minutes. Turn chicken and broil 5 minutes more or until meat is no longer pink inside. Serve with rice garnished with remaining sliced onions.

Note: This can be served without rice as an hors d'oeuvre.

153

CHICKEN BREASTS IN MUSHROOM CHIVE SAUCE

Serves 4 to 6

Great with spinach noodles.

4 whole chicken breasts,
  boned, skinned and halved
3 green onions, chopped
1 clove garlic, minced
1 lb. mushrooms, sliced
6 tablespoons butter
1 cup chicken broth
dash lemon juice
1 cup heavy cream
2 tablespoons butter
2 tablespoons flour
2 tablespoons finely
  chopped fresh chives
parsley for garnish
salt and pepper to taste

• Sauté onions, garlic and mushrooms in 2 tablespoons butter. Cook on high heat until mushrooms are lightly browned. Remove from pan.

• Melt 4 tablespoons butter in pan and sauté chicken until lightly browned. Remove from pan. Add broth and boil until reduced by half. Add lemon juice and cream. Reduce heat.

• In a separate pan, make a roux with 2 tablespoons butter and flour. Add roux to the cream sauce and simmer until thickened. Add chicken and simmer until done. Add mushroom mixture and chives and heat through.

STUFFED CHICKEN LEGS

Serves 4

4 strips bacon, chopped
½ large onion, chopped
2 cloves garlic, minced
1 large stalk broccoli or
  ½ package frozen chopped
  spinach, thawed and well-
  drained
¾ cup shredded mozzarella
  cheese
½ cup dry bread crumbs or
  cracker crumbs
4 whole chicken legs,
  including thighs

• Sauté bacon until crisp and remove from pan; sauté onion and garlic in pan until tender. Cook broccoli until tender; drain.

• Puree broccoli, bacon, onion, garlic, cheese and bread crumbs in blender. Stuff mixture under skin of chicken legs (drumstick and thigh).

• Bake at 375 degrees for 1½ hours; cover for the first 45 minutes.

Note: You can substitute 4 whole chicken breasts for the legs.

CHICKEN SAUTERNE

Serves 4

3 lb. chicken, cut into
  serving pieces
½ cup flour
½ teaspoon salt
¼ teaspoon paprika
½ teaspoon fresh or dried
  oregano
¼ cup butter
½ cup sliced green onion
½ cup sliced fresh
  mushrooms
1 tomato, thinly sliced

● Combine flour, salt, paprika and oregano in a bag. Add chicken and shake to coat. Melt butter in large, flat baking pan. Arrange chicken in pan, skin side down, and bake at 400 degrees for 30 minutes.

● Remove from oven and turn the chicken skin side up. Pour Wine Sauce over chicken and let stand several hours or overnight, refrigerated.

● Sprinkle green onions and mushrooms on top of chicken and bake at 400 degrees for 40 minutes. Arrange sliced tomato down center of dish as garnish and serve.

Wine Sauce

2 tablespoons butter
2 tablespoons flour
2 tablespoons water
1 cube chicken bouillon
1 cup sauterne wine

● Melt butter; add flour and cook 2 minutes. Add water, wine and bouillon cube and cook until thickened.

OVEN CHICKEN LINGUINE

Serves 4 to 6

A surprisingly mild dish. It is important to include the dried chilies.

½ cup butter
1 medium onion, thinly sliced
2 cloves garlic, mashed
1 tablespoon dried basil
¾ teaspoon crushed dried red chilies
3 lb. chicken breast, or thighs
2 packages (10 oz. each) frozen chopped spinach, thawed and squeezed dry
8 oz. dry linguine or spaghetti
½ to 1 cup grated Parmesan cheese
1 small orange, cut in wedges

• Melt butter in 12x15-inch baking pan in 400-degree oven.

• Mix onion, garlic, basil and chilies with butter. Place chicken in the seasoned butter, coating pieces well. Arrange pieces skin side up. Bake, uncovered, until chicken skin is well browned, about 45 minutes.

• Cook linguine; set aside. When chicken is done, remove from pan and keep meat warm while you add spinach to the pan and stir to scrape the browned bits.

• Add linguine and Parmesan to the pan and toss to mix well. Serve with chicken pieces and orange wedges to squeeze over each serving.

WILD DUCK IN WINE

Serves 4

4 small wild ducks, ready
  to cook
2 tablespoons butter
2 tablespoons flour
1 cup chicken broth
¼ cup Burgundy
1 cup sliced fresh
  mushrooms
2 tablespoons chopped onion
1 bay leaf
½ teaspoon salt
dash pepper
snipped parsley

- Simmer ducks in salted water for 20 to 30 minutes. Drain and brown birds in butter in a skillet; transfer ducks to buttered 2-quart casserole.

- Blend flour into pan drippings and cook until bubbly. Add broth and remaining ingredients, except parsley, and simmer 5 minutes. Stir occasionally to prevent burning.

- Pour sauce over ducks and bake at 350 degrees for 1¼ to 1½ hours or until tender. Remove ducks to platter; sprinkle with parsley. Serve with sauce from pan, removing bay leaf and any fat.

TIPSY ROAST WILD DUCK OR GOOSE

Serves 6 to 8

Very good with rice pilaf, stewed prunes and apricots.

2 to 3 well-plucked ducks
  or 1 well-plucked goose
½ cup apricot brandy
salt and pepper
2 to 3 onions, coarsely
  chopped
3 to 4 apples, cored and
  chopped
2 to 3 stalks celery, chopped
½ bay leaf per bird
pinch Italian herbs for each
  bird

- Douse birds, inside and out, with brandy. Place in a roasting pan and stuff each bird with some of each of the remaining ingredients (these are just flavor enhancers, so amounts aren't important).

- Cover and roast in a 250-degree oven for 3 to 4 hours until done and juices run clear. Discard stuffing ingredients and drippings before serving.

WILD DUCK

Serves 6

3 mallards, halved, or
6 whole teal or other
small ducks
1 cup flour
½ teaspoon Italian
seasoning
½ teaspoon poultry
seasoning
1 teaspoon onion powder
1 teaspoon rubbed sage
salt and pepper to taste
¼ cup sherry or Burgundy
(optional)

- Skin rather than pluck ducks and cut into serving-size pieces. Mix remaining ingredients, except wine, and coat ducks. Brown in a heavy pan using just enough oil to prevent sticking.

- Remove browned pieces to a roasting pan, large pieces on the bottom and smaller ones on top. Pour enough hot water into frying pan to cover bottom; scrape to dislodge browned bits. Add wine.

- Pour mixture over ducks, cover and bake at 325 degrees for 1½ hours. Remove ducks from pan. Thin or thicken sauce as necessary. Serve with wild rice.

WILD DUCKS AND GREEN PEPPER SAUCE

Serves 4

Distinctively different served over brown rice.

4 ducks (mallards preferred)
¼ cup flour
1 teaspoon salt
1 teaspoon pepper
¼ teaspoon garlic salt
¼ teaspoon celery salt
½ cup vegetable oil
1 cup chopped onion
1 cup chopped green pepper
½ cup flour
2 cups hot water
2 cups dry red wine (or
increase water to 4 cups)
4 chicken bouillon cubes

- Cut ducks into serving pieces or use just the breasts. Dredge with flour seasoned with salt, pepper and garlic powder. Brown in hot oil in a heavy skillet.

- Remove meat and sauté onion and green pepper in pan; remove vegetables. Add flour and brown it without burning. Mix in hot water, wine and bouillon, stirring constantly.

- Return ducks and vegetables to the sauce and cook over low heat for 1½ hours (or bake at 300 degrees for 1½ hours). Serve with brown rice.

158

FRUIT-STUFFED WILD DUCK

Serves 6

This recipe has been handed down through three generations. A good way to serve duck, either wild or domestic.

6 small wild ducks or
  3 large mallards, cleaned,
  plucked and aged in
  refrigerator 2 days
  uncovered
salt to taste
6 thick slices bacon

- Wipe inside of ducks and salt lightly. Stuff each bird with Apple-Raisin Stuffing. Salt outside of ducks and place them on a rack in a metal roaster.

- Place one slice bacon over each duck and roast at 425 degrees for 1½ hours or until done. If bacon causes smoke, add a little water to the pan.

Apple-Raisin Stuffing

6 tart apples, sliced and
  cored
2 large onions, chopped
½ cup butter
¼ cup raisins
¼ lb. saltine crackers,
  crushed
salt and pepper to taste

- Sauté apples and onions in butter over medium heat; add raisins.

- Mix in enough of saltines to make a moist stuffing (you may not need all the crackers). Season to taste.

Note: The key to good wild duck is the preparation before cooking. They must be cleaned and well-picked before aging; they should then be dry-aged for two days under refrigeration . . . that is, not covered and body cavity open.

BAKED PHEASANT

Serves 4

An easy way to dress up the day's shoot.

2 pheasants, cut up (and
  skinned, if desired)
½ cup flour
1 teaspoon salt
½ teaspoon pepper
¼ cup vegetable oil
1 cup sour cream
1 can (2.8 oz.) French fried
  onions

● Combine flour, salt and pepper in a plastic bag. Shake pheasant pieces in it and brown in hot oil.

● Arrange browned pieces in an oiled baking dish. Top each piece with sour cream and cover all with fried onion rings. Cover dish with foil and bake at 300 degrees for 1 hour.

FRICASSEED FOWL

Serves 4

4 quail or doves or
  1 pheasant prepared for
  cooking and cut into
  pieces
flour
salt and pepper to taste
¼ cup vegetable oil
2 cups chicken broth or
  1 cup water and 1 cup
  white wine

● Dredge bird(s) in flour seasoned with salt and pepper. Brown in oil in a heavy skillet.

● Add broth (or water and wine); cover and cook over low heat 45 to 60 minutes or until tender; turn meat once during cooking. Sauce should be thick enough to serve over rice or mashed potatoes.

RED SNAPPER AU GRATIN

Serves 6

A colorful fish dish even the children will eat.

2 lbs. red snapper fillets
vegetable oil
3 tablespoons margarine
½ lb. fresh mushrooms,
  sliced
2 tablespoons green onion,
  chopped
½ teaspoon salt
1 teaspoon dried basil
¼ teaspoon pepper
1 medium tomato, chopped
1 cup shredded Cheddar
  cheese
1 egg, beaten

• Place fish on lightly oiled rimmed baking sheets. Sprinkle a little oil on each fillet. Bake at 500 degrees for 6 to 8 minutes or until fish flakes. Remove from oven and drain off juices.

• While fish is cooking sauté onions and mushrooms in margarine until liquid evaporates. Remove from heat. Stir in remaining ingredients.

• Spoon mixture evenly over top of each fillet. Broil 5 inches away from heat until cheese melts and is bubbly.

SNAPPER PARMIGIANA

Serves 4

2 tablespoons olive oil
1 cup chopped onion
3 cloves garlic, minced
2 cans (16 oz. each) chopped
  tomatoes
¼ teaspoon salt
¼ teaspoon pepper
dash oregano, basil, mixed
  Italian seasoning
1 lb. red snapper, cut into
  serving-size pieces
½ cup flour
1 egg, beaten
¼ cup grated Parmesan
  cheese
1 cup bread crumbs
4 slices mozzarella cheese

• Sauté onions and garlic in oil. Add tomatoes, undrained, and seasonings. Simmer until sauce is thickened, about 30 minutes.

• Dip fish pieces first in flour, then beaten egg, then in mixture of Parmesan and bread crumbs. Sauté fish in oil. Spoon sauce into bottom of flat baking pan and place fish pieces on sauce. Top each with a slice of mozzarella.

• Bake 10 minutes at 350 degrees until cheese is melted. Serve with pasta.

CHANNEL HOUSE, Depoe Bay

Perched high on a cliff overlooking the jaws of Depoe Bay on the coast, Channel House Restaurant and Inn is probably the only bed-and-breakfast establishment in the state to list whale watching as one of its attractions.

Channel House offers cozy lodging in suites that capitalize on a magnificent view of the Pacific Ocean and the Bay. Fireplaces and private whirlpools are available in some units, as are oceanfront decks.

Guests can sit and watch fishing and charter boats head out to sea in the morning and then back home again at day's end—hopefully with a hold full of freshly caught fish. Often, whales can be spotted just a few hundred yards offshore, feeding on the rich ocean bottom. For those intent on souvenir shopping, an abundance of small specialty shops is just across the street.

Channel House serves a full breakfast, including fresh-baked bread, biscuits, and muffins. Other items on the menu might include a luscious French toast or a delightful quiche brimming with savory ingredients. The dining room decor is charming with its nautical antiques, an antique stove, and an 18th-century oak cooler from a midwest farmers' grocery.

For additional information:
Channel House
P.O. Box 56
Depoe Bay, OR 97341
(503) 765-2140

LING COD FLORENTINE
WITH HOLLANDAISE SAUCE

Serves 4

From the Dining Room of Channel House

2 lb. fresh ling cod fillets
1 package (10 oz.) frozen
   chopped spinach, thawed
   and drained
2 tablespoons finely diced
   onion
1 teaspoon minced garlic
butter
salt, pepper and granulated
   garlic to taste
½ cup flour
1 cup Hollandaise Sauce
   (see index)

● Sauté spinach, onion and garlic in butter. Season with salt, pepper and garlic; set aside.

● Trim ling cod, removing any bones or skin; cut into 3 to 4 oz. pieces. Dredge fillets in flour and brown very quickly in butter over high heat; remove from pan.

● Place fillets in a baking dish. Bake at 400 degrees for 5 to 6 minutes or until fish flakes. Using a warm platter, place fillets on a bed of seasoned spinach mixture and top with Hollandaise Sauce.

163

TU TÚ TUN LODGE, Gold Beach

Tu Tú Tun Lodge successfully combines the congeniality of a small exclusive hideaway with the comforts and conveniences of a resort hotel complex, allowing guests a memorable stay on the famous Rogue River.

The Lodge is big, comfortable, and of relatively new construction. A native stone fireplace dominates the lounge area, where guests relax after a fun-filled day of fishing or touring the river. A recreation room provides facilities for tying flies, playing pool on the beautifully restored antique pool table, or enjoying the melodious strains of a player piano.

Sixteen guest rooms in the adjacent two-story building, also new, enable visitors to enjoy the river from their own private decks. Each room contains two double beds and is rustically decorated with a touch of elegance here and there. Fresh flowers and up-to-date magazines greet each guest's arrival.

Since the Lodge is located just seven miles inland from the Pacific Ocean, fishermen can take advantage of fly fishing on the Rogue or offshore ocean fishing. The famous Rogue River Chinook salmon run occurs in the spring and fall, with steelhead runs in late August through October. Offshore ocean fishing is at its best during July and August. The Lodge can arrange for guides for both river and ocean fishing.

Tu Tú Tun Lodge has its own private dock on the Rogue, and excursion jetboats stop there daily to pick up guests for an exciting scenic trip up the river. Guests may also bring their own boats; ample parking for boat trailers is available.

Nearby hiking trails and the Lodge's beautiful modern swimming pool, pitch-and-putt course, and horseshoe area offer diversions for non-anglers in the family. Horseback riding and golf are also in the area, as are beachcombing and clam digging on the Pacific coast.

The dining room features a relaxed atmosphere, with guests eating family style at round tables. Food is hearty and delicious, featuring homemade soup and bread and entrées such as baked fresh salmon or maybe thick slices of prime rib.

For additional information:
Tu Tú Tun Lodge
96550 North Bank Rogue
Gold Beach, OR 97444
(503) 247-6664

BAKED SALMON WITH CAPER SAUCE

Serves 4 to 6

From the Dining Room of Tu Tú Tun Lodge

fresh salmon
juice of 1 lemon
butter
paprika
¼ cup white wine
capers
lemon swirls
parsley sprigs

- Fillet salmon and cut into individual servings. Place fillets skin side up on a baking pan. Sprinkle with lemon juice and dot with butter. Sprinkle with paprika. Bake at 350 degrees for 10 minutes. Baste with white wine and bake 10 minutes more.

- Serve garnished with a strip of Caper Sauce down center of each fillet, dotted with capers and chopped parsley and surrounded with lemon swirls and parsley sprigs.

(continued)

BAKED SALMON WITH CAPER SAUCE (continued)

Caper Sauce

1 cup mayonnaise
1 cup sour cream
2 tablespoons chopped
  green onions
2 tablespoons chopped
  parsley
3 tablespoons capers,
  drained and halved
⅛ teaspoon salt
⅛ teaspoon white pepper
1 teaspoon lemon juice

● Combine ingredients and chill
  until served.

BAKED WHOLE SALMON   Serves 8 to 10

Fresh from the ocean, what could be better!

1 (7 to 10 lb.) salmon
¾ cup dry white wine
¼ teaspoon dried thyme
¼ teaspoon dried rosemary
½ teaspoon dried basil
¼ teaspoon dried tarragon
celery leaves
3 green onions, minced
2 slices lemon
3 peppercorns
salt

● Put wine and all seasonings in a
  covered saucepan and steep
  without boiling for 30 minutes;
  strain.

● Rinse the salmon; pat dry.
  Remove the tail and lay fish
  lengthwise on a sheet of
  aluminum foil. Pour warm herb-
  flavored wine over and inside the
  fish. Bring foil up over the fish
  and seal by crimping. Be sure no
  liquid can escape.

● Place on a baking sheet and bake
  at 350 degrees 12 to 15 minutes
  per pound, or about 1½ hours.
  Do not overcook. Can be served
  either hot or cold.

SALMON STEAKS WITH MOUSSELINE SAUCE

Serves 6

6 salmon steaks
fish stock or white wine
  diluted with water
parsley and lemon wedges
  for garnish

- Place salmon in a baking pan or fish poacher. Pour enough fish stock or diluted wine over fish to cover it. Bring stock to boiling point, reduce heat and simmer until the salmon flakes easily with a fork.

- Remove fish carefully from pan. Remove skin from fish and transfer fish to a heated platter. Garnish with parsley and lemon wedges. Serve with warm Mousseline Sauce (made from Hollandaise Sauce).

Hollandaise Sauce

Yields ¾ cup

¾ cup butter
3 large egg yolks, well-
  beaten
4 teaspoons fresh lemon
  juice
dash each salt and cayenne
  pepper

- Break butter into 3 pieces; put 1 piece into top of a double boiler. Add egg yolks and lemon juice. Cook over hot water, beating constantly until butter is melted.

- Add second piece of butter; continue beating and cooking until mixture thickens, never allowing water to boil. Add last piece of butter. Stir and cook until thickened. Remove from heat and add seasonings.

Mousseline Sauce

Yields 1 cup

¾ cup Hollandaise Sauce
⅓ cup heavy cream,
  whipped

- Add whipped cream to warm Hollandaise after last piece of butter has been added. Stir and cook over hot, but not boiling, water for one minute.

167

DEPOE BAY SALMON

Serves 4 to 6

A nice departure from plain broiled fish.

2 lbs. salmon steaks
2 tablespoons lemon juice
2 egg whites, beaten stiff
½ cup mayonnaise
½ cup grated Cheddar
  cheese
2 green onions, chopped
½ teaspoon dried rosemary
½ teaspoon pepper
½ teaspoon salt

● Blend egg whites, mayonnaise, cheese and seasonings. Grease a broiler pan and arrange the steaks on it. Brush each with lemon juice. Broil 10 minutes.

● Spread mayonnaise mixture over fish and broil about 2 to 3 minutes longer or until topping bubbles.

SALMON LOAF

Serves 6 to 8

Excellent served with cold Lemon Mayonnaise.

1 lb. fresh salmon, cooked
  (or use canned)
1 egg
¼ cup evaporated milk or
  heavy cream
1 cup soft bread crumbs
½ teaspoon salt
1 teaspoon lemon pepper
2 teaspoons lemon juice
1 teaspoon Worcestershire
  sauce
1 tablespoon melted butter
3 tablespoons minced
  parsley
¼ cup chopped celery
¼ cup chopped onion

● Blend all ingredients together lightly. Spoon into a greased 5x9-inch loaf pan and bake at 300 degrees for 30 minutes. Serve with Lemon Mayonnaise

Lemon Mayonnaise

1 cup mayonnaise, home-
  made preferred
2 tablespoons fresh lemon
  juice
½ teaspoon grated lemon
  peel
½ teaspoon lemon pepper
  seasoning

● Blend all ingredients together; refrigerate.

168

STUFFED FILLET OF SOLE

Serves 8

Perfect for company—can be assembled ahead.

8 sole fillets, about 2 lbs.
4 oz. Swiss cheese, shredded
paprika and parsley

- Prepare Crab Stuffing and spread on fillets. Roll fillets and place seam side down in a buttered, shallow baking dish. Pour Wine Sauce over fish (may be refrigerated at this point).

- Bake at 400 degrees for 25 minutes; sprinkle Swiss cheese over the top and bake 10 minutes longer. Garnish with a little paprika and chopped parsley.

Crab Stuffing

¼ cup chopped onion
¼ cup butter
¼ lb. fresh mushrooms, sliced
8 oz. crab or shrimp
½ cup coarse crumbs of saltine crackers
2 tablespoons chopped parsley
½ teaspoon salt
dash pepper

- Sauté onion in butter until tender but not browned. Stir in mushrooms; cook until done. Add rest of ingredients.

Wine Sauce

3 tablespoons butter
3 tablespoons flour
¼ teaspoon salt
½ cup milk
⅓ cup dry white wine

- Melt butter in a saucepan; stir in flour and salt and cook briefly. Add milk and wine, whisking constantly. Cook, stirring, until sauce is thickened and smooth.

Note: This can also be prepared in individual au gratin dishes.

SALISHAN LODGE, Gleneden Beach

Salishan Lodge—quiet, unobtrusive, spectacular—gently rests on a forested bluff overlooking Siletz Bay and effortlessly evokes praise for its unique integration with the land.

Salishan combines outstanding architecture, imaginative landscaping, and abundant use of natural materials, and does it so winningly that the resort is a consistent winner of the coveted Mobil Travel Guide Five-Star Rating. Guest accommodations sprinkled around the main lodge are oriented for view, privacy, and quiet. Each of the 200 luxurious rooms sports a fireplace, a view balcony, oversized beds, and covered parking right outside the door.

Recreation—both indoor and outdoor—is an integral part of the 750 acres that make up Salishan. The 18-hole championship golf course, indoor and outdoor tennis courts, nature and jogging trails, swimming and hydrotherapy pools, gym, and sauna all assure guests of ample activities throughout their stay. An art gallery, game room, children's playground, and beauty salon are other features geared to make Salishan one of the country's most complete resorts. Other activities within the area include deep sea fishing, beachcombing, and agate hunting.

The informal elegance of Salishan's famed Dining Room restaurant promises outstanding meals featuring abundant seafood delicacies, continental and American cuisine, and a distinguished wine list. During the summer season, guests may also enjoy charcoal-broiled steaks and dancing by candlelight in The Cedar Tree.

For additional information:
Salishan Lodge
Gleneden Beach, OR 97388
(503) 764-3600

FILLET OF SOLE "MARGUERY"   Serves 1

From the Dining Room of Salishan Lodge

4 to 5 oz. fillet of Petrale sole, trimmed and folded skin-side in
1 teaspoon minced shallots
salt and white pepper
1 oz. Oregon or Bay shrimp
3 mushrooms, sliced
1 oz. sauterne
1 oz. Hollandaise Sauce (see index)
2 to 3 mussels, canned imported
parsley and lemon

● Prepare a fish stock from sole bones, onions, parsley stem, bay leaf, salt, water and mussel brine.

● Butter a shallow sauté pan well. Sprinkle minced shallot on bottom of pan. Arrange sole on top. Season lightly with salt and pepper. Distribute shrimp and mushrooms into empty spaces. Add a mixture of ½ wine and ½ fish stock (strained) to barely cover the sole.

● Bring to a quick boil, reduce heat and simmer until done (3 to 4 minutes). Remove fillets with a slotted spatula to a heated platter. Arrange shrimp and mushrooms on or around it.

(continued)

FILLET OF SOLE "MARGUERY" (continued)

- Reduce stock to ⅓ its volume. Heat mussels. Thicken reduced stock with a white roux (flour and butter). Strain sauce.

- Fold in Hollandaise and adjust seasonings (lemon, MSG, salt, etc.). Pour over sole, shrimp, mushroom arrangement. Garnish with mussels, parsley and lemon.

SOLE CALEDONIA
Serves 4

1 lb. sole fillets
½ cup dry white wine
2 tablespoons butter
2 tablespoons flour
1¼ cups half and half
¼ cup dry white wine
1 cup asparagus, cooked
  crisp-tender
1 cup sliced mushrooms
1 cup halved cherry
  tomatoes
slices of avocado, or sliced
  almonds, or buttered
  bread crumbs

- Poach sole in wine 2 to 3 minutes in covered pan. Drain and set aside. In saucepan, melt butter; add flour and cook until frothy. Add half and half, stirring constantly until thickened and bubbly. Add wine.

- Pour half the sauce into a shallow baking pan. Arrange fish over sauce; place the asparagus and mushrooms around the fish. Add rest of the sauce and the tomatoes. Garnish top with avocado slices, sliced almonds, or buttered bread crumbs. Bake at 350 degrees for 20 minutes.

FLORENTINE SOLE

Serves 8

3 packages (10 oz. each) frozen chopped spinach
2 cups sour cream
3 tablespoons flour
½ cup chopped green onions
1 teaspoon lemon juice
2 teaspoons salt
2 lb. sole fillets
2 tablespoons butter
paprika

● Cook spinach; drain well. Blend sour cream with flour, onions, lemon juice and salt. Combine half with spinach and spread over bottom of 10x15-inch baking dish.

● Arrange sole over spinach, overlapping pieces. Dot with butter. Spread remaining sour cream mixture evenly over sole. Sprinkle with paprika. Bake at 375 degrees for 25 minutes.

HALIBUT ROYALE

Serves 4 to 6

In a hurry? Try this!

2 lbs. halibut steaks
1 cup white wine
2 teaspoons salt
¼ cup dry bread crumbs
½ cup sour cream
½ cup mayonnaise
¼ cup minced green onion
½ teaspoon paprika

● Combine wine and salt; pour over halibut. Refrigerate for at least one hour. Drain fish on paper towels. Dip both sides in bread crumbs and place in buttered 2-quart baking dish.

● Combine sour cream, mayonnaise and green onion. Spoon mixture over fish and sprinkle with paprika. Bake at 500 degrees for 15 minutes, or until fish flakes easily with a fork.

HALIBUT WITH SHRIMP SAUCE   Serves 4

Beautiful dish for company.

4 halibut steaks
lemon juice
salt and pepper
3 tablespoons butter
1 medium onion, minced
½ cup white wine

● Dry fish with paper towel. Baste with lemon juice and let stand 10 minutes. Sprinkle with salt and pepper.

● Melt 3 tablespoons butter in frying pan and cook steaks over low heat for 10 minutes. Add onion and cook 2 more minutes. Add a few sprigs of parsley. Pour in wine and simmer 5 minutes. Place fish steaks on serving platter and keep warm till ready to serve. Use fish stock for Shrimp Sauce.

Shrimp Sauce

3 tablespoons butter
3 tablespoons flour
1 cup fish stock
½ cup white wine
3 oz. fresh mushrooms, sliced
4 oz. small shrimp
2 lemons, juiced
1 medium onion, minced
1 egg yolk, beaten

● Melt butter in a saucepan. Add flour and cook until frothy. Pour in warm fish stock and stir until sauce comes to a boil. Add onion and any juice from standing fish.

● Pour in wine and cook over low heat until smooth. Add mushrooms and shrimp; cook 15 minutes over low heat. Add salt and lemon juice to taste.

● Blend a little of the warm sauce into beaten egg yolk and then return mixture to rest of sauce. Reheat sauce and pour over fish.

SHRIMP ETOUFFÉ

Serves 4 to 6

Excellent served over a simple parsleyed rice.

1 medium onion, finely
  chopped
2 green onions, finely
  chopped
3 to 4 cloves garlic, minced
¼ cup finely chopped celery
½ cup butter
2 tablespoons flour
2½ cups water
1 can (10 oz.) tomato purée
2 bay leaves
1 tablespoon Worcestershire
  sauce
4 drops Tabasco sauce
1 teaspoon salt
½ teaspoon sugar
½ teaspoon whole thyme,
  crushed
⅛ teaspoon pepper
1 lb. medium shrimp, peeled
  and cleaned

● In a large skillet, sauté onion, green onions, garlic and celery in butter until tender. Stir in the flour and cook until slightly browned. Do not burn.

● Add water, tomato purée, bay leaves, sauces and seasonings. Simmer, uncovered, for 25 minutes. Stir occasionally. Add shrimp and cook 15 minutes longer.

SHRIMP AU GRATIN

Serves 4

Works equally well with Dungeness crab or scallops too.

2 cups shrimp, peeled and deveined
3 tablespoons butter
¼ cup diced onion
3 tablespoons flour
1½ cups milk
salt and pepper to taste
dash garlic powder
1½ cups shredded sharp Cheddar cheese

● Sauté onions in butter until transparent. Add flour, salt, pepper and garlic powder; stir in the milk. Cook until thickened and smooth.

● Add cheese and cook over low heat until melted and smooth. Fold in shrimp. Simmer over low heat about 5 minutes to cook shrimp. Do not overcook.

● Pour into ungreased 2-quart casserole and spread the Cheese Topping over all. Bake at 350 degrees for 20 to 30 minutes, or until bubbly and topping is lightly browned and crisp.

Cheese Topping

¾ cup fresh bread crumbs
¾ cup shredded sharp Cheddar cheese

● Combine ingredients.

CRAB AND SHRIMP CASSEROLE

Serves 6 to 8

Quick and easy for company.

2 cups cooked rice
1 cup mayonnaise
½ cup milk
½ cup chopped onion
¼ cup chopped green pepper
1 cup fresh crab or canned
1 cup fresh shrimp or canned
1 cup tomato juice
¼ cup slivered almonds

● Mix all ingredients together and place in buttered 9x13-inch baking dish. Bake at 350 degrees for 1 hour.

Mo's SEAFOOD CIOPPINO   Serves 8 to 10

"Mo's" is an Oregon institution, a seafood restaurant famed for its thick, rich clam chowder chockful of clams and bits of ham. Oregonians and visitors alike can enjoy this hearty treat and other equally good fresh seafood delights at several Mo's eateries around the state, including the original Mo's in Newport.

In 1975, Assistance League of Corvallis held its first "Mo's Chowder Luncheon." With the generous assistance of Mo Niemi, owner of Mo's, Assistance League members invited the Corvallis community for a bowl of Mo's hot chowder and a generous slice of a rich homemade dessert (baked by Assistance League members). The community loved it, and the Luncheon has become a November tradition in Corvallis. The Luncheon provides Assistance League with money to support its various philanthropic projects.

¼ cup vegetable oil
1 lb. fresh mushrooms, halved
1 lb. onion, chopped in large chunks
4 green onions, cut in large pieces
2 green peppers, cut in 1-inch chunks
¼ cup chopped fresh parsley
4 bay leaves
1½ tablespoons salt
1 tablespoon pepper
1 tablespoon each rosemary, thyme and garlic
1 can (16 oz.) tomato sauce
2 cups water
2 cans (16 oz. each) tomato purée
4 cups Burgundy wine
steamed or poached fish or shellfish
grated Romano cheese

● Sauté vegetables in oil; add seasonings. Stir in tomato sauce, water, tomato purée and wine. Bring to a boil, reduce heat and simmer for 1 hour.

● Serve the sauce over any steamed or poached fish or shellfish. Top with grated cheese.

BAKED SEAFOOD SALAD

Serves 6 to 8

An especially flavorful seafood combo.

1 cup chopped celery
1¼ cups chopped onion
1 green pepper, chopped
¼ cup butter
3 tablespoons butter
3 tablespoons flour
1½ cups milk
1 teaspoon salt
½ teaspoon Worcestershire
  sauce
dash cayenne pepper
1 cup mayonnaise
½ cup small cooked shrimp
¾ cup crab meat
3 cups cooked rice
1 cup buttered bread
  crumbs

● Sauté vegetables in the ¼ cup butter over low heat until tender. In separate pan, melt 3 tablespoons butter; add flour. Stir in milk and cook until thickened. Add seasonings and cooked vegetables. Stir in mayonnaise, shrimp and crab.

● Butter a 2-quart casserole and line it with the cooked rice. Cover rice with seafood mixture and top with buttered bread crumbs. Bake at 350 degrees for 30 minutes.

SEAFOOD LASAGNE

Serves 6 to 8

An easy dish with wonderful flavor. Good when you are pressed for time.

8 to 10 oz. lasagne noodles
2 cans (10¾ oz. each) cream
  of shrimp soup
1 lb. crab and/or shrimp
2 cups ricotta cheese
8 oz. cream cheese
1 cup chopped onion
2 teaspoons sugar
1 egg
1 teaspoon dried basil
1 teaspoon salt
½ teaspoon pepper
¼ cup sherry
1 tablespoon vegetable oil
4 medium tomatoes, sliced
1 cup shredded Cheddar
  cheese

● Cook noodles, drain and reserve. Mix seafood with soup and heat. Blend ricotta and cream cheese. Add onion, sugar, egg, sherry and spices.

● Oil a 9x13-inch baking pan or casserole and layer ⅓ of the noodles, all of the cheese mixture, ⅓ of the noodles, all the seafood mixture, the remaining noodles, and sliced tomatoes. Bake at 350 degrees for 30 minutes. Top with Cheddar cheese and bake 20 minutes more.

SCALLOPS IN WINE

Serves 6

Dinner in a minute!

1½ lbs. scallops
4 tablespoons butter
2 tablespoons lemon juice
¾ cup dry white wine
parsley and lemon

● Sauté scallops in butter until
they're opaque throughout. Add
lemon juice and wine. Heat
through and serve. Garnish with
parsley and sliced lemon.

SHRIMP AND SCALLOPS GRUYÈRE

Serves 12

1½ lb. cooked shrimp
1½ lb. raw scallops
½ teaspoon salt
2 teaspoons lemon juice
¾ lb. mushrooms, sliced
3 tablespoons butter

● Prepare Cheese Sauce and keep
it warm.

● Poach scallops in water with
lemon juice and salt until opaque.
Remove 1 cup poaching liquid
and add it to Cheese Sauce.

● Sauté mushrooms in 3 tablespoons butter and add to Sauce.
Drain scallops and add with
shrimp to the Sauce. Serve with
rice or pilaf.

Cheese Sauce

1 cup butter
1 cup flour
4 cups milk
1 lb. Gruyère cheese,
shredded
¼ teaspoon garlic powder
½ teaspoon salt
¼ teaspoon white pepper
¼ teaspoon dry mustard
1 tablespoon tomato paste
1½ tablespoons lemon juice

● Melt butter in a saucepan. Add
flour and cook until frothy. Add
milk and cook, stirring
constantly, until thickened. Add
cheese, garlic powder, salt,
pepper, mustard, tomato paste
and lemon juice. Stir until cheese
melts.

CRAB FETTUCCINE

Serves 6

½ lb. crab meat
½ cup butter
1 clove garlic, minced
¾ cup heavy cream
½ cup grated Parmesan
  cheese
½ teaspoon pepper
½ teaspoon salt
12 oz. dry fettuccine,
  cooked and drained
1 tablespoon chopped
  parsley

● Melt butter in skillet; add garlic and sauté. Blend in crab, cream, cheese, salt and pepper. Heat, stirring constantly until blended. Add to noodles. Toss lightly and serve immediately. Garnish with chopped parsley.

CLAMS IN SHELLS

Serves 6

½ cup chopped green onions
½ lb. mushrooms, sliced
1 tablespoon butter
1 tablespoon flour
¼ cup heavy cream
¼ cup white wine or
  vermouth
2 tablespoons grated
  Parmesan cheese
2 cups chopped or minced
  clams (drained, if canned)
3 egg yolks, beaten
1 tablespoon lemon juice
salt and pepper to taste
½ cup fine bread crumbs
¼ cup grated Parmesan
  cheese
2 tablespoons butter, melted
6 mushroom caps, sautéed

● Sauté green onions and mushrooms in 1 tablespoon butter. Mix in flour, cream, white wine or vermouth and cook over medium heat until bubbly. Add grated Parmesan cheese and clams. Bring mixture to a simmer.

● Blend some of the hot mixture with the beaten egg yolks and return to saucepan, stirring constantly. Season with lemon juice, salt and pepper.

● Mix bread crumbs, Parmesan cheese and butter. Spoon clam mixture into six 5-inch baking shells and top with crumb mixture. Broil 6 inches from heat for 5 minutes or until bubbly and golden brown. Garnish with sautéed mushrooms.

STEAMED CLAMS ORIENTAL

Serves 4 to 6

½ cup chopped green onions
1 teaspoon ground ginger
6 cloves garlic, minced
2 tablespoons olive oil
2 tablespoons soy sauce
1 tablespoon sugar
2 tablespoons sherry or sake
2 tablespoons cornstarch
1 cup water
3 dozen hard-shell clams,
  scrubbed clean (discard
  any not tightly closed)
4 tablespoons vegetable oil

● Combine green onions, ginger, garlic and olive oil in a small saucepan. Add soy sauce, sugar and sherry. Mix together cornstarch and water, add to the sauce and bring all to a simmer. Cook until thickened and clear.

● Heat the 4 tablespoons vegetable oil in a skillet. Add clams and cook until shells open partway. Add sauce, cover and cook until shells are completely open. Serve immediately.

CLAM FRITTERS

Serves 2

1 can (6½ oz.) chopped
  clams, with juice
1 cup flour
1 teaspoon baking powder
½ teaspoon salt
1 egg, beaten
3 tablespoons melted butter
2 tablespoons oil

● Combine all ingredients except oil. Heat oil and drop batter by spoonfuls to fry until crispy and cooked through. Drain on paper towels. Serve with tartar sauce or fresh lemon.

OVEN-BAKED OYSTERS
Serves 2

6 medium-size fresh oysters
½ clove garlic, minced
juice of 1 lemon
1 teaspoon oregano, crushed
1 teaspoon sweet basil,
  crushed
salt and pepper
¼ cup olive oil
1 teaspoon chopped fresh
  parsley
dried bread crumbs
chopped fresh parsley

● Distribute oysters and garlic over bottom of a glass pie plate. Sprinkle with lemon juice, then oregano and basil. Season with salt and pepper.

● Spoon oil over oysters and sprinkle with parsley. Top with a light covering of bread crumbs. Shake dish to blend ingredients. Bake at 500 degrees for 10 minutes. Serve, spooning pan liquid over the top. Sprinkle with parsley.

YAQUINA BAY BAKED OYSTERS
Serves 4

A very basic recipe with a great result.

1 pint fresh oysters, small
  or extra-small preferred
1 egg
2 to 4 tablespoons milk
1 to 2 cups saltine cracker
  crumbs
½ cup melted butter
onion salt
paprika

● Rinse and drain oysters. Beat egg and milk together. Use no salt or pepper. Pour melted butter in a baking dish large enough to hold all the oysters in a single layer.

● Dip oysters in the egg mixture and then in cracker crumbs, coating both sides. Place in buttered pan and turn once to coat both sides. Lightly season with onion salt and paprika. (Oysters may be refrigerated for up to 5 hours at this point.) Bake at 400 degrees for about 15 minutes, or until plumped and golden brown.

Side Dishes

SIDE DISHES

RICE
Three-Grained Pilaf, 185
Confetti Rice, 185
Green Chili Rice, 186
Brown Rice Croquettes, 186
Hazelnut Rice, 186
Rice Milanese, 187
Far East Rice Casserole, 187

POTATOES
Stuffed Baked Potatoes, 189
Kartoffel Kloesse, 190
Rosemary Potatoes, 190
"Sinful" Potatoes au Gratin, 191
Pommes Dauphine, 191

MISCELLANEOUS
Pasta with Four Cheeses, 192
Jalapeno Grits, 192
Country Noodle Casserole, 193
Oyster Stuffing, 194
Hawaiian Pineapple Pudding, 194

THREE-GRAIN PILAF

Serves 6

A very hearty dish—good with barbecued meats.

¼ cup butter
⅓ cup chopped almonds
1 large onion, chopped
1 large carrot, chopped
1 large clove garlic, chopped
1 cup fresh mushrooms, sliced
⅓ cup barley
⅓ cup brown rice
⅓ cup bulgur wheat
2½ cups chicken broth
¼ cup sherry
½ teaspoon salt
dash pepper
½ teaspoon oregano
¾ teaspoon basil
⅓ cup chopped parsley

- In a large fry pan, sauté nuts in butter until toasted. Remove nuts and add onion, carrot, garlic and mushrooms; sauté until tender. Add grains and cook until lightly browned.

- Add broth, sherry, salt, pepper, oregano and basil. Bring to a boil and simmer, covered, for 45 minutes. Remove from heat and let stand 10 minutes. Toss with reserved nuts and parsley and serve.

CONFETTI RICE

Serves 6 to 8

Colorful and elegant side dish.

1 cup raw or converted rice
2½ cups chicken broth
½ teaspoon salt
¼ cup butter
10 mushrooms, sliced
1 to 2 stalks broccoli, peeled and chopped
1 cup cherry tomatoes, halved
½ cup grated Parmesan cheese
½ cup heavy cream
¼ cup toasted pine nuts or almonds

- Cook rice in chicken broth with salt. Sauté mushrooms in butter. Cook broccoli briefly in small amount of water until tender yet crisp.

- Add broccoli and mushrooms to the rice; gently stir in tomatoes, cheese and cream. Cook over medium heat just until tomatoes are heated through, about 2 minutes.

- Serve garnished with nuts.

GREEN CHILI RICE

Serves 4 to 6

A real crowd-pleaser.

½ cup raw rice
1 can (4 oz.) green chilies
1 cup sour cream
8 oz. Monterey jack cheese,
  shredded
2 tablespoons milk

- Cook rice as directed on package; combine with remaining ingredients in a buttered casserole. Bake at 325 degrees for 40 minutes.

BROWN RICE CROQUETTES

Serves 6 to 10

2 tablespoons butter
1 bunch green onions,
  chopped, using half the
  green tops
1 clove garlic, minced
2 cups chicken broth
1 cup brown rice, uncooked
¼ teaspoon salt
½ cup grated Parmesan
  cheese
1 egg
½ cup dry bread crumbs
oil

- Melt butter in a saucepan; add onion and garlic and sauté until soft. Add broth and bring to boil; add rice and salt. Cook 30 minutes or until liquid is absorbed. Cool.

- In a mixing bowl, beat egg and cheese. Add rice mixture and mix well. Shape mixture into patties and dip them into bread crumbs, coating both sides. Heat ½-inch oil in a skillet. Fry patties 4 to 5 minutes per side.

HAZELNUT RICE

Serves 6

Terrific with barbecued meats.

2 tablespoons butter
½ cup finely chopped celery
½ cup finely chopped onion
2½ cups chicken broth
1 teaspoon salt
1 cup brown rice, preferably
  California brown rice
¼ cup chopped hazelnuts,
  toasted and skins rubbed
  off
2 tablespoons butter
  (optional)

- Sauté celery and onion in butter until transparent. Add chicken broth and bring to a boil.

- Add rice and salt; cover and reduce heat. Simmer for 40 to 50 minutes, or until rice is fluffy and tender. Add hazelnuts and additional butter.

RICE MILANESE

Serves 4 to 6

¼ cup butter
¼ cup finely chopped onion
1 cup uncooked rice
2 cups chicken broth
½ cup Marsala wine
1 teaspoon salt
¼ teaspoon saffron
2 tablespoons hot water
¼ cup grated Parmesan
  cheese

● Melt butter in a 1½-quart heavy saucepan; add onion and cook until lightly browned. Stir in the rice and cook slowly until lightly browned, stirring frequently.

● Add broth, wine and salt and bring to a boil. Cover pan, reduce heat to low and allow to simmer for 18 minutes. Turn off the heat and let rice steam, covered.

● Meanwhile, dissolve saffron in hot water. When rice is fluffy and dry, add saffron, mixing well. Serve topped with grated cheese.

FAR EAST RICE CASSEROLE

Serves 8

5 tablespoons vegetable oil
1 medium onion, chopped
1 medium green pepper,
  chopped
2 stalks celery, chopped
1½ teaspoons garlic salt
½ teaspoon pepper
6 cups cooked rice
6 tablespoons soy sauce
1 can (8 oz.) sliced water
  chestnuts
1 can (10¾ oz.) condensed
  cream of mushroom soup
1 cup sour cream
blanched almonds

● Brown onion, green pepper, and celery in oil; add garlic salt and pepper. Combine with remaining ingredients, except nuts, in a buttered casserole. Top with nuts and bake at 350 degrees for 30 minutes.

MORRISON'S LODGE, Merlin

Even though it enjoys a reputation as a first-class fisherman's lodge, Morrison's Lodge on the Rogue River is a treat for anyone who relishes the idea of vacationing by a gorgeous rushing river.

Outstanding fall and winter steelheading on the Rogue used to be the primary reason for staying at Morrison's, but the Lodge's facilities have been expanded to provide enjoyable family vacations throughout summer and fall. Activities available include swimming (river or pool), river rafting, tennis, hiking, gold panning, rockhounding, and just plain relaxing in the sun. Golfers can even practice their shots on a putting green.

Morrison's offers one-day raft trips to guests, as well as three- and four-day trips into the wilderness section of the Rogue. River trips can include camping out or staying at different lodges along the river each night.

Morrison's retains licensed fishing guides who will take fishermen in drift boats on 9- and 10-mile trips on the river. Fishing equipment is furnished on guided trips, but anglers may take their own rods if desired. Back at the Lodge, facilities are available to take care of the catch (chill, freeze, or smoke).

Accommodations include rooms in the Lodge or cottages along the river. Meals may be cooked in cottages, or guests may opt to eat at the Lodge (fall and winter guests eat all meals at the Lodge). Cottages are "just like home," with two bedrooms, living room, dining area, kitchen, bath, and carport.

Gourmet meals in the Lodge's dining room are served family style and are planned for hearty outdoor appetites. A typical fall dinner might include a relish tray of homemade specialties, crepes, spinach salad, prime rib with Yorkshire pudding, broccoli soufflé, and chocolate mousse.

For additional information:
Morrison's Lodge
8500 Galice Rd.
Merlin, OR 97532
(503) 476-3825
(503) 476-3027

STUFFED BAKED POTATOES

Serves 12

From the Dining Room of Morrison's Lodge

6 baking potatoes
1 cup freshly grated
  Romano cheese
12 slices bacon, fried and
  crumbled
½ cup thinly sliced green
  onion
1 teaspoon salt
freshly ground pepper to
  taste
1½ cups sour cream, or
  more if needed
½ cup butter
additional grated Romano
  cheese
minced parsley
paprika

● Bake potatoes at 425 degrees until done. Halve each potato lengthwise and scoop out pulp; reserve skins. Blend pulp with cheese, bacon, onions, salt, pepper, and enough sour cream to moisten well. Mix just until blended.

● Fill reserved skins with potato mixture. Dot with butter and sprinkle with extra grated cheese, parsley and paprika. Bake at 350 degrees for about 20 minutes.

KARTOFFEL KLOESSE

Serves 10

These potato croquettes can be made ahead and reheated with the sauce.

9 medium potatoes
3 eggs, well-beaten
1 cup flour
⅔ cup dry bread crumbs
½ teaspoon grated nutmeg
1 teaspoon salt

- Boil potatoes, unpeeled, until soft. Peel and rice the potatoes; spread on a towel for a few minutes to dry and then place in a bowl and add salt.

- Stir in eggs, flour, bread crumbs and nutmeg. Mix thoroughly. Form into balls (mixture should be dry).

- Drop balls into gently boiling, salted water. When they rise to the surface, allow them to boil 3 minutes. Test for doneness by cutting one in half; the center should be dry. Remove balls from water and serve with Sauce.

Onion Butter Crumb Sauce

½ lb. butter
½ cup bread crumbs
1 teaspoon chopped onion

- Melt butter; add crumbs and onion. Cook 10 minutes and serve.

ROSEMARY POTATOES

Serves 6

A great accompaniment to any hearty roast meat.

3 baking potatoes
3 cloves garlic, chopped
4 3-inch fresh rosemary sprigs, or 2 tablespoons dried rosemary
2 to 3 tablespoons olive oil
salt and pepper to taste

- Pour olive oil into a 12-inch au gratin dish or other ovenproof dish. Arrange fresh rosemary sprigs and chopped garlic over the bottom.

- Cut potatoes into thick slices and arrange them over seasonings. Sprinkle with salt and pepper and bake at 375 degrees for 1 hour, turning once during the cooking. Potatoes should be crispy and brown when done.

"SINFUL" POTATOES AU GRATIN   Serves 6

Forget the calories; these are delicious!

2 lbs. potatoes, peeled and
thinly sliced
¼ cup butter, cut in small
pieces
1½ cups heavy cream
salt and pepper
1 cup shredded Swiss cheese

- Butter a shallow baking dish and arrange layers of potatoes, sprinkling each layer with salt, pepper, cheese and butter.

- Pour cream over the assembled dish and bake at 325 degrees for 1 hour or until tender.

POMMES DAUPHINE   Serves 8

A classic recipe.

½ cup butter
1 cup water
1 teaspoon salt
1 cup flour
4 eggs
dash grated nutmeg
2½ cups mashed potatoes
vegetable oil for deep-frying

- Combine butter, water and salt in a large saucepan. Heat to boiling, then add flour all at once.

- Remove from heat and add eggs, one at a time, beating well after each one. Season with nutmeg and add mashed potatoes. (Mixture may be refrigerated at this point, if desired.)

- Heat oil in a deep saucepan to 375 degrees. Drop potato mixture by rounded tablespoonfuls into hot oil and fry until golden. Drain croquettes and keep warm while frying remaining potatoes.

Note: Croquettes can be baked at 350 degrees for 45 minutes, if preferred.

PASTA WITH FOUR CHEESES

Serves 6

An impressive entrée or side dish.

8 oz. spinach pasta, any
  shape
3 tablespoons butter
1½ tablespoons flour
1 cup cream
½ cup chicken broth
dash ground nutmeg
⅓ cup shredded fontina
  cheese
⅓ cup crumbled Gorgonzola
  cheese
⅓ cup shredded Gouda or
  mild Cheddar cheese
⅓ cup grated Parmesan
  cheese
chopped chives and parsley

● Melt butter in a large skillet; add flour and cook briefly. Add cream and broth and cook until bubbly and thickened. Add nutmeg and all cheeses except the Parmesan. Cook over low heat until cheeses are melted.

● Meanwhile, cook pasta in salted boiling water. Drain well and mix with the sauce. Add Parmesan and toss again. Serve on a warm platter garnished with chopped chives and parsley.

JALAPENO GRITS

Serves 6

Try this! Even if you "hate" grits.

1 tube (6 oz.) jalapeno cheese
1 tube (6 oz.) garlic cheese
4 cups water
1 teaspoon salt
1 cup uncooked grits
¼ cup butter

● Chop cheeses into small cubes. Bring salted water to a boil and slowly add grits, stirring constantly. Bring to a boil again and cook over medium heat for 4 to 5 minutes, stirring often.

● Add cheeses and butter, stirring until cheese is melted and well blended. Pour into ungreased 1½-quart casserole and bake at 350 degrees for 30 minutes.

COUNTRY NOODLE CASSEROLE

Serves 8

Hearty enough to use as a main dish too.

½ lb. bacon
1 lb. very fine noodles
3 cups cottage cheese
3 cups sour cream
2 cloves garlic, crushed
¾ cup grated Parmesan cheese
2 onions, minced
2 tablespoons Worcestershire sauce
dash cayenne pepper
1 tablespoon salt
3 tablespoons prepared horseradish
¼ cup grated Parmesan cheese
¼ cup sour cream

● Fry bacon until crisp; drain and crumble. Cook noodles as directed until just tender. Drain well.

● Combine remaining ingredients, except ¼ cup Parmesan cheese and ¼ cup sour cream, in a large bowl. Add noodles and bacon and toss well. Place in a buttered 3½-quart casserole.

● Cover and bake at 350 degrees for 30 to 40 minutes. Remove cover and top with mixture of remaining Parmesan cheese and sour cream. Broil until golden.

OYSTER STUFFING

Yields 8 to 10 cups

An old recipe with a moist consistency. Original recipe said, "Never use fresh oysters." This makes enough to stuff a large turkey and have some left for a casserole.

5 cans (8 oz. each) small
   oysters
½ gallon milk
1 cup butter
1 lb. saltine crackers
ground pepper

● Scald milk with liquid from the oysters. Melt butter in hot milk.

● Cut oysters into small pieces and add to milk (remove green stomachs from oysters, if desired). Crumble crackers into milk mixture. Add pepper to taste. Mixture should be juicy. Let stuffing stand before filling the bird cavity.

HAWAIIAN PINEAPPLE PUDDING

Serves 6

A good side dish with ham. Also tasty for dessert or a brunch dish.

4 eggs
½ cup sugar
3 tablespoons flour
½ teaspoon salt
1 can (15 oz.) crushed
   pineapple in its own juice
4 slices white bread, cubed
¼ cup butter, melted

● Combine eggs, sugar, flour and salt; add pineapple, including the juice, and mix well.

● Pour into a 9x9-inch casserole and top with bread cubes. Drizzle with melted butter. Bake at 350 degrees for 1 hour. Cover with foil if the top becomes too brown. Serve upside down on a plate.

Vegetables

VEGETABLES

ARTICHOKE CASSEROLE

Serves 4

An unusual combination of ingredients for a quick, tasty side dish.

1 package (10 oz.) frozen artichoke hearts, drained and sliced (or use canned artichokes)
2 eggs, hard-boiled, peeled and sliced
½ cup stuffed green olives, sliced
¼ cup water chestnuts, sliced
½ cup grated American cheese
1 can (10¾ oz.) condensed cream of mushroom soup
¼ cup milk
½ cup buttered bread crumbs

● Layer artichokes, eggs, olives, chestnuts and cheese in a 1½-quart casserole. Combine soup and milk; pour over casserole. Top with buttered crumbs. Bake at 350 degrees for 25 minutes or until bubbly and lightly browned.

CHINESE ASPARAGUS

Serves 4

1 lb. fresh asparagus, cut in 2-inch pieces
¼ cup butter
1 cup sliced, fresh mushrooms
4 green onions, chopped
1 tablespoon sliced pimiento
1 cup chicken stock
salt and pepper to taste

Béchamel Sauce

3 tablespoons butter
3 tablespoons flour
1 cup milk
salt and pepper to taste

● Sauté asparagus stalks in butter; when tender yet crisp, add asparagus tips, mushrooms, onions, pimiento, chicken stock and seasonings.

● When mushrooms are cooked, add enough Béchamel Sauce to thickly coat vegetables. Serve.

● Sauté butter and flour in a small saucepan for a few minutes. Add milk and cook until thickened and smooth, stirring constantly.

ENHANCED BAKED BEANS

Serves 18

The humble bean in exalted disguise.

2 cans (28 oz. each) baked
beans
2 lb. bulk sausage
8 slices bacon, browned and
crumbled
2 large onions, chopped
2 stalks celery, chopped
1½ teaspoons basil
1 tablespoon chopped
parsley
¼ cup chutney, chopped
¼ cup soy sauce
1 can (28 oz.) tomatoes, cut
into small pieces
2 teaspoons salt
1 cup molasses
¼ cup vinegar

● Brown sausage; drain off fat and
add bacon, onion, celery. Add to
beans with remaining ingredients
and simmer one hour. Drain off
some of the excess liquid and
reserve it for later.

● Place beans in a crock pot. Cook
on high for one hour, then cook
on low approximately 12 hours.
(Or, beans may be placed in an
ovenproof casserole and baked at
350 degrees for 1½ hours.) Add
reserved liquid, if necessary,
during cooking to keep beans
juicy.

PROVISIONAL BEANS

Serves 8

An easy dish for a tailgate picnic.

1 can (15 oz.) pork and beans
1 can (14 oz.) butter beans
or white lima beans,
drained (or use 2 cans
pork and beans)
6 slices bacon, cut in 1-inch
pieces
1 green pepper, chopped
1 medium onion, chopped
½ cup sliced fresh
mushrooms or 4 oz.
canned
½ cup catsup
¼ cup mild prepared
mustard
⅓ cup maple syrup
1 teaspoon oregano
¼ teaspoon ground cloves
2 bay leaves

● Fry bacon slowly until clear but
not crisp. Remove from pan and
fry green pepper and onion in
drippings until glazed. Add with
remaining ingredients and
reserved bacon to beans in a
large earthenware pot; bake at
350 degrees for 45 to 60 minutes.
Remove bay leaves before
serving.

GREEN BEAN RING MOLD

Serves 12 to 16

Very pretty when filled with cooked carrots.

1 lb. mushrooms, finely
minced
1 cup minced yellow onions
¼ cup butter
2 lbs. fresh whole green
beans or 3 packages
(10 oz. each) frozen whole
4 eggs, beaten
1 cup shredded Gruyère or
Swiss cheese
¼ cup bread crumbs
1 teaspoon salt
½ teaspoon pepper
¼ teaspoon grated nutmeg

● Sauté mushrooms and onions in foaming butter over high heat until mushrooms are dry. Cook fresh green beans in boiling water for 7 minutes or frozen beans half the time that package directs; drain.

● Beat eggs and add mushroom-onion mixture, beans, cheese, bread crumbs, salt, pepper and nutmeg. Pack mixture into oiled 10-inch ring mold. Place mold in pan of boiling water in a 350-degree oven and bake 30 minutes.

● Remove mold from water bath and let stand 5 minutes; unmold by running a knife around edge of pan and inverting it over serving dish.

● Serve hot with Lemon Butter. (Mold may be kept in hot water bath for 30 minutes at 200 degrees; or, if baked ahead and refrigerated, bring to room temperature and reheat for 15 minutes at 350 degrees in water bath.)

Lemon Butter

1 cup butter, melted and hot
2 tablespoons chopped
parsley
4 tablespoons lemon juice

● Combine ingredients and serve hot.

199

CURRIED LIMA BEANS

Serves 6

A vegetable dish dressed for a party.

2 packages (10 oz. each)
frozen baby lima beans
4 slices bacon, diced
1 medium onion, minced
1 small clove garlic, mashed
1 teaspoon curry powder
1 can (10¾ oz.) condensed
cream of mushroom soup
2 tablespoons sherry
½ cup sour cream
1 can (2.8 oz.) French-fried
onion rings

- Cook lima beans in small amount of boiling salted water until barely tender. Drain.

- Fry bacon until crisp; remove from pan. Add onions, garlic and curry and sauté 5 minutes. Stir in soup, sherry, beans, bacon and sour cream; heat, but do not boil.

- Place in 1½-quart casserole and top with onion rings. Bake, uncovered, at 325 degrees for 10 to 15 minutes.

BROCCOLI CASSEROLE

Serves 4

1 lb. fresh broccoli or 1
package (10 oz.) frozen
3 tablespoons butter,
melted
12 to 14 Ritz crackers,
crumbled
1 egg, beaten
1 cup milk
salt and pepper

- Wash and chop broccoli. Cook in boiling, salted water until done. Drain, leaving moist. Mix remaining ingredients and add to broccoli.

- Bake in buttered 1-quart casserole at 300 degrees until firm but not hard (about 25 minutes).

Note: Chopped spinach may be substituted for the broccoli.

WINTER VEGETABLES AU GRATIN   Serves 8

A colorful dish which can be prepared ahead and baked at the last minute.

1 lb. carrots, sliced
  diagonally
1½ lbs. broccoli, trimmed
1 medium cauliflower,
  broken into florets

- Cook each vegetable separately in salted water. Plunge into cold water and drain.

- Pour half the Sauce into shallow 3-quart casserole. Add vegetables and mix gently. Top with remaining Sauce and sprinkle with sesame seeds. Bake at 375 degrees for 30 minutes.

Cheese Sauce

5 tablespoons butter
5 tablespoons flour
2¾ cups milk
1 tablespoon Dijon mustard
1 teaspoon salt
½ teaspoon pepper
1½ cups shredded Swiss
  cheese
2 tablespoons chopped
  parsley
¼ cup toasted sesame seeds

- Melt butter; add flour and cook, stirring constantly, until bubbly. Gradually stir in milk and cook until thickened. Stir in mustard, salt, pepper, cheese and parsley.

CRATER LAKE LODGE, Crater Lake

The deepest lake in the United States and one of the world's scenic wonders, Crater Lake serves as a fitting backdrop for Crater Lake Lodge.

Crater Lake National Park is Oregon's only national park, and as such it receives numerous visitors each year. The lake is believed to have been formed thousands of years ago when the top of Mount Mazama collapsed and was swallowed up inside the mountain. The huge "bowl" thus created gradually filled with water. Still later a small volcano formed in the center of the lake when lava erupted from the interior of Mount Mazama. A 2-hour boat tour around the lake's 25-mile shoreline enables visitors to gain full appreciation of this scenic wonder.

The sprawling rustic Lodge blends harmoniously with its natural surroundings and offers numerous lodging choices for groups and families. The spacious lobby and main dining room are full of wood and stone and convey a feeling of warmth and friendliness.

Hiking is a favorite activity here, with hikers enjoying the more than 500 kinds of flowering plants, ferns, and flowers in the meadows and on the slopes of the volcano. Camping in the nearby wilderness is also popular.

The Lodge dining room features a gourmet-style menu, with entrées ranging from king crab and salmon to New York steak or a light quiche. Fresh pies and desserts are baked daily on the premises. College students from around the Northwest staff the Lodge facilities throughout the summer and add to the friendly atmosphere.

For additional information:
Crater Lake Lodge
Crater Lake, OR 97604
(503) 594-2511

STIR-FRY VEGETABLES   Serves 8

From the Dining Room of Crater Lake Lodge

1 lb. broccoli
1 lb. zucchini
1 lb. carrots
6 oz. onions
6 oz. mushrooms
3 tablespoons olive oil
1 clove garlic, crushed
1 teaspoon salt
1 teaspoon pepper
1 tablespoon Italian
  seasoning
1 tablespoon soy sauce

● Wash vegetables, dry and let crisp in refrigerator. Cut broccoli into 1-inch pieces. Cut zucchini and carrots into ½-inch slices and onion and mushrooms into ¼-inch slices.

● In a wok or large frying pan, heat olive oil with garlic, salt, pepper and Italian seasoning. Add vegetables and cook, stirring constantly, until vegetables are tender but still slightly crunchy. Stir in soy sauce and serve.

SURKAL
(SHOW CRAUTE)

Serves 8 to 10

A sweet-sour cabbage dish to go with ham or game.

1 large cabbage, red or
  white, sliced thin
3 tablespoons butter
3 tablespoons flour
1 teaspoon salt
1½ teaspoons caraway seed
2 cups beef broth
1 tablespoon vinegar
1 tablespoon sugar

● Melt butter in large saucepan;
  alternately layer in pan the sliced
  cabbage and a mixture of flour,
  salt and caraway.

● Pour broth over cabbage and
  simmer, covered, until cabbage is
  soft, about 1½ hours. Stir occasionally to prevent sticking. Just
  before serving, add sugar and
  vinegar, cooking enough to
  dissolve sugar.

GLAZED CARROTS AND GRAPES

Serves 8

A refreshing combination . . . in taste and color!

4 cups sliced fresh carrots
  or 3 packages (10 oz. each)
  frozen carrots in butter
3 tablespoons butter (omit
  with frozen carrots)
3 tablespoons brown sugar
3 tablespoons vodka
1½ teaspoons cornstarch
2 teaspoons water
1½ cups seedless green
  grapes

● Cook carrots with butter until
  tender; drain. Add sugar and
  vodka.

● Mix cornstarch and water until
  smooth and add to carrots; bring
  to a boil, stirring constantly.
  Just before serving, add grapes
  and heat through.

CARROTS IN HORSERADISH SAUCE

Serves 6

2½ lb. fresh whole carrots
½ cup mayonnaise
1 tablespoon minced onion
1 tablespoon prepared
  horseradish
salt and pepper
¼ cup fine cracker crumbs
2 tablespoons butter
paprika
chopped parsley

- Cook whole carrots in salted water until just tender; reserve ½ cup of the liquid. Cut carrots into ¼-inch strips and arrange in a shallow 9x9-inch baking dish.

- Combine cooking liquid, mayonnaise, onion, horseradish and salt and pepper to taste.

- Just before baking, pour sauce over carrots. Sprinkle with cracker crumbs and paprika and dot with butter.

- Bake, uncovered, at 375 degrees for 15 to 20 minutes. Garnish with parsley.

CARROTS IN WINE SAUCE

Serves 6

8 medium carrots
3 tablespoons butter
1 bunch green onions, thinly
  sliced, including some
  tops
¼ teaspoon salt
1 tablespoon sugar
1 tablespoon water
4 teaspoons flour
⅔ cup milk or cream
3 tablespoons white wine
finely chopped parsley

● Peel and slice carrots; sauté with onions in butter for 3 minutes over medium-high heat.

● Add salt, sugar and water. Cover and simmer until carrots are tender yet crisp. Sprinkle with flour and cook, stirring, until sauce is bubbly.

● Remove from heat and stir in cream or milk and wine. Return to heat and cook until thickened. Garnish with parsley and serve immediately.

Note: You may substitute sherry or orange juice and 1 teaspoon grated orange peel for the wine.

CARROTS AMBROSIA

Serves 8

24 small whole carrots,
  trimmed
½ cup butter
½ cup sugar
3 to 4 oranges, peeled and
  sliced
½ teaspoon salt
chopped parsley

● Cook carrots in small amount of salted water until tender. Drain and add butter, sugar, orange slices and salt.

● Simmer until carrots are glazed. Garnish with parsley before serving.

FAR EAST CELERY

Serves 6

4 cups celery, cut into 1-inch pieces
1 can (5 oz.) water chestnuts, sliced and drained
1 can (10¾ oz.) condensed cream of chicken soup
1 jar (2 oz.) diced pimiento
½ cup soft bread crumbs
¼ cup slivered almonds, toasted
2 tablespoons butter, melted

● Cook celery in salted water 8 minutes; drain and mix with water chestnuts, soup and pimiento in 1-quart casserole.

● Toss bread crumbs with butter and almonds and sprinkle over casserole. Bake at 350 degrees 35 minutes.

SWISS CORN BAKE

Serves 4 to 6

An easy make-ahead for busy days.

3 cups fresh corn kernels, or same amount of frozen or canned
1 can (5½ oz.) evaporated milk
1 egg, beaten
2 tablespoons chopped onion
½ teaspoon salt
dash pepper
1 cup shredded Swiss cheese
½ cup soft bread crumbs
1 tablespoon butter, melted

● Cook fresh or frozen corn; drain. Combine corn, milk, egg, onion, salt and pepper and ¾ cup of the cheese. Mix well and pour into greased 1½-quart baking dish.

● Toss bread crumbs with butter and remaining cheese. Sprinkle over corn mixture and bake at 350 degrees for 25 to 30 minutes.

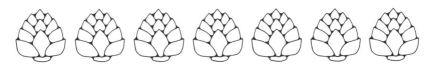

JOT'S RESORT, Gold Beach

Two spectacular natural attractions help ensure the popularity of Jot's Resort: the Oregon coast and the Rogue River.

Jot's is a 100-unit vacation complex situated on the north shore of the Rogue, a famous Oregon fishing river. Jot's Sports Shop caters to anyone interested in the great outdoors, providing deep sea charters and guided salmon and steelhead fishing trips.

For those interested in striking out on their own, Jot's rents boats and equipment for fishing, crabbing and clam digging. Guests can view the scenic Rogue Wilderness Area on jetboat trips that depart daily from the Resort.

Jot's Rod 'n Reel Restaurant has enjoyed a reputation for fine gourmet dining for more than 30 years. Featuring fresh local seafood, top-quality steaks, and unusual specialty dishes, the Rod 'n Reel has developed a devoted following for its fine cuisine.

For additional information:
Jot's Resort
P.O. Box "J"
Gold Beach, OR 97444
(503) 247-6676

STUFFED EGGPLANT PARMESANA   Serves 4

From the Dining Room of Jot's Resort

2 eggplants
2 eggs
½ cup shredded mozzarella
 cheese
3 tablespoons grated
 Parmesan cheese
1 tablespoon granulated
 garlic
3 tablespoons chopped
 parsley
1 tomato, finely chopped
salt and pepper to taste
4 slices mozzarella cheese

● Halve eggplants lengthwise and scoop out pulp, leaving ½-inch thick shells. Boil pulp 5 minutes and drain. Mix pulp with remaining ingredients except mozzarella slices.

● Parboil shells 5 minutes. Carefully lift from water and drain. Stuff shells with cheese mixture. Place in a deep buttered baking dish and top with mozzarella slices. Bake at 375 degrees for 35 to 40 minutes.

ROCK SPRINGS GUEST RANCH, Bend

In a small hidden valley about 10 miles northwest of Bend is Rock Springs Guest Ranch, a family-oriented dude ranch that provides all the trappings of the Old West with enough amenities to make it popular with the most demanding visitor.

Rock Springs caters to families by employing counselors who provide a recreation program for five-to-12-year-olds for part of each day. Kids take part in such varied activities as horseback riding, evening hayrides, hiking, crafts, swimming, and trips to the nearby High Desert Museum.

Guests come from all over the world to enjoy this authentic Old West setting and the variety of activities offered. Horses are a big part of many guests' vacations, and the 55 horses at Rock Springs allow the novice and the seasoned rider to find a mount that's exactly right.

Guided horseback rides are available twice each day, and most areas of the 1200-acre Ranch are accessible by horseback. The riding trails are spectacular, with the majestic Cascade mountains providing a dream background.

Other activities on the Ranch include tennis and volleyball on lighted courts, swimming in the heated pool, country dancing, and just relaxing. Fishermen can also take advantage of nearby high lakes and the Deschutes, Metolius, and Crooked Rivers for superb trout fishing.

Cozy knotty-pine cabins are scattered among the pines and feature fireplaces and comfortable furnishings. With just 15 units on the Ranch, guests soon get to know each other and make new friends.

Buffet-style meals are served in the rustic knotty-pine lodge. Rib-sticking good food puts everyone in a convivial mood, and guests often gather around the piano after dinner for an old-fashioned sing-along.

For additional information:
Rock Springs Guest Ranch
64201 Tyler Road
Bend, OR 97701
(503) 382-1957

AVOCADO RATATOUILLE

Serves 4 to 6

From the Dining Room of Rock Springs Guest Ranch

1 small eggplant, chopped
salt and lemon pepper to
 taste
¼ cup vegetable oil
1 medium onion, diced
½ small green pepper, finely
 diced
2 tablespoons vegetable oil
1 medium zucchini, chopped
2 medium tomatoes,
 chopped
3 cloves garlic, finely diced
½ cup spicy tomato sauce
2 medium avocados,
 chopped
1 cup diced Monterey jack
 cheese
¼ cup unsalted sunflower
 seeds

● Season eggplant with salt and lemon pepper; sauté in ¼ cup vegetable oil until partially cooked. Set aside in a large bowl.

● Sauté onion and green pepper in 2 tablespoons oil until partially done. Add zucchini and cook 3 minutes. Add tomatoes, garlic and tomato sauce to zucchini and cook until warm.

● Remove from heat and add to eggplant mixture. Gently stir in avocado and cheese. Pour into 9x13-inch casserole. Sprinkle with sunflower seeds and bake at 325 degrees for 30 minutes.

SAUCY EGGPLANT

Serves 4

A Hungarian version of eggplant in tomato sauce.

1 medium eggplant
1 egg, beaten
flour
oil

- Peel eggplant and slice ⅓-inch thick. Dip each slice in beaten egg, then in flour. Brown in oil and place on paper towels to drain.

- Place half of eggplant in casserole in single layer. Cover with half the Sauce; repeat layers. Bake at 350 degrees for 30 minutes.

Tomato Sauce

1 can (15 oz.) tomatoes
1 can (8 oz.) tomato sauce
2 tablespoons lemon juice
¼ teaspoon salt
¼ teaspoon paprika
¼ teaspoon garlic powder
1 teaspoon sugar
½ teaspoon Worcestershire sauce

- Combine all ingredients and simmer 30 to 40 minutes.

Note: Grated cheese may be added as a topping.

EGGPLANT AND TOMATO CASSEROLE

Serves 8

An interesting side dish even for those who may be hesitant about eggplant.

2 lb. eggplant, peeled and
   cubed to make 8 cups
2 cups water
1 teaspoon salt
2 eggs
½ cup fine, dry bread
   crumbs
2 tablespoons chopped onion
1 teaspoon salt
¼ teaspoon pepper
1 teaspoon dried basil
2 tablespoons butter
3 medium tomatoes, sliced
⅓ cup grated Parmesan
   cheese

- Cook eggplant in salted water until tender, about 5 minutes. Drain and mash slightly with back of a spoon.

- Beat eggs and add bread crumbs, onion, salt, pepper and ½ teaspoon basil. Stir in mashed eggplant and spread in greased 9x13-inch baking dish. Dot with 1 tablespoon butter.

- Arrange tomatoes in rows over eggplant. Sprinkle with ½ teaspoon basil, more salt and pepper and remaining butter. Top with cheese and bake at 375 degrees for 20 minutes.

TAKE IT EASY RANCH RESORT,
Fort Klamath

A paradise for fishermen—or for anyone who just wants to relax and get away from it all—is the Take It Easy Ranch Resort in the beautiful Wood River Valley in Southern Oregon.

The unspoiled beauty of lush green meadows, tall timber, and the majestic Cascade Mountains makes a fitting setting for "outstanding fly fishing" in two springfed creeks on the Ranch and in nearby rivers and lakes. The Ranch provides guide service for both float and wade trips on the Williamson River, famed for its 3- to 16-pound trout.

Take It Easy Ranch Resort sports a complete Fly Shop for all flyfishing needs plus rod and wader rentals. The Fly Tying Room houses tying tables, vices, and tools to enable every fly fisherman to ready his gear for successful fishing. Fly casting and fly tying lessons are available, as are fly fishing schools for larger groups.

Accommodations on the Ranch are all new, attractive cabins with comfortable modern furnishings and full baths. Cabins are set in the woods overlooking Fort Creek, "just a short cast from a rising trout."

Guests who are interested in just relaxing and not much fishing enjoy the Ranch's recreation room, which houses pinball machines, a pool table, ping pong and dart games. Crater Lake National Park is just 15 miles away, and Upper Klamath Lake and Agency Lake are nearby for water sport enthusiasts.

The main lodge houses the dining room, where guests enjoy great homestyle cooking in a colorful rustic atmosphere. A big stone fireplace and hunting and fishing trophies add a touch of authenticity to this outdoor-oriented resort.

For additional information:
Take It Easy Ranch Resort
P.O. Box 408
Fort Klamath, OR 97626
(503) 381-2328

PARMESAN MUSHROOMS WITH SOUR CREAM
Serves 8

From the Dining Room of Take It Easy Ranch

2 lb. mushrooms, sliced
¼ cup finely diced onion
butter or margarine
1½ to 2 cups sour cream
½ cup grated Parmesan
  cheese
3 tablespoons sherry

- Sauté sliced mushrooms and onions in butter until soft and liquid has evaporated.

- Combine sour cream, Parmesan and sherry. (Use 2 cups sour cream if mixture is very thick.) Add mushrooms to sour cream mixture. Cook over low heat until heated through. Serve warm.

215

WALLA WALLA ONION CASSEROLE   Serves 6

Walla Walla Sweet onions, famous in the Northwest, are extremely mild in flavor. Any mild white onion may be used.

4 to 5 large Walla Walla
  Sweet onions, sliced thin
¼ cup butter
2 cups cooked rice
1 cup shredded Swiss cheese
⅔ cup half & half
dash salt
¼ cup grated Parmesan
  cheese

● Melt butter in large skillet; add onions and cook over medium heat until transparent but not brown. Remove from heat.

● Mix together onions, rice, cheese, half & half and salt; put into 2-quart shallow casserole and top with Parmesan cheese. Bake at 325 degrees for 1½ hours.

SWEDISH RUTABAGAS   Makes 6 cups

A unique way to serve an often-overlooked vegetable.

8 medium rutabagas
⅓ cup sour cream
1 tablespoon oil
1 tablespoon butter
1 teaspoon salt
⅛ teaspoon freshly grated
  nutmeg
parsley

● Steam rutabagas for 20 minutes or until soft; peel and cut into cubes. Mash with sour cream, oil, butter and seasonings until fluffy. Garnish with parsley.

CREAMED SPINACH

Serves 6

Popeye would've loved this!

2 lb. fresh spinach, stemmed
and chopped or
2 packages (10 oz. each)
frozen
2 tablespoons butter
2 tablespoons flour
1 cup sour cream
1 teaspoon minced onion
½ teaspoon lemon juice
salt and pepper to taste

● Cook spinach and drain thoroughly; set aside.

● In a small saucepan, melt butter and blend in flour. Add sour cream, onion, lemon juice, salt and pepper. Cook until mixture thickens slightly, stirring constantly.

● Add the drained spinach and heat through; do not boil. Serve immediately.

SPINACH SUPREME

Serves 4

2 bunches fresh spinach
2 tablespoons butter
1 tablespoon lemon juice
¼ teaspoon dry mustard
½ cup sliced fresh
mushrooms
¼ cup thinly sliced red
onions
coarsely ground pepper

● Cook spinach until tender; remove to heated platter.

● Melt butter in saucepan; stir in lemon juice and mustard. Add mushrooms and onions and sauté until tender; pour over spinach. Sprinkle with pepper and serve.

ZUCCHINI WITH MOZZARELLA

Serves 8

Even children will eat zucchini when it's prepared this way.

3 medium zucchini, sliced
1 large onion, thinly sliced
3 medium tomatoes,
  chopped
1 can (15 oz.) tomato sauce
1 teaspoon oregano
1 teaspoon marjoram
1 teaspoon basil
8 oz. mozzarella cheese,
  shredded
¼ cup grated Parmesan
  cheese
1 tablespoon chopped
  parsley
paprika

- In lightly buttered 2-quart baking dish, layer half the zucchini, onion, tomatoes and tomato sauce. Sprinkle with half herbs and mozzarella. Repeat layers.

- Top with Parmesan, parsley and a few dashes of paprika. (Can be refrigerated at this point, covered.) Bake at 350 degrees for 1½ hours or until zucchini is tender.

ZUCCHINI PUFF

Serves 6 to 8

Finished dish is similar to a soufflé.

4 cups shredded zucchini
4 eggs
¼ cup biscuit mix
1 cup shredded Cheddar
  cheese
1 tablespoon chopped
  parsley
1 tablespoon dried onion
  flakes
2 tablespoons grated
  Parmesan cheese
garlic salt, salt and pepper
  to taste

- Drain zucchini in a colander for 1 hour; press out all juice. Beat eggs slightly in large bowl and add zucchini and remaining ingredients.

- Pour mixture into a 2-quart casserole and bake at 350 degrees for 25 to 30 minutes. Serve immediately.

Breads

BREADS

YEAST BREADS

QUICK BREADS

FRENCH TOAST AND PANCAKES

BREAD SPREADS

SWISS EGG BRAID

Yields 2 loaves

Fine-grained, light yellow loaves . . . very pretty!

1 package dry yeast
¼ cup warm water
1 tablespoon sugar
2 cups milk, scalded and
  cooled
1½ cups flour
1 teaspoon salt
¼ cup sugar
3 eggs, beaten
5 cups flour
½ cup shortening, melted
  (or use oil)
1 egg yolk
poppy seeds or sesame
  seeds (optional)

- Make a sponge by dissolving yeast in warm water. Add 1 tablespoon sugar and the milk. Mix in 1½ cups flour, stirring until smooth. Let rest in warm place for about 1 hour.

- Stir the sponge down and add salt, ¼ cup sugar, eggs, 2 cups of the flour, and shortening or oil. Mix until smooth. Gradually add remaining flour until dough can be kneaded. Knead well and let rise until double, about 1 hour.

- Divide dough into halves. Divide each half into thirds and braid each loaf.

- Grease 2 5x9-inch loaf pans and place a braided loaf in each. Let rise until doubled, about 45 minutes. Brush with egg yolk and sprinkle with poppy or sesame seeds.

- Bake at 325 degrees for 45 to 50 minutes. Remove from pans and cool on racks.

CHEESE AND WINE BREAD

Yields 1 loaf

Great with soup on a cold night.

3 cups flour
1 package dry yeast
½ cup dry white wine
½ cup margarine
2 teaspoons sugar
1 teaspoon salt
3 eggs
4 oz. Monterey jack cheese, cubed

● In large mixer bowl, combine 1½ cups of flour and the yeast.

● In a saucepan, heat wine, margarine, sugar, and salt until warm (115 to 130 degrees). Add to dry mixture in bowl. Add the eggs and beat at low speed for ½ minute, scraping the sides of the bowl; beat at high speed for 3 minutes. By hand, stir in cheese and enough extra flour to make a soft dough.

● Turn out onto lightly floured surface; knead until smooth and elastic. Place in a lightly greased bowl, turning once to grease all surfaces. Cover and let rise in a warm place until double in bulk, about 1½ hours.

● Punch dough down; cover and let rest 10 minutes. Shape into an 8-inch round loaf and place in a greased 9-inch pie pan. Cover and let rise until doubled, about 40 minutes. Bake at 375 degrees for 40 minutes, covering with foil after the first 20 minutes.

CRACKED WHEAT BREAD

Yields 2 loaves

Good for sandwiches or toast.

1 package dry yeast
¼ cup warm water
½ cup firmly packed brown
  sugar
2 teaspoons salt
2½ cups hot water
¼ cup vegetable oil
2 cups whole wheat flour
½ cup cracked wheat
5 cups white flour

• Dissolve yeast in warm water. In a large mixing bowl, dissolve brown sugar and salt in hot water. Add oil, whole wheat flour, cracked wheat and 2 cups white flour. Stir in yeast and mix well. Add remaining flour to form a dough that leaves sides of bowl.

• Let dough rest 20 minutes; knead until smooth. Place in greased bowl, turning dough so top is greased. Cover and let rise in warm place until doubled, about 1½ hours.

• Punch dough down and divide in half. Let rest 10 minutes. Shape into 2 loaves and place in 2 well-greased 5x9-inch loaf pans.

• Let rise in warm place for 45 minutes or until dough is well-rounded above the pans. Bake at 375 degrees for 45 minutes.

LAKE CREEK LODGE, Sisters

Amidst sweet-scented pines in the invigorating air of Central Oregon, Lake Creek Lodge beckons all who would enjoy a vacation in a charming country inn.

Located in the middle of the Metolius Recreation Area, Lake Creek Lodge is especially attractive to families who like outdoor activities. The nearby spring-fed Metolius River presents some of the best fishing anywhere, while Lake Creek pond is stocked and ready for kids to try their hands at trout fishing.

Lake Creek stables offer hand-picked horses for riding along wooded forest trails or mountain streams. Also available are tennis, swimming, hiking, cycling, shuffleboard, horseshoes and, for the kids, weekly wienie roasts and hayrides. Nearby golf courses and crystal clear lakes offer more summer activities, while winter weather offers skiing at nearby Hoodoo Ski Bowl or Mt. Bachelor (Bend).

Lodging includes picturesque knotty-pine-paneled cabins which are really little homes, complete with living rooms, kitchens, and screened porches. Smaller cottages are also available.

The Lodge is a popular gathering place in all kinds of weather—dress is informal, hospitality is gracious. The dining room offers outstanding food served country buffet style—fresh salmon, country fried chicken, sizzling steaks, roast lamb. A different entrée every night and homemade breads and desserts bring hungry diners back again and again.

For additional information:
Lake Creek Lodge
Sisters, OR 97759
(503) 595-6331

WHEAT BREAD

Yields 4 loaves

From the Dining Room of Lake Creek Lodge

2 packages dry yeast
1 cup warm water
4 cups water, room temperature
3 tablespoons sugar
2 teaspoons salt
2 cups whole wheat flour
9 to 10 cups white flour

● Dissolve yeast in 1 cup warm water. Add yeast mixture, sugar and salt to the 4 cups water. Stir in whole wheat flour and 4 cups of white flour; beat until very smooth.

● Gradually beat in additional 5 to 6 cups white flour to make a firm dough; knead until smooth and elastic. Place dough in a well-greased bowl and let rise 1 hour. Punch down and knead for about 1 minute.

● Divide dough into four equal parts. Shape into loaves and place in greased 9x5-inch loaf pans. Let rise until just above edges of pans. Bake at 350 degrees for 1 hour or until golden brown.

Note: To make raisin bread, replace whole wheat flour with white flour and add 1 lb. raisins.

CINNAMON CURRANT OATMEAL BREAD

Yields 2 loaves

Makes excellent toast and freezes well.

2 packages dry yeast
⅓ cup warm water
1½ cups warmed milk
½ cup white or brown sugar
2 teaspoons salt
⅓ cup shortening
5 to 6 cups flour, sifted
2 eggs, beaten
1 cup currants or raisins
1½ cups uncooked quick or
  old-fashioned oatmeal
⅓ cup brown or white sugar
1 tablespoon ground
  cinnamon

● Soften yeast in the warm water. In a large bowl, pour the milk over ½ cup sugar, salt and shortening. Cool to lukewarm. Beat in half of the flour and all of the eggs.

● Stir in the yeast, currants and oatmeal. Add enough more flour to make a stiff dough. Turn out onto a lightly floured board and knead until smooth and silky, about 10 minutes. Place in a well-greased bowl and let rise until double in bulk. Divide dough into two parts. Let rest 10 minutes.

● Combine ⅓ cup sugar and ground cinnamon. Roll each half of dough into an 8x15-inch rectangle and spread each with half the sugar-cinnamon mixture. Roll each to form a loaf and place in a greased 5x9-inch bread pan, seam side down.

● Brush loaves lightly with melted shortening, cover and let rise until doubled, about 45 minutes. Bake at 400 degrees for 10 minutes. Reduce oven temperature to 375 degrees and continue baking for 35 to 45 more minutes. Cool on racks.

SLAVIC BREAD

Yields 2 round loaves

A very dark, heavy bread. Good for sandwiches and for appetizers with pickled herring and caviar.

2½ cups white flour
2 cups shredded whole bran cereal
2 packages dry yeast
1 tablespoon sugar
1 tablespoon instant coffee powder
1 tablespoon salt
2 teaspoons onion powder
1 teaspoon crushed fennel seed (optional)
2½ cups water
½ cup molasses
¼ cup vegetable oil
1 square unsweetened chocolate
4 cups medium rye flour
1 cup white flour, more or less
1 egg white
1 tablespoon water

● In large mixing bowl, combine first 8 ingredients.

● In a medium saucepan, heat water, molasses, oil and chocolate until very warm (120 degrees). Add warm liquid mixture to dry ingredients in bowl and beat 3 minutes. Stir in the rye flour.

● Knead on board covered with white flour, working in additional flour until dough is smooth, about 5 minutes. Place in a greased bowl, cover and let rise 45 to 60 minutes until nearly doubled. Punch dough down and divide in half.

● Shape into two round loaves and place on greased baking sheets. Cover and let rise 30 to 45 minutes until nearly doubled.

● Brush loaves with a mixture of egg white and 1 tablespoon water. Bake at 375 degrees for 45 to 55 minutes, or until crust is dark brown and loaves sound hollow when tapped. Remove from pans and cool on racks.

REFRIGERATOR POTATO ROLLS
Yields 4 to 5 dozen rolls

Dough may be prepared from one to several days ahead.

⅔ cup shortening, melted
¼ cup sugar
1 teaspoon salt
1 cup scalded milk
1 cup mashed potatoes
1 package dry yeast
¼ cup warm water
2 eggs, beaten
6 to 7 cups flour

● Combine melted shortening, sugar, salt and milk with mashed potatoes. Cool to lukewarm.

● Soften yeast in water and add to potato mixture. Add eggs and 1½ cups of flour; mix well. Add enough of remaining flour to form a soft dough; knead until smooth and satiny.

● Place in an oiled bowl, turning dough to cover with oil; cover with a towel and let dough rest 20 minutes. Cover and refrigerate several hours or overnight.

● When ready to use, punch down dough. Shape into rolls and place on greased baking pans. Let rise 2 hours or until doubled in size. Bake at 400 degrees for 10 to 12 minutes.

Note: This dough can be used as a sweet roll dough by increasing the sugar to ½ cup.

NO-KNEAD ROLLS

Yields 24 rolls or 2 loaves

Low in calories and cholesterol!

1 package dry yeast
½ cup warm water
1 tablespoon sugar
4 cups flour, unsifted
1½ teaspoons salt
1 cup water
2 tablespoons oil
1 egg white, beaten
sesame or poppy seeds

● Dissolve yeast in ½ cup warm water. Add sugar and let rest until foamy. Add flour, salt, additional 1 cup water and oil. Mix until dough forms a firm ball. Cover and let rise 10 minutes. Press dough down and let rise 10 minutes; repeat 5 times.

● Roll out on a floured board and cut into 24 squares. Form each into a roll by pulling corners of dough underneath; place on a greased baking sheet. Brush rolls with beaten egg white and sprinkle with sesame or poppy seeds.

● Let rise until double, about 45 minutes. Bake at 350 degrees for 25 to 30 minutes.

Note: This dough may be formed into two long loaves and baked as French bread. For variations, add 1 teaspoon dill weed and 1 tablespoon chopped onion, or 1 cup shredded cheese.

ROMEO INN, Ashland

The excitement of Oregon's nationally acclaimed Shakespearean Festival is a fitting contrast to the restful atmosphere awaiting guests at Romeo Inn.

Tucked away in the small mountain town of Ashland, the Inn is a beautifully charming Cape Cod house whose spaciousness warmly invites guests to feel at home and relax during their stay. The bed-and-breakfast establishment is set amidst tall pines on half an acre of land commanding a panoramic view of the valley.

The four bedrooms at the Inn are large and furnished for guests' comfort, with king-size beds and private baths. Guests may enjoy the swimming pool or jacuzzi or, on cooler days, may prefer to sit by the fire in the reading room and catch up on the latest best-seller.

Activities in the nearby area include fishing, hiking, skiing, and attending the outstanding presentations of the Shakespearean Theatre. Many specialty shops throughout the town make browsing and shopping a discovery-filled pastime.

A complimentary full breakfast awaits guests each morning at Romeo Inn, served in the dining room or on the patio. The heady aroma of fresh-baked breads or Belgian waffles gently beckons guests from their beds.

For additional information:
Romeo Inn
295 Idaho St.
Ashland, OR 97520
(503) 488-0884

COLOSSAL CINNAMON ROLLS Yields 12 large rolls

From the Dining Room of the Romeo Inn

1 tablespoon yeast
½ cup water
1 cup warm milk
½ cup honey
2 cups whole wheat flour
⅔ cup dry instant mashed
  potatoes
⅔ cup warm water
4 cups unbleached white
  flour
2 teaspoons salt
ground cinnamon
1 cup brown sugar

● Combine yeast and ½ cup water; set aside until foamy. Mix dry potatoes and ⅔ cup warm water. Add milk, honey, whole wheat flour and mashed potato mixture to yeast. Let stand 1 hour or until bubbly.

● Mix in white flour and salt; knead to form a soft dough. Let rise until double in bulk, about 1 hour.

● On a floured board, roll dough into a rectangle about ½-inch thick. Brush with water, sprinkle with cinnamon and then brown sugar. Roll up, jellyroll fashion; seal edges and cut into 12 equal pieces.

● Arrange cut side up on a greased jellyroll pan and let rise 45 minutes to an hour. Bake at 350 degrees for 20 minutes or until light brown. Ice with powdered sugar icing.

HAZELNUT TWIST SWEET ROLLS

Yields 24 rolls

The orange and hazelnuts make a great flavor combination.

2 packages dry yeast
¼ cup warm water
⅓ cup butter, softened
¾ cup scalded milk
¼ cup sugar
2 teaspoons salt
2 teaspoons grated orange
   rind
2 eggs
4 to 4½ cups flour

● Soften yeast in warm water. Combine butter and milk in a large bowl. Add sugar, salt, orange rind, eggs and yeast mixture. Gradually add flour to form a stiff dough.

● Knead dough 3 to 5 minutes and place in a well-greased bowl to rise for about 30 minutes, covered. Turn out onto floured board and knead just to release air. Let rest a few minutes, then roll out to a 12x22-inch rectangle.

● Spread Hazelnut Filling along half of the dough on the 22-inch side. Fold the other half over the filling and cut into 1-inch strips. The strips should be 1x6 inches.

● Twist each strip 4 or 5 times. Place one end on a greased baking sheet and curl the twist around to make a circle; tuck the end under the roll. Continue until all strips are formed.

● Cover and let rise until double in bulk. Bake at 375 degrees for 15 minutes.

Hazelnut Filling

⅓ cup butter, softened
1 cup powdered sugar
1 cup ground hazelnuts

● Cream butter and sugar and blend in the hazelnuts.

ORANGE BUTTER PAN ROLLS

Yields 24 rolls

Breakfast rolls at their best.

1 package dry yeast
¼ cup warm water
¼ cup sugar
1 teaspoon salt
2 eggs
½ cup sour cream
6 tablespoons butter, melted
2¾ cups flour, or more if needed
2 tablespoons butter
¾ cup sugar
¾ cup coconut, toasted if desired
2 teaspoons grated orange rind
¼ cup coconut

● Soften yeast in water. Stir in ¼ cup sugar, salt, eggs, sour cream and melted butter. Add enough flour to form a stiff dough. Let rise about 2 hours.

● Combine ¾ cup sugar, ¾ cup coconut and the orange rind.

● Divide the dough in half and roll each half into a 12-inch circle. Brush each with 1 tablespoon melted butter; sprinkle each with half the sugar mixture. Cut each circle into 12 wedges. Roll each wedge to form a crescent, beginning with the wide edge.

● Place rolls in a buttered 9x13-inch baking pan and let rise until double, about 1 hour. Bake at 350 degrees for 25 to 30 minutes. Leave in the pan and pour glaze over while still warm. Sprinkle with remaining ¼ cup coconut.

Orange Glaze

½ cup sugar
¼ cup sour cream
1 tablespoon orange juice
2 tablespoons butter

● Combine ingredients in a saucepan and boil 3 minutes. Cool.

WHOLE GRAIN BREADSTICKS

Yields 48 breadsticks

This dough also makes a delicious pizza crust.

3 cups white flour
2¼ teaspoons salt
3 packages dry yeast
¾ cup wheat germ
1½ tablespoons honey
6 tablespoons vegetable oil
1¾ cups hot water (120 degrees)
2 to 2¼ cups whole wheat flour
1 egg
1 tablespoon water
sesame seeds or poppy seeds

● In a large bowl, stir together white flour, salt, yeast and wheat germ. Add honey, oil, and gradually beat in hot water; beat 2 minutes.

● Add about 1½ cups whole wheat flour and beat 2 minutes more. Beat in enough whole wheat flour to form a stiff dough. Turn onto floured board and knead until smooth.

● Cut dough into quarters and each quarter into 12 pieces. Roll each piece into a 12-inch rope and arrange 1 inch apart on greased baking sheets. Cover and let rise 15 minutes or until slightly puffy.

● With a soft brush, paint each breadstick with mixture of egg and 1 tablespoon water. Sprinkle with seeds. Bake at 375 degrees for 15 minutes or until brown.

WHOLE WHEAT ENGLISH MUFFINS

Yields 10 muffins

Healthy and delectable.

1 package dry yeast
¼ cup water
¾ cup milk, scalded and
  cooled
¼ cup shortening,
  melted and cooled
1 tablespoon honey
1 egg
1 teaspoon salt
2 cups whole wheat flour
1 cup white flour
½ cup cornmeal

● Dissolve yeast in water. Set aside.

● Combine cooled milk, shortening, honey, egg, salt and softened yeast. Stir in whole wheat flour and knead in white flour. Pat out on floured board to ½-inch thickness and cut into 2½-inch rounds. Let rise 1 hour, covered.

● Heat griddle to medium-hot and sprinkle with a little cornmeal. Cook muffins on each side until light brown, about 7 minutes. Split cooked muffins and toast.

PUMPKIN MUFFINS

Yields 24 muffins

Good for lunchbox treats.

⅓ cup shortening
1⅓ cups sugar
2 eggs
1 cup prepared pumpkin
1⅔ cups flour, sifted
1 teaspoon salt
½ teaspoon ground cloves
½ teaspoon ground
  cinnamon
¼ teaspoon baking powder
1 teaspoon baking soda
⅓ cup water
½ cup raisins or chopped
  nuts (optional)

● Cream together shortening and sugar. Add eggs and pumpkin and beat well.

● Sift together dry ingredients and add in thirds alternately with water. Add raisins or nuts.

● Fill paper-lined muffin tins two-thirds full and bake at 350 degrees for 20 to 25 minutes.

BAKER'S BAR M RANCH, Adams

Nestled in the quiet Blue Mountains of northeastern Oregon, Baker's Bar M Ranch is the ideal spot for a close-to-nature western vacation.

The center of the Bar M is the hand-hewn log Ranch House built in 1864 as a stopover freight and stage station. The rustic House now provides lodging for guests upstairs, with fireside lounge, dining room, and kitchen downstairs. Other overnight accommodations include the nearby Homestead Annex with suites, and separate cabins by a brook or a lake.

The Ranch is strategically located on the Umatilla River, 31 miles east of Pendleton. Guests are encouraged to take the 30-second walk from the Ranch House to the river, toss in a line, and maybe pull out a rainbow trout or two.

Horses are a big part of any western ranch, and this is especially true at the Bar M. Experienced riders and new dudes can ride as much or as little as they like over the Ranch's 2500 acres, using the Ranch's mountain-raised saddle horses.

Other activities at the Bar M include swimming in the large pool fed with natural water from nearby warm springs, square dancing, volleyball, basketball, and evening entertainment in the Ranch House. Some guests relish the opportunity to just relax and enjoy the invigorating mountain air, while others prefer to pitch in and help with the chores.

The Bar M dining room features home-cooked meals served family style in the Ranch House. With beef, pork, vegetables, and berries raised right on the Ranch, Bar M foods are as fresh as they are delicious. And the informal family setting allows guests to really get to know each other.

For additional information:
Baker's Bar M Ranch
Route 1
Adams, OR 97810
(503) 566-3381

BAR M BISCUITS
Serves 6

From the Dining Room of Bar M Ranch

1 egg, beaten
⅔ cup milk
2 cups flour
1 tablespoon sugar
½ teaspoon salt
2 teaspoons baking powder
½ cup lard
oil

● Combine egg and milk in a bowl. Set aside. Sift together flour, sugar, salt and baking powder in a medium bowl; cut in lard until fine. Combine with egg mixture and stir well with a two-tined fork. Mixture will be very moist.

● Turn out onto a well-floured board and knead several times. Pat to a circle ¾-inch thick. Cut biscuits, roll each in oil and arrange on a baking sheet.

● Bake at 450 degrees for 10 minutes. Reduce heat to 400 degrees and bake for 10 more minutes.

COUNTRY PEAR MUFFINS

Yields 24 muffins

3½ cups flour
⅔ cup sugar
4 teaspoons baking powder
1 teaspoon baking soda
1 teaspoon ground
  cinnamon
1 teaspoon freshly grated
  nutmeg
½ teaspoon salt
1 teaspoon grated lemon
  peel
2 eggs
1⅓ cups buttermilk
½ cup vegetable oil
2 cups finely chopped,
  peeled and cored pears

● Blend in a large bowl the flour, sugar, baking powder, soda, cinnamon, nutmeg, salt and lemon peel. In a smaller bowl, blend eggs, buttermilk and oil. Stir egg mixture into dry ingredients and blend just to moisten. Fold in pears.

● Spoon batter into greased muffin tins and sprinkle with Sesame Seed Topping. Bake at 400 degrees for 20 to 25 minutes.

Sesame Seed Topping

2 tablespoons sesame seeds
2 tablespoons sugar
½ teaspoon ground
  cinnamon
½ teaspoon grated nutmeg

● Mix ingredients together.

BEER MUFFINS

Yields 8 to 12 muffins

The beer imparts an interesting flavor, similar to sourdough.

2 cups biscuit mix
2 tablespoons sugar
6 oz. beer, room temperature

● Mix all ingredients together and knead about 6 times. Drop by tablespoonfuls into greased muffin pans. Bake at 400 degrees for 20 minutes.

238

BLUEBERRY BUNS

Yields 20 small buns

1 cup water
½ cup butter or margarine
¼ teaspoon salt
1 teaspoon sugar
⅛ teaspoon ground
cinnamon
1 cup flour
4 eggs
½ cup blueberries, fresh
or frozen

● In a medium saucepan bring water, butter, salt and sugar to a boil. Add cinnamon and flour all at once and beat over low heat for 1 minute, or until mixture leaves the sides of the pan. Remove from heat and beat 2 more minutes.

● Beat in eggs, one at a time, beating well after each. Stir in blueberries (well-drained, if frozen).

● Drop by teaspoonfuls about 2 inches apart on greased baking sheets. Bake at 375 degrees for 30 to 35 minutes. Frost with Lemon Frosting while still warm.

Lemon Frosting

1 tablespoon butter
1½ tablespoons heavy
cream
1 cup sifted powdered sugar
½ teaspoon fresh lemon
juice
½ teaspoon vanilla

● Melt butter in a small saucepan. Add cream and remove from heat. Stir in powdered sugar and flavorings.

KAH-NEE-TA, Warm Springs

Rising unexpectedly from a bluff of red clay in the middle of the Warm Springs Indian Reservation is a striking contemporary structure known as Kah-Nee-Ta.

Here, where the sun shines more than 300 days a year, the Warm Springs, Wasco, and Paiute Indians have shared this half-million acre paradise since an 1855 treaty. The centerpiece, Kah-Nee-Ta, is a resort designed to cater to every discriminating taste.

The lodge itself is a dramatic, multi-level structure with a massive artistic fireplace, warm earthtone furnishings, and rich wood carvings. Visible just outside is an enormous pool, deliciously inviting a dip into its aquamarine depths.

The resort's hotel is built in an unusual arrowhead shape, with deluxe rooms, saunas, and eateries. Each room has a private balcony with an outstanding view of the harshly beautiful country.

Two miles from the lodge is the Village, where guests may stay in cottages, teepees or in their own RV's. Highlighting the area are a restaurant, snack bar, play area, and a gigantic pool fed by the warm waters of an ancient natural spring.

Activities available at Kah-Nee-Ta include horseback riding, bicycling, miniature golf, tennis, golf, and white water rafting. Good fishing in nearby lakes and rivers is a favorite pastime of many.

Dining in the lodge's Juniper Room may feature game hen baked in clay or Kah-Nee-Ta's famed Indian fry bread with blackberry jam. Twice a week, the resort features a buffalo and salmon bake, an authentic Northwest Indian delight.

For additional information:
Kah-Nee-Ta
P.O. Box K
Warm Springs, OR 97761
1-800-831-0100 (OR)
(503) 553-1112 (Elsewhere)

INDIAN FRY BREAD
Serves 8 to 10

From the Dining Room of Kah-Nee-Ta Resort

3 cups flour
2 tablespoons baking
powder
1 tablespoon sugar
1 teaspoon salt
1 teaspoon lard
2 cups cold water
(approximate)
oil

● Mix dry ingredients; cut in the lard. Add enough water to make a thick dough and knead well.

● Heat oil in deep-fryer to 350 degrees. Break off handfuls of dough and fry until golden brown. Drain and serve warm.

STRAWBERRY RHUBARB COFFEE CAKE

Serves 12 to 15

3 cups flour
1 cup sugar
1 teaspoon baking powder
1 teaspoon baking soda
1 teaspoon salt
1 cup butter or margarine
1 cup buttermilk
2 eggs, slightly beaten
1 teaspoon vanilla

● Prepare Strawberry-Rhubarb Filling.

● In a large bowl, stir together flour, sugar, baking powder, soda and salt. Cut in butter to form fine crumbs.

● Beat together buttermilk, eggs and vanilla; add to dry ingredients. Stir to moisten. Spread half the batter in a greased 13x9-inch baking pan; spoon Filling over batter. Spread remaining batter over Filling.

● Sprinkle Sugar Topping over cake and bake at 350 degrees for 40 to 45 minutes.

Strawberry-Rhubarb Filling

3 cups fresh or frozen rhubarb, cut into 1-inch pieces
16 oz. frozen sliced, sweetened strawberries, thawed
2 tablespoons lemon juice
1 cup sugar
⅓ cup cornstarch

● Cook fruit, covered, for about 5 minutes. Add lemon juice. Combine sugar and cornstarch and add to fruit mixture. Cook, stirring, for 4 to 5 minutes until thickened and clear. Cool.

Sugar Topping

¾ cup sugar
½ cup flour
¼ cup butter

● Cut ingredients together in a small bowl till crumbly.

APRICOT BREAKFAST PASTRY

Serves 20

Impressive, easy, and you can make 24 hours ahead.

2 cups flour
½ teaspoon salt
1 cup butter
1 cup sour cream
10 oz. apricot jam
⅔ cup chopped walnuts
1 cup coconut

● Combine flour and salt, then cut in butter as for a pie crust. Mix in sour cream. Refrigerate overnight. Remove and let stand at room temperature for 1 hour.

● Cut dough in half and roll each half into a 10x15-inch rectangle. Spread each with ½ of the jam, coconut, and nuts. Roll up jelly-roll style, beginning with the long edge.

● Place each roll on a greased baking sheet and bake at 350 degrees for 45 minutes. Cool; then sprinkle with powdered sugar and slice.

BLUEBERRY TEA CAKE

Serves 8 to 10

2 cups sifted flour
2 teaspoons baking powder
½ teaspoon salt
½ cup butter, softened
¾ cup sugar
1 egg
½ cup milk
2 cups blueberries, fresh
  or frozen

- Sift together flour, baking powder and salt. Cream together butter and sugar. Add egg and milk to butter mixture and beat until smooth.

- Add dry ingredients; fold in blueberries. Spread in a greased and floured 8- or 9-inch round cake pan. Sprinkle with Crumb Topping and bake at 375 degrees for 40 to 45 minutes.

Crumb Topping

½ cup sugar
¼ cup flour
½ teaspoon ground
  cinnamon
¼ cup butter

- Cut butter into dry ingredients until it forms coarse crumbs.

HAWAIIAN BREAD

Yields 3 loaves

Makes a lovely treat with tea.

2 cans (15 oz. each) crushed
  pineapple in heavy syrup
10 oz. coconut
4 eggs, beaten until light
1½ cups sugar
4 cups flour
2 teaspoons salt
2 teaspoons baking soda

- Combine pineapple and coconut. Add eggs and sugar and mix well. Mix in flour, salt, and baking soda.

- Pour into 3 greased 5x9-inch loaf pans. Bake at 325 degrees for 45 minutes.

OREGON ZUCCHINI FRUIT BREAD

Yields 2 loaves

A healthful favorite that freezes well.

3 eggs
1 cup vegetable oil
2 cups sugar
2½ cups shredded, raw
  zucchini
1 tablespoon vanilla
2 cups whole wheat flour
1 cup white flour
½ teaspoon baking powder
1 teaspoon baking soda
1 teaspoon salt
1 tablespoon ground
  cinnamon
1 cup chopped walnuts
1 cup chopped dates
1 cup raisins

● Beat eggs until light and foamy. Add oil, sugar, zucchini and vanilla.

● Mix dry ingredients together and add to egg mixture, stirring to blend. Stir in nuts, dates and raisins and pour into 2 greased 5x9-inch loaf pans.

● Bake at 325 degrees for 1 hour. Cool in pans for 10 minutes before turning out onto racks.

HAZELNUT PUMPKIN BREAD

Yields 3 loaves

Hazelnuts add a rich flavor and new texture to this old favorite.

3 cups sugar
1 cup vegetable oil
4 eggs
2 cups prepared pumpkin
1 cup water
4 cups flour
½ teaspoon baking powder
2 teaspoons salt
2 teaspoons baking soda
1 teaspoon each ground
cinnamon, ground cloves,
grated nutmeg, ground
allspice
2 cups chopped hazelnuts
1 cup raisins

● Blend together sugar, oil, eggs and pumpkin; mix well. Sift together dry ingredients and add alternately with water to pumpkin mixture. Stir in nuts and raisins.

● Divide batter among 3 greased 5x9-inch loaf pans and bake at 350 degrees for 1 hour or until done.

ORANGE NUT BREAD

Yields 1 loaf

zest* of 3 oranges, sliced
fine
1 cup sugar
½ cup water
3 cups flour
1 tablespoon baking powder
½ cup firmly packed brown
sugar
1 teaspoon salt
1 egg, beaten
1 cup milk
1 cup slivered nuts

● Boil the orange zest in a little salted water until tender; drain. Combine sugar, water and prepared orange zest. Boil 10 minutes; cool.

● Sift dry ingredients and add egg, milk, nuts and sugar-zest syrup. Place in a greased 5x9-inch loaf pan and bake at 300 degrees for 15 minutes.

● Increase heat to 350 degrees and bake 60 minutes. Test with toothpick for doneness.

*Zest is orange part of rind.

BANANA PUMPKIN BREAD

Yields 1 loaf

½ cup shortening
1 cup sugar
2 eggs
1 banana, mashed
¼ cup prepared pumpkin
1¼ cups flour
¾ teaspoon baking soda
¼ teaspoon salt
1 teaspoon ground
　cinnamon
½ cup chopped nuts

● Cream shortening and sugar in a medium bowl until fluffy. Add eggs, one at a time, beating well after each. Stir in mashed banana and pumpkin.

● Sift together dry ingredients and add to egg mixture. Stir in nuts and pour into a greased 5x9-inch loaf pan. Bake at 350 degrees for 45 minutes.

HONEY BREAD

Yields 1 loaf

Delicious thinly sliced, toasted and served with cream cheese mixed with orange marmalade.

1 cup honey
1 cup milk
1 cup firmly packed brown
　sugar
2 teaspoons ground
　cinnamon
1 teaspoon baking soda
½ teaspoon salt
3½ cups flour

● Beat honey, milk and brown sugar until well blended. Mix together dry ingredients and add to honey mixture.

● Pour into a well-greased 5x9-inch loaf pan and bake at 250 degrees for 2½ hours, or until it tests done with a toothpick.

BAKED FRENCH TOAST

Serves 4 to 6

Perfect when you have overnight guests.

3 eggs
⅔ cup milk or cream
1 teaspoon vanilla
¼ teaspoon ground
  cinnamon
6 to 8 slices stale French
  bread, thickly sliced
¼ cup butter

• In a large shallow pan, mix eggs, milk, vanilla, and cinnamon. Place bread slices in a single layer in pan and allow them to soak up the liquid. (Can be refrigerated overnight at this point.)

• In another large baking pan, melt butter in a 400-degree oven. Arrange bread in a single layer in pan and bake for 15 minutes. Turn bread over and bake another 10 minutes, or until the underside is golden.

HAWAIIAN FRENCH TOAST

Serves 4

Elegant but easy!

4 eggs
2 teaspoons vanilla
1 tablespoon maple syrup
1 tablespoon plain yogurt
1 tablespoon sugar
1 can (8 oz.) crushed
  pineapple, drained
¼ cup milk
8 slices day-old French
  bread
¼ cup butter or margarine
powdered sugar and
  shredded coconut

• Place eggs, vanilla, syrup, yogurt, sugar, pineapple and milk in a blender and whirl until smooth. Place bread slices in a shallow dish and pour the egg mixture over, turning bread once. Allow mixture to saturate.

• Melt 1 tablespoon butter in a frying pan over medium heat. Add a few slices of the bread and cook until browned, turning to cook both sides. Place on a warm platter in a low oven while cooking the remaining slices in the remainder of the butter. Serve dusted with powdered sugar and coconut.

LEMON PANCAKES

Serves 4

Refreshing change for a breakfast standby.

1 cup flour
¼ cup sugar
¼ teaspoon salt
1 cup milk
2 tablespoons oil or melted
 butter
3 egg yolks
3 egg whites
grated rind of 2 lemons

● Sift dry ingredients together. Gradually add milk and beat until smooth. Beat egg yolks slightly and add with oil and lemon rind to milk mixture.

● Beat egg whites until stiff but not dry; fold into batter. Bake on a hot griddle immediately.

APPLE PANCAKES

Serves 4 to 6

2 cups flour
1 teaspoon soda
1 tablespoon sugar
1 teaspoon salt
½ teaspoon ground
 cinnamon
2 eggs
2 cups buttermilk
¼ cup butter, melted
1 firm apple, pared, cored
 and grated

● In mixing bowl, combine dry ingredients. Mix together eggs, buttermilk, butter and grated apple. Stir into dry ingredients just to moisten. Thin batter with milk if necessary, depending on juiciness of apple.

● Drop by ¼ cupfuls onto a hot griddle. Turn when bubbles appear on the surface. Serve with maple syrup and lots of butter.

THE ADOBE, Yachats

Right next to the Pacific Ocean in the small resort community of Yachats is a purposefully secluded resort that capitalizes on quiet and relaxation—The Adobe.

The original builders of this resort motel handcrafted adobe bricks and used them to adorn the guest rooms, along with clear and knotty pine. All the original rooms have carports, private baths, fireplaces, and most important of all, spectacular views of the ocean. Two newer annexes offer larger rooms, some with lanais and fireplaces.

Many guests at The Adobe spend much time exploring the beach and tidepools, hunting agates on the beach, surf casting, and kite flying. Others may choose to relax in their warmly furnished rooms and enjoy the closeness of the ocean and its changing moods.

Between April and October, guests may relish a visit to the famous silver smelt runs nearby. The mating season of the silver smelt brings thousands of these delicious tiny fish to the sandy coves of Yachats, where eager fishermen await them with special nets. Yachats is one of the few places in the world where these sea-run smelt come into shore.

Dining at The Adobe offers guests a sweeping panoramic view of the ocean from the semi-circle dining room. In this romantic setting, diners can indulge in delicious gourmet dinners of fresh seafoods and tender steaks, and breakfasts of unique pancakes, omelettes, and egg dishes.

For additional information:
The Adobe
P.O. Box 219
Yachats, OR 97498
(503) 547-3141

CREAM CHEESE HOT CAKES
Serves 4

From the Dining Room of The Adobe

8 oz. cream cheese, softened
2 tablespoons flour
2 eggs
1 teaspoon sugar
1 teaspoon butter, melted
powdered sugar

● Blend all ingredients except powdered sugar. Prepare grill with vegetable cooking spray. Make dollar-size cakes. Serve sprinkled with powdered sugar.

Note: Especially nice served with a fruit salad.

HERBED BUTTER

Yields 1 cup

A wonderfully fragrant topping.

1 cup butter
¾ teaspoon poppy seed
¾ teaspoon sesame seed
¾ teaspoon caraway seed
¾ teaspoon dill weed
¾ teaspoon celery seed
¾ teaspoon summer savory
¾ teaspoon finely chopped
  chives or green onion tops
¾ teaspoon finely chopped
  parsley
¾ teaspoon minced garlic
¼ cup minced onion

● Melt butter and add remaining
  ingredients. Spread over French
  bread or over vegetables.

GOLDEN CHEESE SPREAD

Yields 1½ cups

A good accompaniment to soups and salads.

1 cup shredded sharp
  Cheddar cheese
1 cup mayonnaise
¼ cup grated onion
⅓ cup grated Parmesan
  cheese
French bread

● Mix ingredients together and
  spread on loaf of French bread
  split horizontally.

● Wrap crust side of each half in
  foil, leaving topping side open.
  Bake at 400 degrees until cheese
  is melted and lightly browned,
  about 10 minutes.

Desserts

DESSERTS

CAKES
Apple Lemon Cake, 255
Banana Pecan Layer Cake, 256
Banana Cake, 257
Carrot Walnut Cake, 258
Blueberry Lemon Loaf Cake, 259
Chocolate Buttermilk Dessert Cake, 260
Chocolate Beet Cake, 260
Chocolate Walnut Cake, 261
Alta's Sourdough Chocolate Cake, 263
Oregon Prune Cake, 264
Oregon Plum Cobblecake, 265
Strawberry Roll, 266
Pumpkin Nut Roll, 267
Poppy Seed Cake, 269

COOKIES AND BARS
Chocolate Mint Drops, 270
Oatmeal Macaroon Cups, 271
Cheesecake Cookies, 271
Hazelnut Squares, 272
Red Raspberry Squares, 272
Chocolate Caramel Squares, 273
Favorite Brownies, 274
Swedish Brownies, 274
Creamy Chocolate Layers, 275

PIES AND TARTS
Hazelnut Angel Pie, 276
Open Face Apple Pie, 276
Marbled Chocolate Rum Pie, 277
Raspberry Ice Cream Pie, 278
Mile-High Strawberry Pie, 279
Apple Pie Slices, 280
Apfel Kuchen, 281
Butter Crust Fresh Fruit Tart, 282
Oregon Blackberry Tart, 283
Hazelnut Fruit Tart, 284
Strawberry Tea Tarts, 285
Peach Tarts, 286

DESSERTS
Crusty Peach Cobbler, 286
Blueberry Flummery, 287
Blueberry Apple Crisp, 287
Blackberry Crisp, 288
Rhubarb Pastry, 288
Banana Puffs, 289
Carrot Pudding, 290
Cranberry Pudding with Butter
   Sauce, 291
Hazelnut Cheesecake, 291
Cheesecake, 293
Orange Cranberry Torte, 294
Raspberry Walnut Torte, 295
Sans Rival, 296
Chocolate Peppermint Torte, 297
Chocolatissimo, 299
Chocolate Mousse Torte, 300
Elegant Chocolate Torte, 301
Chocolate Ice Cream Cake, 303
Chocolate Intolerance, 305
Fresh Peach Ice Cream, 306
Frozen Delight, 307
Fresh Lemon Freeze, 308
Popcorn Cake, 308

APPLE LEMON CAKE

Serves 12 to 15

A superb cake that improves with age.

4 cups coarsely chopped,
  peeled apples
1¾ cups sugar
2 eggs
½ cup vegetable oil
2 teaspoons vanilla
2 cups flour, sifted
2 teaspoons baking soda
1 teaspoon salt
2 teaspoons ground
  cinnamon
½ cup chopped walnuts

● Combine apples and sugar; set aside. In a large bowl mix eggs, oil, and vanilla. Beat one minute at medium speed.

● Combine dry ingredients and add alternately to egg mixture with the apple mixture. Stir in walnuts.

● Pour into greased and floured 9x13-inch baking pan and bake at 350 degrees for 45 to 50 minutes. Cool. Drizzle Lemon Glaze over cooled cake.

Lemon Glaze

1 cup powdered sugar
1½ tablespoons lemon juice
½ teaspoon vanilla
1 tablespoon light corn
  syrup

● Blend ingredients until smooth.

BANANA PECAN LAYER CAKE   Serves 12 to 16

An elegant dessert from a family recipe.

2¼ cups sugar
1 cup butter, softened
3 large egg yolks, well-
  beaten
3 egg whites
3 cups cake flour
1½ teaspoons baking soda
1½ cups mashed ripe
  bananas
6 tablespoons buttermilk
1 cup coarsely chopped
  pecans

● Cream butter and sugar until light and fluffy. Add beaten egg yolks and mix well.

● Sift together dry ingredients. Mix buttermilk and mashed bananas.

● To butter mixture, alternately add the dry mixture and butter-milk mixture, beginning and ending with the dry ingredients. Add chopped pecans.

● Beat egg whites until they hold a peak; gently fold them into the batter. Divide batter among three 9-inch round cake pans which have been greased and lined with waxed paper.

● Bake at 350 degrees 25 to 35 minutes or until cake tester comes out clean. Cool cake layers in pans on rack for 10 minutes; remove from pans. Cool completely, then frost. If possible, frost with Fluffy White Frosting several hours before serving.

Fluffy White Frosting

2 cups sugar
⅔ cup water
⅔ teaspoon cream of tartar
⅔ cup egg whites
2 teaspoons vanilla

● Mix sugar, water and cream of tartar in a saucepan. Cover and bring to boil; boil for 3 minutes. Wipe side of pan with clean, wet cloth wrapped on a fork to remove sugar crystals.

● Boil syrup slowly until it reaches soft ball stage (242 degrees) or spins a thread. Beat egg whites in large bowl until stiff but still glistening.

(continued)

BANANA PECAN LAYER CAKE (continued)

- Pour hot syrup very slowly into beaten egg whites while beating continuously. Beat until frosting holds its shape when a spatula is passed through it. Add vanilla and beat again until frosting dulls slightly.

BANANA CAKE   Serves 8 to 12

The unique filling makes this cake a winner.

1½ cups sugar
½ cup butter
2 eggs, beaten
1 teaspoon vanilla
1¾ cups flour
1 teaspoon baking soda
1 teaspoon baking powder
½ teaspoon salt
4 tablespoons sour milk or
   buttermilk
1 cup mashed banana
1 cup chopped nuts

- In a large mixer bowl, cream sugar, butter, eggs and vanilla until fluffy. On low speed, mix in flour, soda, baking powder and salt alternately with sour milk. Fold in bananas and nuts.

- Pour into 3 greased and floured 8-inch round cake pans and bake at 350 degrees for 25 to 30 minutes or until tester comes out clean. Cool.

- Fill with Feather Filling and frost with favorite seven-minute frosting (or see recipe for Fluffy White Frosting on opposite page).

Feather Filling

1 cup flour
1 cup boiling water
½ cup butter, softened
1 cup sugar
1 cup chopped nuts
1 teaspoon vanilla

- Pour boiling water over dry flour and work into a ball. Cool in refrigerator. Meanwhile, cream butter, sugar and nuts together. Add cooled flour mixture and vanilla.

CARROT WALNUT CAKE

Serves 12

Moist and full of zest.

3 cups flour
2 teaspoons baking powder
1 teaspoon baking soda
1 teaspoon ground cinnamon
½ teaspoon salt
1 cup butter, softened
1 cup firmly packed light
  brown sugar
1 cup sugar
4 eggs
2 tablespoons each grated
  lemon peel and grated
  orange peel
2 tablespoons each lemon
  juice and orange juice
1 lb. carrots, peeled and
  grated medium fine
1 cup chopped walnuts
1 cup seedless raisins
chopped walnuts

● Sift flour with baking powder, soda, cinnamon and salt. Set aside. In a large bowl, beat butter with sugars until light and fluffy. Add eggs, one at a time, beating well after each.

● Combine grated peels and juices. With mixer on low speed, add flour mixture alternately with juice mixture, beginning and ending with flour mixture. Beat just until smooth.

● Gently stir in grated carrots, nuts and raisins, mixing well. Pour into a lightly greased and floured 10-inch tube pan. Bake at 350 degrees for 60 minutes or until cake tester comes out clean. Cool in pan on rack for 20 minutes.

● Turn cake out of pan and spread glaze over top of warm cake, letting it run down the sides. Sprinkle top edge with chopped walnuts. Refrigerate until ready to serve.

Creamy Lemon Peel Glaze

8 oz. cream cheese, softened
1 tablespoon lemon juice
1 teaspoon grated lemon
  peel
1½ cups powdered sugar

● Combine all ingredients and beat until smooth.

BLUEBERRY LEMON LOAF CAKE Serves 8 to 10

Makes a delightful ending to a salmon barbecue.

2 cups flour
1½ teaspoons baking
  powder
¼ teaspoon salt
½ cup butter or margarine
1 cup sugar
2 eggs
⅓ cup milk
½ cup chopped nuts
2 teaspoons grated lemon
  peel
1 cup blueberries, fresh if
  possible

- Sift flour, baking powder and salt. Set aside. Beat butter with sugar until fluffy. Add eggs, one at a time, beating well after each.

- Add dry mixture alternately with milk, ending with dry ingredients. Stir in nuts, lemon peel and berries.

- Grease a 9x5-inch loaf pan. Pour in batter and bake at 350 degrees for 1 hour or until done. While cake is baking, prepare Syrup. Pour Syrup over cake while still warm.

Syrup

¼ cup lemon juice
⅓ cup sugar

- Combine ingredients in saucepan and cook 1 minute until sugar is dissolved.

CHOCOLATE BUTTERMILK DESSERT CAKE

Serves 18

2 cups sugar
2 cups flour
½ teaspoon salt
1 teaspoon soda
1 cup margarine
3 tablespoons cocoa
1 cup water
½ cup buttermilk or sour milk
1 teaspoon vanilla
2 eggs, beaten

● Mix together sugar, flour, salt and soda. Bring to a boil margarine, cocoa and water. Pour cocoa mixture over sugar-flour mixture and blend well. Add buttermilk, vanilla and eggs.

● Pour into greased 10x15-inch jellyroll pan. Bake at 350 degrees for 25 minutes. Spread Chocolate Nut Topping on warm cake.

Chocolate Nut Topping

3 tablespoons cocoa
½ cup margarine
6 tablespoons milk
1 lb. powdered sugar
1 teaspoon vanilla
1 cup nuts, chopped

● Bring to boil 3 tablespoons cocoa, margarine and milk. Remove from heat and add rest of ingredients. Beat well.

CHOCOLATE BEET CAKE

Serves 8

A surprise ingredient adds richness of flavor and color.

3 eggs, beaten
1½ cups sugar
1 cup vegetable oil
3 jars (4½ oz. each) baby food strained beets
2 oz. unsweetened chocolate, melted
1¾ cups flour
1 teaspoon baking soda
½ teaspoon salt
1 teaspoon vanilla

● Add sugar, oil, beets and melted chocolate to eggs and beat thoroughly. Sift dry ingredients together and add to egg mixture; stir together and add vanilla.

● Bake in two greased and floured 8-inch round cake pans at 350 degrees for 30 to 35 minutes. Cool on racks and frost with favorite chocolate frosting.

CHOCOLATE WALNUT CAKE

Serves 10 to 12

A whole wheat cake that's rich and wonderful.

4 tablespoons cocoa
1 teaspoon baking soda
½ cup boiling water
½ cup shortening
1 cup firmly packed brown sugar
1 cup sugar
2 egg yolks, beaten
1 cup buttermilk
¾ cup chopped walnuts
½ teaspoon salt
1½ cups sifted flour (sift 3 times)
1 cup whole wheat flour
1 teaspoon vanilla
2 egg whites, beaten to soft peaks

● Mix together cocoa, baking soda and boiling water. Set aside to cool. Cream together shortening and sugars until fluffy. Add egg yolks and buttermilk.

● Stir in nuts, salt and flours. Add the cooled cocoa mixture and vanilla. Fold in the beaten egg whites. Pour into three greased and floured 9-inch round cake pans.

● Bake at 350 degrees for 35 to 45 minutes or until springy when touched. Frost with Chocolate Mocha Frosting between layers and on top, but not on sides. Sprinkle nuts over the top.

Chocolate Mocha Frosting

2½ tablespoons butter
1½ tablespoons cocoa
1 lb. powdered sugar, sifted
2 tablespoons hot coffee
1 to 2 tablespoons rum or brandy
¾ cup chopped walnuts, for garnish

● In a medium bowl, cut butter into cocoa and 1 cup of the powdered sugar. Add a little of the hot coffee and beat until smooth. Add rest of sugar and coffee and enough rum or brandy to make a smooth frosting.

BLACK BUTTE RANCH, Black Butte

The quiet and serenity of Black Butte Ranch make it instantly appealing for vacationers who want to get away from it all—but want to do it in style.

A non-commercial, family-oriented recreational community, Black Butte Ranch is comprised of 1830 acres of green meadow and ponderosa pine timberland on the eastern slopes of the Central Oregon Cascade Mountains. The land was a family-owned cattle ranch until 1970, and Ranch guests now pedal their bikes through the big meadow which still grazes some 350 head of cattle.

Black Butte Ranch guests can enjoy a myriad of activities during their stay: biking, swimming, tennis, golf, flyfishing, hiking. During the summer the Lodge lake is a favorite canoeing spot; in winter, the frozen lake serves as a wonderland setting for ice skaters. Always in the background are snowcapped mountains encircling the Ranch.

A recreation barn offers activities for kids throughout the summer and on weekends and holidays in the winter: arts and crafts, field trips, movies, video games, sports activities. Kids of all ages participate, from the pre-schooler on through the high schooler.

Just 15 minutes from the Ranch is Hoodoo Ski Bowl, for downhill and cross country skiing. The nearby Deschutes and Metolius Rivers offer outstanding sport for anglers. With so many mountains nearby, mountain climbing and backpacking are favorite activities for many.

Guests stay in condominiums or in private homes available through the Ranch rental program. Accommodations are available to suit every group size.

The Ranch's Lodge is a contemporary structure that capitalizes on a commanding view of the Three Sisters Mountains. The dining room is known for its intimacy as well as its outstanding gourmet food, including seafood and beef entrées. In summer months, casual fare is available at the Pool Place.

For additional information:
Black Butte Ranch
P.O. Box 8000
Black Butte Ranch, OR 97759
(503) 595-6211

ALTA'S SOURDOUGH CHOCOLATE CAKE

Serves 8 to 10

From the Dining Room of Black Butte Ranch

½ cup thick sourdough
   starter
1 cup warm water
¼ cup dry skim milk
1½ cups flour
½ cup cocoa
1 cup sugar
½ cup shortening
½ teaspoon salt
1½ teaspoons soda
1 teaspoon vanilla
1 teaspoon ground
   cinnamon
2 eggs

● Mix together starter, warm water, dry milk, flour and cocoa. Let stand in a warm place 2 to 3 hours or until the mixture smells yeasty.

● In a separate bowl, cream together sugar, shortening, salt, soda, vanilla and cinnamon. Add eggs, one at a time, beating well after each.

(continued)

ALTA'S SOURDOUGH CHOCOLATE CAKE (continued)

- Add the creamed mixture to the sourdough mixture. Mix on low speed of mixer for 1 to 2 minutes.

- Bake in greased and floured Bundt pan or 2 round cake pans at 350 degrees for 25 to 30 minutes. Be sure cake is done before removing from oven. Cool on racks and frost with Mocha Icing.

Mocha Icing

5 tablespoons butter, softened
3 tablespoons cocoa
2½ cups powdered sugar
2 teaspoons instant coffee granules
3 tablespoons hot water
1 teaspoon vanilla

- Dissolve coffee granules in hot water; cool. Cream butter and add cocoa; add sugar gradually, alternating with the coffee. Cream well and flavor with vanilla. Add more sugar, if necessary.

OREGON PRUNE CAKE   Serves 10 to 12

2 cups sugar
1 cup vegetable oil
2 eggs
1 cup chopped cooked prunes
1 cup chopped walnuts
1 teaspoon baking soda
2 cups sifted flour
2 teaspoons each ground cinnamon, ground cloves, ground allspice, grated nutmeg
½ teaspoon salt
1 cup buttermilk
powdered sugar

- Mix together sugar, oil, eggs, prunes and walnuts. Sift together dry ingredients. Alternately add dry ingredients and buttermilk to the prune mixture.

- Bake in a greased 10-inch tube pan at 325 degrees for 45 to 60 minutes. Cool in the pan. Remove from pan and dust with powdered sugar.

OREGON PLUM COBBLECAKE

Serves 12

Good for a brunch or a light dessert.

½ cup butter, softened
¾ cup sugar
1 egg, beaten
2 cups flour
1½ teaspoons baking soda
½ teaspoon salt
½ teaspoon ground
  cinnamon
1 cup buttermilk
1 teaspoon vanilla
1 teaspoon grated lemon
  peel
2 cups chopped fresh plums
flour
whipped cream or ice cream

● Cream together butter and sugar. Add egg and beat well.

● Sift dry ingredients together and add alternately with buttermilk to the creamed mixture. Add vanilla and lemon peel. Gently blend in chopped plums which have been lightly floured to absorb any extra juice.

● Pour into a 9x13-inch pan. Sprinkle Topping over batter and bake at 350 degrees for 35 to 40 minutes. Serve with whipped cream or ice cream.

Topping

1 teaspoon ground cinnamon
¼ cup butter, softened
½ cup sugar

● Mix ingredients together until crumbly.

STRAWBERRY ROLL

Serves 8 to 10

A beautiful springtime dessert; can be made ahead and frosted just before serving.

6 eggs, separated
4 tablespoons sugar
3 tablespoons sifted flour
pinch salt
1 teaspoon vanilla
2 tablespoons powdered
  sugar
2½ cups crushed
  strawberries*
1 cup heavy cream, whipped
  and sweetened
toasted sliced almonds
mint leaves (optional)

● Grease a 12x18-inch jellyroll pan. Line with parchment paper; butter the paper. Combine egg yolks with 4 tablespoons sugar and beat until thick and lemon-colored.

● Beat egg whites until stiff. Gradually and carefully fold the flour, salt and vanilla into the egg yolk mixture. Fold in egg whites.

● Spread the cake mixture over bottom of pan. Bake at 350 degrees for 12 to 14 minutes.

● Remove cake from oven and sprinkle with 1 tablespoon powdered sugar. Loosen from pan and turn out on waxed paper, sugared side down. Carefully remove paper from bottom of cake.

● Sprinkle cake with remaining tablespoon powdered sugar and spread crushed strawberries on top. Roll up cake from the long edge and place on a platter.

● When cake has cooled, frost with whipped cream. Decorate with almonds down the center. Mint leaves can garnish the platter.

*If the berries are juicy, drain off some of the juice before filling the roll.

PUMPKIN NUT ROLL

Serves 10 to 12

An exquisite and impressive dessert for fall.

3 eggs
1 cup sugar
⅔ cup prepared pumpkin
1 teaspoon lemon juice
¾ cup flour
1 teaspoon baking powder
1 teaspoon ground ginger
1 teaspoon ground cinnamon
½ teaspoon ground nutmeg
½ teaspoon salt
1 cup chopped walnuts
powdered sugar

● Beat eggs for 5 minutes on high speed. Gradually beat in sugar. Stir in pumpkin and lemon juice.

● Sift together flour, baking powder, ginger, cinnamon, nutmeg and salt. Fold into pumpkin mixture. Pour into greased and floured jellyroll pan. Top with nuts and bake at 375 degrees for 15 minutes.

● Turn cake out onto a towel sprinkled with powdered sugar. Starting with long side, roll towel and cake up. Let cool. Unroll. Spread Cream Cheese Filling over cake and reroll. Chill before serving.

Cream Cheese Filling

1 cup powdered sugar
8 oz. cream cheese, softened
2 tablespoons milk
4 tablespoons butter,
  softened
1 teaspoon vanilla

● Beat all ingredients until smooth.

267

THE INN OF THE SEVENTH MOUNTAIN,
Bend

Strategically situated in the heart of Central Oregon's multi-faceted recreation area is a resort that's popular in both winter and summer—The Inn of the Seventh Mountain.

Beautifully contemporary in design, the Inn is set amidst pine-scented forests, sparkling clear rivers, and white-capped mountains. Its diverse range of activities and recreational programs makes it a favorite destination for the entire family.

Many guests take advantage of the Inn's close proximity to one of Oregon's famed skiing mountains, Mt. Bachelor, just 14 miles away and open for skiing from November to August. Other winter activities include sleigh rides, ice skating, swimming in the heated pool, snowmobile tours, and cross country ski trips.

Throughout the rest of the year, the Inn offers tennis, mini-golf, roller skating, arts and crafts classes, bicycling, and aerobics. Professionally guided adventure trips in the summer and fall include whitewater rafting, canoe float trips, horseback trail rides, windsurfing school, fishing trips, and moped tours.

The Inn offers a wide variety of accommodations, from lodge rooms to full condominium apartments. Many feature fireplaces and fully equipped kitchens.

Three restaurants at the Inn allow visitors to choose their own style of fare: The Baron's Deli, snacks and quick-service meals; The Poppy Seed, budget-minded sit-down meals; and El Crab Catcher, full-course dinners of seafood, beef, and chicken entrées and Mexican delights.

For additional information:
The Inn of the Seventh Mountain
P.O. Box 1207
Bend, OR 97709
1-800-452-6810 (OR)
1-800-547-5668 (Other Western states)
(503) 382-8711 (Elsewhere)

POPPY SEED CAKE
Serves 12

From the Dining Room of The Inn of the Seventh Mountain

4½ cups flour
1 package dry yeast or
  1 oz. compressed
1 cup lukewarm milk
¼ cup sugar
6 tablespoons butter,
  softened
1 egg
grated zest of 1 lemon
pinch salt
powdered sugar

● Sift flour into a bowl. Dissolve yeast in warm milk. Make a well in the flour and pour yeast mixture into it. Dust with a little flour and let ferment in a warm place for 15 minutes.

● Add sugar, egg, softened butter, lemon zest and salt. Work all into a dry dough; cover and set aside to rise again. When double in bulk, punch dough down. Roll out into a circle and line a 9-inch springform pan with it.

(continued)

269

POPPY SEED CAKE (continued)

- Spoon Poppy Seed Filling over dough. Cover with Butter Streusel Topping. Bake at 350 degrees for 45 minutes. When cool, drizzle with powdered sugar frosting.

Poppy Seed Filling

6 oz. freshly ground poppy
   seeds
1 cup milk
½ cup sugar
1 egg
2 tablespoons butter
grated zest of 1 lemon
fine bread crumbs, if
   required

- Soak poppy seeds in milk over low heat; remove from heat. Add sugar, lemon zest and butter; cool. If filling is not thick enough, add a small amount of bread crumbs.

Butter Streusel Topping

¾ cup sugar
⅞ cup butter
2¼ cups flour

- Mix butter and sugar well. Add flour and crumble to make coarse crumbs.

CHOCOLATE MINT DROPS
Yields 54 cookies

A mint-filled drop cookie for a brown bagger's treat.

3 cups flour
1 teaspoon soda
½ teaspoon salt
1 cup sugar
½ cup firmly packed brown
   sugar
1 cup butter, softened
2 eggs
1 teaspoon vanilla
2 packages (6½ oz. each)
   chocolate mint candy
   wafers
54 walnut halves

- Combine all ingredients except candy wafers and walnuts in a large mixer bowl and blend well. Drop by scant teaspoonfuls 2 inches apart onto ungreased baking sheets.

- Press candy wafer on each cookie and top with another scant teaspoon of dough. Seal dough to completely enclose candy. Press a walnut half onto top of each. Bake at 375 degrees for 9 to 12 minutes.

OATMEAL MACAROON CUPS

Yields 4 dozen

3 cups quick-cooking rolled oats
2 cups flaked coconut or 1 cup chopped nuts and 1 cup flaked coconut
1 cup flour
1½ cups firmly packed brown sugar
1 cup butter
⅓ cup honey

● In a large mixing bowl, combine oats, coconut and flour. Combine remaining ingredients in a heavy saucepan and bring to boil. Pour over dry ingredients; blend well.

● Drop dough by teaspoonfuls into greased miniature muffin cups (or foil baking cups on cookie sheet). Bake at 350 degrees for 12 to 15 minutes or until well-browned. Cool in pans.

CHEESECAKE COOKIES

Yields 16 to 20 bars

A boon to tight schedules, these must be frozen at least two days before they are served.

½ cup butter
⅓ cup firmly packed brown sugar
1 cup flour
½ cup finely chopped walnuts
¼ cup sugar
8 oz. cream cheese, softened
1 egg
2 tablespoons milk
1 tablespoon lemon juice
½ teaspoon vanilla

● Cream butter and brown sugar together; add flour and walnuts. Mix to make crumb mixture; reserve 1 cup for topping. Press remainder in bottom of 8x8-inch pan and bake at 350 degrees for 12 to 15 minutes.

● Blend sugar and cream cheese. Add egg, milk, lemon juice and vanilla. Spread over baked crust. Sprinkle with remaining crumb mixture.

● Bake for 25 minutes. Cool; cut into squares. Wrap and freeze for at least two days.

HAZELNUT SQUARES
Yields 18

3 tablespoons warm raspberry jam or apricot jam
¾ cup hazelnuts
3 tablespoons butter
½ cup firmly packed brown sugar
1 tablespoon heavy cream
¾ teaspoon lemon juice
1 teaspoon vanilla

- Prepare Shortbread Crust. Spread jam over the warm crust. Toast hazelnuts, rub with a towel to remove the skins; chop.

- Melt butter, add sugar, cream and lemon juice; bring to a boil and boil till sugar is dissolved. Remove from heat and add vanilla and hazelnuts.

- Spread over jam layer and bake 15 minutes more at 350 degrees. Cut while warm.

Shortbread Crust

½ cup butter, softened
¼ cup sugar
1¼ cups flour
1 egg yolk

- Combine ingredients in a bowl with a pastry blender. Pat into a 9x9-inch baking pan. Bake at 350 degrees for 15 minutes.

RED RASPBERRY SQUARES
Yields 12 dozen

2 cups flour
½ teaspoon salt
2 teaspoons baking powder
1 cup butter
2 eggs
1 tablespoon milk
1¾ cups mashed raspberries
½ cup butter
1½ cups sugar
2 cups unsweetened coconut
2 eggs, beaten
small bonbon papers

- Sift flour, salt and baking powder into a bowl. Cut in 1 cup butter with a pastry blender. Add eggs and milk to form a soft dough.

- Pat dough into a greased jellyroll pan. Cover with mashed raspberries. Melt ½ cup butter with sugar over medium heat. Add coconut and beaten eggs. Spread over raspberry layer.

- Bake at 350 degrees for 35 minutes. Cool and cut into 1-inch squares. Serve in tiny bonbon papers.

CHOCOLATE CARAMEL SQUARES Yields 30

½ cup butter
⅔ cup firmly packed brown
  sugar
2 tablespoons light corn
  syrup
1 can (14 oz.) sweetened
  condensed milk
1 teaspoon vanilla
8 oz. Hershey chocolate bar

- Prepare Shortbread Base.

- Stir butter, brown sugar, corn
  syrup, and milk in a saucepan
  over low heat until sugar
  dissolves and butter melts. Bring
  to boil, stirring constantly; boil
  7 minutes.

- Add vanilla and beat well for 3
  to 5 minutes and pour over
  Shortbread Base. Let cool. Melt
  and spread chocolate bar over
  filling. Cool and cut into cookie-
  size squares.

Shortbread Base

1¼ cups flour
½ teaspoon salt
½ cup (scant) powdered
  sugar
½ cup butter

- Sift flour and salt, add sugar and
  rub in butter. Knead well. (This
  may be done in the food
  processor.) Press into bottom of a
  greased 7x11-inch baking dish.
  Bake at 325 degrees for 20
  minutes. Let cool.

FAVORITE BROWNIES

Yields 1 dozen

The aroma from these brownies will drive chocoholics wild.

4 oz. unsweetened chocolate
½ cup butter
2 cups sugar
4 eggs
1 teaspoon vanilla
1 cup flour
½ cup chopped walnuts
powdered sugar (optional)

• Melt chocolate and butter; add sugar and eggs, one at a time. Beat well. Add vanilla.

• Blend in flour and nuts. Pour into a greased 9-inch square baking pan. Bake at 350 degrees for 20 to 25 minutes; center will not be completely set. Cool before cutting. Dust with powdered sugar, if desired.

SWEDISH BROWNIES

Yields 2 dozen

Even the texture says "chocolate."

1 cup sugar
½ cup butter, softened
1 teaspoon vanilla
4 eggs
1 cup flour
1 teaspoon baking powder
½ teaspoon salt
1 can (16 oz.) chocolate
   syrup
6 oz. chocolate chips
powdered sugar

• Cream butter, sugar, vanilla and eggs until mixed. Add dry ingredients. Add chocolate syrup.

• Grease and flour a 9x13-inch baking pan and pour in mixture; sprinkle with chocolate chips.

• Bake for 30 minutes at 350 degrees. Let cool 10 minutes and cut into squares. Dust with powdered sugar.

CREAMY CHOCOLATE LAYERS

Yields 24 bars

1 cup semi-sweet chocolate
chips
3 oz. cream cheese
⅓ cup evaporated milk
½ cup chopped walnuts
2 tablespoons sesame seeds
¼ teaspoon almond extract

● Prepare Crumb Crust. Reserve.

● In a saucepan combine chocolate
chips, cream cheese and
evaporated milk. Melt over low
heat, stirring constantly. Remove
from heat. Stir in remaining
ingredients and blend well. Set
aside.

● Press half of Crumb Crust mixture in greased 7x11-inch pan.
Spread with chocolate filling and
sprinkle rest of crumb mixture
over the filling. Bake at 375
degrees for 20 to 25 minutes.
Cool; cut into bars.

Crumb Crust

1½ cups flour
½ teaspoon baking powder
¼ teaspoon salt
¾ cup sugar
½ cup butter, softened
1 egg
¼ teaspoon almond extract

● Cut butter into dry ingredients;
stir in lightly beaten egg and
flavoring. Mix until crumbly.

275

HAZELNUT ANGEL PIE

Serves 8 to 10

A heavenly finale to dinner.

1 cup hazelnuts
3 egg whites
¼ teaspoon salt
1 teaspoon vanilla
½ cup firmly packed brown
  sugar
½ cup white sugar
1 cup vanilla wafer crumbs
1 cup heavy cream
2 tablespoons powdered
  sugar
1 tablespoon hazelnut
  liqueur
fresh fruit or berries

● Toast hazelnuts and remove skins by rubbing them with a towel; grind or chop fine in a blender or food processor.

● Beat egg whites with salt; add vanilla. Continue beating, adding the white and brown sugars slowly. Beat until sugars are dissolved. Fold in ground nuts and vanilla wafer crumbs.

● Bake in a well-buttered 9-inch pie pan at 325 degrees for 30 minutes. Cool. Whip the cream and flavor with powdered sugar and hazelnut liqueur. Fill baked pie shell with whipped cream and garnish with fresh fruit or berries.

OPEN FACE APPLE PIE

Serves 6 to 8

An old recipe which still tastes great today. Serve warm or cold.

1 9-inch deep-dish unbaked
  pie shell
4 to 5 apples, peeled, cored
  and sliced (Gravenstein or
  Transparent)
1 cup sugar
¼ cup flour
¼ teaspoon salt
1 cup heavy cream
ground cinnamon

● Place sliced apples in the unbaked pie shell. Mix together sugar, flour and salt and sprinkle over apples.

● In a saucepan, bring cream to the boiling point; pour over apples. Sprinkle generously with cinnamon. Bake at 375 degrees for 45 minutes, or until apples are soft and the pie is firm.

MARBLED CHOCOLATE RUM PIE   Serves 8 to 10

A visual treat—and delicious, too.

1 envelope unflavored
  gelatin
¼ cup sugar
⅛ teaspoon salt
3 egg yolks
1 cup milk
¼ cup rum
12 oz. semi-sweet chocolate
  chips
3 egg whites
½ cup sugar
⅛ teaspoon cream of tartar
1 cup heavy cream
¼ cup sugar
1 teaspoon vanilla

- Prepare Chocolate Pie Shell.

- In top of a double boiler, combine gelatin, ¼ cup sugar, salt, egg yolks, milk and rum. Cook until slightly thickened. Remove from heat and stir in chocolate chips until melted. Refrigerate until thick.

- Beat egg whites until foamy. Add ½ cup sugar and cream of tartar; beat until stiff. Fold into chocolate-rum mixture.

- Whip the cream with ¼ cup sugar and vanilla until stiff. Alternate layers of chocolate-rum filling and whipped cream in the pie shell. Run a knife through the mixtures for a marbled effect. Chill until served.

Chocolate Pie Shell

1½ cups flour
½ cup shortening
2 tablespoons cocoa
½ teaspoon salt
1 to 2 tablespoons cold
  water

- Cut shortening into flour, cocoa and salt. Toss with enough water to form a dough. Roll out for single crust or press into 9-inch pie pan. Prick with a fork and bake at 450 degrees for 10 to 12 minutes. Cool.

RASPBERRY ICE CREAM PIE
Serves 6 to 8

Waits in the freezer, ready for the last-minute addition of the Raspberry Topping.

1½ cups fresh raspberries
6 tablespoons sugar
3 tablespoons water
3 tablespoons light corn
  syrup
1½ tablespoons cornstarch
1½ tablespoons water
1 tablespoon lemon juice
1½ quarts vanilla ice cream,
  softened

- Prepare Pastry and reserve.

- In a small saucepan, combine berries, sugar, water and corn syrup. Mix cornstarch and water together and stir into berry mixture. Cook over medium heat, stirring and mashing the berries until mixture is thickened and boiling. Remove pan from heat and stir in lemon juice. Cool.

- Spoon ⅓ of the ice cream into the cooled pie shell. Top with half the sauce. Repeat layers, ending with ice cream on top. Freeze until hard.

- Remove pie from freezer and swirl Meringue over ice cream, covering completely to the edge. Bake at 450 degrees for 2 to 3 minutes to brown. Return the pie to the freezer immediately. To serve, cut pie and pour Fresh Raspberry Topping over individual servings.

Pastry

1 cup flour
2 tablespoons sugar
6 tablespoons butter
1 egg yolk, beaten

- Combine flour, sugar and butter with a pastry blender until fine and crumbly. Stir in egg yolk and work with your fingers until mixture is no longer crumbly and forms a ball.

- Press dough into a 9-inch pie pan. Bake at 325 degrees for 20 to 30 minutes or until light golden brown. Cool.

(continued)

RASPBERRY ICE CREAM PIE (continued)

Meringue

3 egg whites
1 cup marshmallow cream
1 teaspoon vanilla

● Beat egg whites until stiff. Beat in marshmallow cream, one spoonful at a time. Blend in vanilla.

Fresh Raspberry Topping

2 cups fresh raspberries, puréed
⅓ cup sugar
1 cup whole raspberries

● Combine puréed berries and sugar. Cover and chill until needed. Just before serving, stir in the whole berries.

MILE-HIGH STRAWBERRY PIE   Serves 8 to 10

The crumbs in this crust recipe are great to have on hand for other desserts, too. The filling is from an Oregon strawberry farmer.

2 egg whites
2 cups fresh strawberries, or 10 oz. frozen strawberries, room temperature
1 cup sugar
pinch salt
1 tablespoon lemon juice
1 cup heavy cream, whipped
whole fresh berries

● Prepare Crumb Crust. Freeze one crust for another pie (do *not* divide recipe in half; results are not as good).

● Beat egg whites until fluffy. Add berries, sugar, salt and lemon juice; beat 15 minutes at high speed. Carefully fold in whipped cream and spoon the filling into prepared crust. Freeze until ready to serve. Garnish with fresh whole berries.

Crumb Crust

1 cup flour
¼ cup firmly packed brown sugar
½ cup butter, melted
½ cup chopped walnuts

● Mix ingredients well and spread in a shallow pan. Bake at 350 degrees for 20 minutes, stirring occasionally. Cool crumbs and press into two 9-inch pie pans.

APPLE PIE SLICES

A different approach to apple pie; nice to have in the freezer.

2½ cups flour
3 tablespoons sugar
1 cup shortening
1 teaspoon salt
1 egg
⅔ cup milk

- To make the crust, cut shortening into flour, sugar and salt. Combine egg and milk; stir into flour mixture.

- Roll out half the dough between two sheets of waxed paper to fit a jellyroll pan. Reserve the other half to top the dessert.

- Spread Apple Filling over crust in pan. Roll out remaining dough and cover the filling. Seal edges well and bake at 375 degrees for 30 minutes. Cool and frost with Cream Cheese Frosting.

Apple Filling

6 large apples, peeled, cored and sliced
1 teaspoon ground cinnamon
2 tablespoons quick-cooking tapioca
1½ cups sugar

- Mix all ingredients together.

Cream Cheese Frosting

3 oz. cream cheese, softened
1 teaspoon vanilla
6 tablespoons butter, softened
1 tablespoon cream
1¾ cups powdered sugar, sifted

- Mix well to make a smooth frosting. Add a little more cream if needed.

APFEL KUCHEN

Serves 10 to 12

A unique cross between a pie and a cake.

½ cup butter, softened
⅔ cup sugar
1 egg
1 teaspoon vanilla
2 cups flour
2 teaspoons baking powder
1 to 2 tablespoons milk
8 apples, peeled and sliced
  paper-thin
5 tablespoons sugar
½ cup raisins
2 teaspoons ground
  cinnamon

● Cream butter well. Add ⅔ cup sugar, egg and vanilla. Gradually add flour and baking powder. Add milk sparingly to form a stiff dough. Knead with hands.

● Roll out half the dough and line bottom and halfway up sides of greased and floured 9- or 11-inch springform pan. Combine apples, 5 tablespoons sugar, raisins and cinnamon. Spoon into crust-lined pan.

● Roll out top layer of dough. Cover the filling, tucking dough in around filling to make a tight seal.

● Bake at 325 degrees for 45 to 50 minutes. Remove from oven; remove sides of pan and cool. Glaze with Creamy Lemon Glaze.

Creamy Lemon Glaze

1 cup powdered sugar
3 oz. cream cheese, softened
1 tablespoon lemon juice

● Combine ingredients until smooth.

BUTTER CRUST FRESH FRUIT TART

Serves 6 to 8

You can make this crust ahead and freeze; the fillings are quick and fresh.

1 cup flour
2 tablespoons powdered
  sugar
½ cup butter

- Make a shortbread crust by sifting flour and sugar together into mixing bowl. With pastry blender, cut in butter until mixture resembles cornmeal. Chill 30 minutes. Spread in a 9-inch tart pan or pie pan and press firmly onto bottom and up sides.

- Bake at 425 degrees for 10 to 12 minutes until golden brown. Cool on a rack.

- Fill with either of the following fillings and serve.

Strawberry Filling

3 cups whole strawberries
1 cup seedless raspberry
  jelly, melted
¼ to ½ cup finely chopped
  toasted pistachios
sweetened whipped cream

- Arrange berries over crust.

- Brush melted jelly over tops of berries. Scatter nuts over top. Serve with sweetened whipped cream.

Blueberry Filling

1 cup sour cream
2 cups fresh blueberries
1 cup red currant jelly,
  melted
2 tablespoons chopped
  toasted walnuts

- Spread sour cream over crust.

- Arrange berries over sour cream and spread melted currant jelly over berries. Top with chopped walnuts and serve.

OREGON BLACKBERRY TART   Yields 9-inch tart

Served with softened vanilla ice cream, this is a sinfully luscious dessert.

1 cup flour
¼ cup butter
¼ cup sugar
¼ teaspoon baking powder
½ teaspoon grated lemon
  peel
pinch salt
1 egg
2 cups fresh blackberries
  or other cane berries,
  fresh or frozen
2 tablespoons sugar
sweetened whipped cream or
  softened vanilla ice cream

- Blend first 7 ingredients with a mixer or food processor. Press dough onto the bottom and 1½ inches up sides of a 9-inch spring-form pan.

- Chill crust for 10 to 15 minutes. Bake at 400 degrees for 10 minutes or until light golden brown. Cool and release sides of pan.

- Arrange berries in baked shell and sprinkle the 2 tablespoons sugar over the top. Pour Black-berry Glaze over all and chill. Serve with sweetened whipped cream or softened vanilla ice cream.

Blackberry Glaze

2 cups fresh blackberries,
  or other cane berries,
  fresh or frozen
¾ cup sugar or to taste
3 tablespoons cornstarch
¼ teaspoon salt

- In a large saucepan, crush the berries. Add sugar, cornstarch and salt and mix well. Heat until thickened and clear.

HAZELNUT FRUIT TART

Serves 8

A showpiece dessert that can be made ahead in stages.

3 tablespoons finely ground hazelnuts or almonds
3 tablespoons finely ground vanilla wafer crumbs
¼ cup firmly packed brown sugar
2 tablespoons butter
2 eggs
1 cup sugar
1 cup flour
1 teaspoon brandy or rum
½ cup milk
1 tablespoon butter
2 tablespoons brandy or rum
3 to 4 cups fresh fruits of choice (select fruits for flavor and color)
¾ cup apple jelly
sweetened whipped cream

- Butter and flour an 11-inch flan pan. Mix together nuts, wafer crumbs, brown sugar and 2 tablespoons butter. Press lightly onto flat surface of pan only.

- Beat eggs until foamy. Gradually add sugar and beat until thick. Stir in flour and 1 teaspoon brandy or rum.

- Bring milk and 1 tablespoon butter to simmer; blend into batter. Pour batter into prepared pan. Bake on lowest rack at 350 degrees for 25 minutes.

- Cool 5 minutes and invert onto wire rack. Some of the nut mixture may stick to the pan; scrape it off and fill in uneven places. Drizzle with remaining brandy or rum. Let cool. (Can be made ahead to this point and stored at room temperature, tightly wrapped in plastic wrap.)

- Arrange fruits on top of nut layer in concentric rings, one kind of fruit per ring for a colorful array. Heat apple jelly until bubbly and spread over fruit, filling in small spaces between fruit. Chill 30 minutes to 4 hours. Top with whipped cream and serve.

STRAWBERRY TEA TARTS

Yields 10 to 12

Pastry (enough for two 9-inch crusts)
3 oz. cream cheese, softened
½ cup powdered sugar
1 cup heavy cream
1 quart fresh strawberries, sliced

- Roll out pastry and cut to fit 2-inch tart pans. To prevent crust from slipping, fill each tart shell with dry beans. Bake at 350 degrees for 8 to 10 minutes or until lightly browned. Remove beans. Cool.

- Beat together cream cheese, powdered sugar and cream to the consistency of whipped cream. Fill each cooled tart shell half full.

- Arrange sliced berries over cheese filling. Spoon Strawberry Glaze over berries. Chill to set and serve.

Strawberry Glaze

1 cup crushed strawberries
1 tablespoon cornstarch
½ cup sugar
1 tablespoon lemon juice

- Combine ingredients in a saucepan and cook over medium heat until thickened and clear.

PEACH TARTS

Yields 6 4-inch tarts

6 fresh or canned peach
halves
6 (4-inch) individual tart
shells, unbaked
⅓ cup firmly packed brown
sugar
1 tablespoon cornstarch
¼ teaspoon salt
¼ teaspoon ground
cinnamon
1 egg
1 cup sour cream
sweetened whipped cream

- Place a peach half in each tart
shell. Combine next 6 ingredients
with a mixer and pour over tarts,
distributing evenly. Bake at 375
degrees for 15 minutes.

- Divide Nut Topping over tarts
and bake 10 minutes more. Serve
topped with sweetened whipped
cream.

Nut Topping

½ cup chopped pecans
¼ cup firmly packed brown
sugar
2 tablespoons butter,
softened
1 tablespoon light corn
syrup

- Combine ingredients, blending
well.

CRUSTY PEACH COBBLER

Serves 8

The aroma will bring them running.

3 cups sliced fresh peaches
2 teaspoons grated lemon
peel
3 tablespoons lemon juice
2 tablespoons quick-cooking
tapioca
1½ cups sifted flour
2 teaspoons baking powder
¼ teaspoon salt
⅓ cup butter
1 egg, beaten
⅓ to ½ cup milk
¾ cup sugar
½ cup water
2 tablespoons butter

- Arrange peach slices in a shallow
7x11-inch baking dish and mix
with lemon juice, grated peel and
tapioca. Sift dry ingredients
together. Cut in ⅓ cup butter
until mixture forms coarse
crumbs.

- Combine egg and milk and stir
into flour mixture, mixing just
until moistened; spoon over
peaches.

- Bring ¾ cup sugar, water and 2
tablespoons butter to a boil and
pour over the batter. Bake at 375
degrees for 45 minutes or until
crusty and brown.

BLUEBERRY FLUMMERY

Serves 4 to 6

4 cups fresh blueberries
1 cup sugar
2 tablespoons lemon juice
1 teaspoon grated lemon
rind
1 teaspoon freshly grated
nutmeg
8 slices bread, crusts
removed
½ cup butter, melted
sweetened whipped cream
nutmeg and powdered sugar

- Cook berries, sugar, lemon juice, lemon rind and nutmeg in a medium saucepan over low heat. Stir until sugar is dissolved. Simmer 10 minutes.

- Cut bread into strips and brush with melted butter. Line a buttered 1½-quart baking dish with some of the strips. Pour in ⅓ of the berry mixture. Continue layering the strips of bread and the berry mixture.

- Bake at 350 degrees for 20 minutes. Chill. Serve with sweetened whipped cream and a dash of nutmeg and powdered sugar on top.

BLUEBERRY APPLE CRISP

Serves 6 to 8

3 cups blueberries
3 cups very tart apples,
peeled, cored and sliced
1 cup firmly packed brown
sugar
1 cup flour
¾ cup sugar
1 teaspoon baking powder
¾ teaspoon salt
1 egg
⅓ cup butter, melted
½ teaspoon ground
cinnamon
rich cream

- Butter a 7x11-inch baking dish and mix together blueberries and sliced apples in the dish. Cover with brown sugar.

- In another bowl, mix together flour, sugar, baking powder, salt and beaten egg until mixture becomes crumbly. Sprinkle over the fruit.

- Top with melted butter and cinnamon. Bake at 350 degrees for 30 minutes until top is golden brown. Serve warm with cream.

Note: Other fresh berries may be substituted for the blueberries.

BLACKBERRY CRISP

Serves 8

Top with cream for an old-fashioned dessert.

4 cups fresh blackberries
1 tablespoon lemon juice
2 tablespoons sugar
⅓ cup flour
1 cup oatmeal
½ cup firmly packed brown sugar
1 teaspoon ground cinnamon
⅓ cup butter, melted

● Place blackberries in a greased 9x13-inch baking dish. Sprinkle with lemon juice and sugar. Combine remaining ingredients and spread over berries. Bake at 375 degrees for 30 to 35 minutes.

RHUBARB PASTRY

Serves 8 to 9

Greet spring with rhubarb and cream.

2 cups sliced fresh rhubarb
2 tablespoons butter
4 tablespoons flour
1½ cups sugar
2 eggs
1 cup heavy cream

● Prepare Cookie Crust.

● Spread rhubarb over the crust. Combine remaining ingredients and pour over rhubarb. Bake at 350 degrees for 1 hour or until set.

Cookie Crust

½ cup butter, softened
1 tablespoon sugar
1 egg yolk
1 cup flour
¼ teaspoon salt
½ teaspoon vanilla

● Mix ingredients together and pat into a 9-inch cake pan.

BANANA PUFFS

Serves 6

⅔ cup shortening
2 cups flour
½ teaspoon salt
2 to 3 tablespoons cold
  water
6 bananas
6 tablespoons white or
  brown sugar

- Make a pie crust by cutting shortening into flour and salt. Gradually mix in water, using just enough to moisten. Set aside.

- Peel bananas and cut in half lengthwise. Cover one cut side with 1 tablespoon sugar and top with the other half of banana.

- Roll out dough to ⅛-inch thickness; cut into 6 pieces. Wrap bananas in dough and seal well. Place on a baking sheet seam side down. Prick each pastry with a fork and bake at 400 degrees for about 15 minutes. Serve with Vanilla Sauce.

Vanilla Sauce

2 cups water
1 cup sugar
¼ teaspoon salt
1 tablespoon butter
1 tablespoon cornstarch
1 teaspoon vanilla

- Combine ingredients in small saucepan and boil until thick as cream.

289

CARROT PUDDING

Serves 12

A rich holiday pudding for a traditional touch.

1 cup finely grated carrots
1 cup flour
1 cup sugar
1 cup chopped walnuts
1 cup seedless raisins
1 cup finely ground beef
  suet
1 tablespoon milk
1 teaspoon ground cinnamon
1 teaspoon baking soda
1 egg
pinch salt

- Mix all ingredients together well and pour into a greased and floured pudding mold. Cover mold tightly and steam for 3 hours in a water bath on top of the stove. Make sure no water can get into the pudding during the steaming.

- Let pudding cool slightly and unmold. Serve warm with Hard Sauce. The pudding will keep well in refrigerator for up to three weeks.

Hard Sauce

1 cup powdered sugar,
  sifted
⅓ cup butter, softened
¼ teaspoon salt
1 teaspoon vanilla or rum

- Cream together the sugar and butter until smooth. Add salt and vanilla or rum.

Note: Can be made in a one-pound coffee can and sealed with foil.

CRANBERRY PUDDING WITH BUTTER SAUCE

Serves 8 to 10

The famous Oregon coast cranberries in a marvelous dessert.

2 cups fresh cranberries, cut
  into halves
1½ cups flour
½ cup light molasses
½ cup boiling water
2 teaspoons baking soda
¼ teaspoon salt

- Gently mix flour through the berries. Combine molasses, water and soda. Add salt and molasses mixture to berries.

- Pour mixture into a greased pudding mold and steam for 2½ hours. Serve warm or cooled, with Butter Sauce.

Butter Sauce

1 cup sugar
½ cup butter
½ cup heavy cream
1 teaspoon vanilla

- Slowly heat sugar, butter and cream in a double boiler until sugar is dissolved. Add vanilla. Beat well before serving.

HAZELNUT CHEESECAKE

Serves 8 to 10

A rich cheesecake which forms a crust during baking.

16 oz. cream cheese,
  softened
4 eggs, beaten
1 cup sugar
½ cup heavy cream
1 tablespoon hazelnut
  liqueur
½ cup ground toasted
  hazelnuts
sweetened whipped cream
1 tablespoon hazelnut
  liqueur

- In a large mixer or food processor, beat cream cheese, eggs, sugar and cream until very smooth. Stir in 1 tablespoon liqueur and ground hazelnuts.

- Pour into an 8-inch springform pan and bake at 350 degrees until lightly browned and puffy, about 1 hour. The center should be slightly firm when touched. Cool and serve with sweetened whipped cream flavored with hazelnut liqueur.

EMBARCADERO RESORT HOTEL AND MARINA, Newport

Oregon's only marina-resort, Embarcadero, is perched on a sun-filled hillside to take full advantage of a spectacular view of the Pacific Ocean and Yaquina Bay.

The strikingly contemporary architecture of the Resort attractively complements the bustling marina filled with sailboats and fishing boats that provide constant activity in the Bay. Spacious rooms and suites, most with kitchens and fireplaces, are tastefully decorated and are oriented toward a view of the Bay.

Embarcadero's recreation facilities include an indoor heated pool, a giant whirlpool bath, and a sauna. Guests can enjoy the outdoor crab cooker and barbecue pit for parties or special events, or they may make use of the Resort's private docks for fishing and crabbing.

The Resort provides mooring facilities for boats of most sizes, plus rental of crab rings, clamming gear, fishing equipment, and small boats for the Bay. Also available are charter fishing and sailing excursions.

Other activities in the area include beachcombing, golf, agate hunting, and browsing through Newport's Old Town area of galleries and specialty shops. Interesting nearby attractions are the

Mark O. Hatfield Marine Science Center, Spouting Horns Geyser, the Undersea Gardens, the Oregon Sea Lion Caves, and the Wax Museum.

Gourmet dining in Embarcadero's Moorage Restaurant centers on an exciting view of the marina and Yaquina Bay. An elaborate Champagne Brunch on Sundays features an array of exquisite foods.

For additional information:
Embarcadero
1000 SE Bay Blvd.
Newport, OR 97365
1-800-452-8567 (OR)
(503) 265-8521 (Elsewhere)

CHEESECAKE
Serves 8 to 10

From the Dining Room of Embarcadero

1 cup graham cracker crumbs
2 tablespoons powdered sugar
½ cup butter, melted
16 oz. cream cheese, softened
1 cup sugar
4 large eggs
2 teaspoons vanilla
pinch salt

- Mix together graham cracker crumbs, powdered sugar and butter; press into bottom and sides of 8-inch springform pan. In a food processor or mixer, combine cream cheese, sugar, eggs, vanilla and salt; mix until smooth.

- Pour into prepared crust and bake at 325 degrees for 1¼ to 1½ hours, or until cake tester comes out clean. Cool 15 minutes. Spoon Sour Cream Topping over cake and bake 5 minutes more. Chill overnight before removing outer ring of springform pan.

Sour Cream Topping

1 cup sour cream
1 tablespoon sugar
½ teaspoon vanilla

- Blend ingredients together.

ORANGE CRANBERRY TORTE   Serves 12 to 16

A wonderful new finale to Thanksgiving dinner.

2¼ cups sifted flour
1 cup sugar
¼ teaspoon salt
1 teaspoon baking powder
1 teaspoon baking soda
1 cup chopped walnuts
1 cup diced pitted dates
1 cup fresh cranberries,
　whole
grated rind of 2 oranges
2 eggs, beaten
1 cup buttermilk
¾ cup vegetable oil
1 cup orange juice
1 cup sugar
sweetened whipped cream

● Sift together into a bowl the flour, 1 cup sugar, salt, baking powder and baking soda. Stir in nuts, dates, cranberries and orange rind.

● Combine eggs, buttermilk and oil. Add to flour-fruit mixture. Stir until blended. Pour into well-greased 10-inch tube pan and bake at 350 degrees for 1 hour.

● Let torte cool in pan for 20 minutes or until just warm. Remove from pan and place on rack positioned over a bowl. Combine orange juice and sugar; pour over cake. Pour any drippings over the cake again.

● Cover with foil. Refrigerate until ready to serve (cake keeps very well refrigerated). To serve, slice and top with sweetened whipped cream.

RASPBERRY WALNUT TORTE   Serves 12 to 15

Very rich—serve in small wedges.

1½ cups raspberry
  preserves
4 eggs
¾ cup firmly packed brown
  sugar
2 cups chopped walnuts
½ cup flaked coconut
2 tablespoons flour
¼ teaspoon baking powder

● Prepare Walnut Pastry.

● Pat pastry onto bottom and up sides of a 9-inch springform pan. Spread preserves over bottom. Beat eggs and sugar at high speed until light and mixture forms a ribbon when dripped from beaters.

● Combine walnuts, coconut, flour and baking powder in another bowl. Fold gently into egg mixture. Pour into pastry-lined pan and bake at 350 degrees for 45 to 60 minutes. Cool, remove from pan and pour Lemon Icing over cake.

Walnut Pastry

½ cup unsalted butter,
  softened
⅓ cup sugar
1 egg
1¼ cups cake flour
1 cup chopped walnuts

● Cream butter and sugar until fluffy; beat in the egg. Combine flour and walnuts and stir into the creamed mixture. Blend well but do not overmix. Refrigerate 2 hours.

Lemon Icing

1½ cups powdered sugar
4 teaspoons lemon juice
4 to 5 teaspoons water

● Combine ingredients until smooth.

SANS RIVAL

Serves 8 to 10

An interesting mocha meringue which can be frozen.

8 egg whites
½ teaspoon cream of tartar
1¼ cups sugar
1 teaspoon vanilla
1 tablespoon cocoa powder
  or instant coffee granules
¼ teaspoon salt
½ cup finely chopped nuts

- Beat egg whites until frothy. Add cream of tartar and beat until stiff. Gradually add sugar and remaining ingredients except nuts.

- Line two 12x15-inch baking sheets with foil. Grease well with a light oil. Spread the mixture in four 8-inch circles on the cookie sheets; sprinkle with nuts.

- Bake at 225 degrees for 1 hour and 40 minutes. Turn off oven and let meringues cool completely in oven.

- Spread Coffee Custard Filling between all layers of the meringue and over the top. Sprinkle chopped nuts over top. Can be wrapped in foil and frozen at this point. Thaw before serving.

Coffee Custard Filling

⅔ cup sugar
½ cup water
6 egg yolks
1 cup butter, softened
2 tablespoons instant coffee
  granules
1 teaspoon vanilla
2 tablespoons finely
  chopped nuts

- Make a syrup of sugar and water. Boil until sugar is dissolved. Set aside. Beat egg yolks until thick and lemon-colored. Add syrup, beating constantly. Chill.

- Cream butter until fluffy and add chilled egg yolk mixture. Dissolve coffee granules in vanilla. Add to butter mixture and beat well.

296

CHOCOLATE PEPPERMINT TORTE   Serves 10

The perfect combination of flavors for a party dessert.

½ cup butter, softened
¾ cup sugar
3 oz. unsweetened chocolate,
  melted
1 teaspoon vanilla
¾ teaspoon peppermint
  extract
3 eggs
½ cup heavy cream,
  whipped
grated unsweetened
  chocolate or chocolate
  curls

- Prepare Chocolate Crust and reserve.

- Beat butter until creamy. Gradually add sugar, beating until light and fluffy. Beat in melted chocolate and flavorings. Add eggs, one at a time, beating for 3 minutes after each egg. Fold in whipped cream and spoon into cooled crust.

- Sprinkle with chocolate garnish. Cover and chill at least 4 hours or overnight. Remove sides of pan before serving.

Chocolate Crust

1 cup chocolate wafer
  crumbs
2 tablespoons butter, melted

- Mix crumbs and butter. Lightly press into a 9-inch springform pan. Bake at 350 degrees for 7 minutes. Cool.

JACKSONVILLE INN, Jacksonville

Jacksonville Inn, located in the first gold rush town in Oregon, enjoys a unique distinction: Not only is the Inn a national historic landmark, but so is the town.

The Inn was built in 1863 and is one of the town's earliest permanent structures. Many materials used in the building were gleaned locally and help perpetuate the nostalgic romance of an earlier era. The walls of the dining area and lounge are built of sandstone quarried nearby; specks of gold dust are scattered throughout the mortar. The massive supporting beams in the Inn were transported from an early-day sawmill on the upper Umpqua River.

History buffs flock to this Old West town and are rewarded with sights that hearken to an earlier way of life. A full day is necessary to take advantage of a good browse through the Jacksonville Museum and the town's many unusual shops.

In summer, the world-famous Peter Britt Music Festival brings visitors keen on enjoying summer sunshine and outstanding musical talent. Other attractions in the nearby area include the Ashland Shakespearean Festival; hunting, fishing, and rafting in the Rogue Valley; a scenic tour to Crater Lake and the Oregon Caves; and winter skiing at Mt. Ashland.

The Inn's Dinner House is justifiably famous for its seven-course gourmet meals. Specialties include entrées such as veal scallopini, prime rib, fresh seafood, and an irresistible dessert tray. Overnight guests receive a complimentary breakfast with freshly baked pastries from the Inn's kitchen.

For additional information:
Jacksonville Inn
175 E. California St.
Jacksonville, OR 97530
(503) 899-1900

CHOCOLATISSIMO
Serves 10 to 12

From the Jacksonville Inn Dinner House

1 lb. unsalted butter,
  softened
2 cups sugar
16 oz. semi-sweet chocolate,
  melted
16 eggs, separated
½ cup orange marmalade
1 oz. semi-sweet chocolate,
  grated

- Grease bottoms only of two 9-inch springform pans. Beat butter and sugar together; add melted chocolate. Add egg yolks, one at a time, and beat on low speed for about 20 minutes.

- In a separate bowl, with clean beaters, beat egg whites until stiff. Fold whites into batter. Pour ¾ of batter into prepared pans. Bake at 325 degrees for 50 minutes; cool.

- Remove from pans. Spread marmalade between the layers and top with remaining uncooked batter. Sprinkle grated chocolate over top and refrigerate overnight.

CHOCOLATE MOUSSE TORTE

Serves 12

You can make this ahead, freeze it, then thaw overnight in refrigerator.

1 lb. semi-sweet chocolate
2 eggs
4 egg yolks
1 pint heavy cream
6 tablespoons powdered
   sugar
4 egg whites, room
   temperature
1 pint heavy cream
sugar

● Prepare Chocolate Crust and reserve.

● Melt semi-sweet chocolate in top of double boiler over simmering water. Let chocolate cool to lukewarm (95 degrees) then add whole eggs and mix well. Add yolks and mix until thoroughly blended. Whip 1 pint cream with powdered sugar until soft peaks form.

● Beat egg whites until stiff but not dry. Stir a little of the cream and whites into the chocolate mixture to lighten. Fold in remaining whipped cream and beaten whites until completely incorporated. Turn into prepared crust and chill at least 6 hours or overnight (or can freeze torte at this point).

● Whip remaining pint of cream until quite stiff. Sweeten to taste. Loosen sides of pan. Remove torte and spread whipped cream over the top. Garnish with Chocolate Leaves.

Chocolate Crust

3 cups chocolate wafer
   crumbs
½ cup unsalted butter,
   melted

● Combine crumbs and butter. Press onto bottom and completely up the sides of 10-inch springform pan. Refrigerate 30 minutes.

(continued)

300

CHOCOLATE MOUSSE TORTE (continued)

Chocolate Leaves

8 oz. semi-sweet chocolate
1 tablespoon vegetable
 shortening
camellia or other waxy
 leaves

● Melt chocolate and shortening in top of double boiler. Using spoon, generously coat underside of leaves. Chill or freeze until firm. Separate leaves from chocolate by gently pulling away stem end.

ELEGANT CHOCOLATE TORTE   Serves 8 to 12

Reminiscent of a light, chocolate cheesecake.

8 oz. cream cheese, softened
½ cup sugar
1 teaspoon vanilla or
 almond extract
2 eggs, separated
6 oz. semi-sweet chocolate
 chips, melted
1 cup heavy cream, whipped
½ cup pecans or almonds,
 chopped
sweetened whipped cream

● Prepare Chocolate Crust and reserve.

● Combine cream cheese, ¼ cup sugar and vanilla, mixing until well blended. Add egg yolks and melted chocolate. Beat egg whites until soft peaks form, then gradually beat in ¼ cup sugar. Fold into chocolate mixture.

● Fold in whipped cream and nuts. Pour over crumb crust and freeze. Let torte soften before serving. Pipe with additional sweetened whipped cream, if desired.

Chocolate Crust

1½ cups chocolate wafer
 crumbs
⅓ cup margarine, melted

● Combine crumbs and margarine. Press onto the bottom of a 9- or 10-inch springform pan. Bake at 325 degrees for 10 minutes. Cool.

301

HOLIDAY FARM, Blue River

Located on the banks of the picturesque McKenzie River, Holiday Farm is a resort as rich in history as it is in modern amenities.

The resort's main restaurant, The Farmhouse, started out as a stagecoach stop in the 1870's—hungry, weary passengers would alight for a bite to eat before continuing on their journey on the McKenzie stagecoach. The automobile has replaced the stagecoach, but The Farmhouse still stands (refurbished), and guests at Holiday Farm can still enjoy excellent meals there.

The McKenzie River location allows this resort to offer its guests great fishing for the famed rainbow trout, a fighting fish that will challenge any angler. Guests either fish from the banks of the river or participate in guided trips arranged through Holiday Farm.

Holiday Farm's cottages overlook the river, and enthusiastic fishermen can even fish right off the porch of their cottages. Cottages vary in size and room combinations, but all are modern and have patios on the riverbank. Two larger houses are also available for rent, one dubbed the "Hoover House," since Herbert Hoover and his family used to stay in it.

Just one-half mile from Holiday Farm is a championship 18-hole golf course, Tokatee. Located on the 90-acre Farm are two small lakes just right for swimming and fishing for the kids. Within a few miles of the resort are two large lakes for water sports, as well as many streams, waterfalls, and hiking trails.

Diners at Holiday Farm can enjoy meals in The Farmhouse, with its old-fashioned charm and cozy fireplaces. They may also eat in the Lodge, with its large patio overlooking the McKenzie—a delightful spot for breakfast and lunch. Both restaurants are known for outstanding hearty meals.

For additional information:
Holiday Farm
Blue River, OR 97413
(503) 822-3715

CHOCOLATE ICE CREAM CAKE   Serves 10 to 12

From the Dining Room of Holiday Farm

1 package (3-roll) chocolate
  creme-filled cookies
⅓ cup melted butter
1½ quarts vanilla ice cream,
  softened
1 pint hot fudge sauce,
  heated
1 quart frozen non-dairy
  topping, defrosted
salted peanuts

● Spray 8x12-inch baking pan with vegetable spray. Place cookies in a plastic bag and crush with a rolling pin. Spread them on bottom of baking pan and pour butter over top. Press cookies to form a crust.

● Spread the ice cream over crust; pour hot fudge sauce over ice cream. Freeze until chocolate sauce has cooled, about 30 minutes.

● Spread non-dairy topping over chocolate and top with peanuts. Return to freezer until ready to cut and serve.

THE VALLEY RIVER INN, Eugene

Along the banks of the gently flowing Willamette River, the Valley River Inn offers "the best of Oregon, all in one place."

Natural beauty and warmth are apparent to guests as soon as they step inside the lobby and view the towering wooden beams which were crafted from trees that grew in a nearby forest. Rich warm wood, earthtone decor, and quiet carefree elegance reflect the Oregon spirit at its best. Accommodations include spacious rooms or suites, beautifully decorated with wood furniture and plush chairs and beds.

Guests can relax and enjoy a stroll along the banks of the Willamette, or the more energetic may opt for a run along the 7½-mile jogging trail or a brisk swim in the Inn's pool. The Inn will also make arrangements for a guided trip down the Willamette or McKenzie Rivers or a tour of the University of Oregon campus.

Other guests may enjoy the proximity of shopping at nearby Delta Village or the totally covered 101-store Valley River Center. Both are within walking distance of the Inn.

Dining in the Inn's Sweetwaters Restaurant is an experience in fine cuisine, with a view of the river to set the mood. The menu features a variety of rotisserie entrées, as well as classic Northwest favorites.

For additional information:
The Valley River Inn
P.O. Box 10088
Eugene, OR 97440
687-0123 (Eugene/Springfield)
1-800-452-8960 (OR)
1-800-547-8810 (Elsewhere)

CHOCOLATE INTOLERANCE   Serves 10 to 12

From the Dining Room of The Valley River Inn.

¾ gallon rich chocolate ice
cream, softened but not
melted
1½ cups chopped brownies
Bittersweet fudge sauce,
heated

● Prepare Graham Cracker Crust
and Meringue before assembling
dessert.

● Line bottom of a 10-inch springform pan or two 8-inch springform pans with Graham Cracker
Crust mixture. Spoon in half the
ice cream. (Do not let ice cream
melt or it will crystallize when
refrozen.)

● Arrange chopped brownies over
ice cream; spoon in remaining
ice cream. Cover dessert with a
thick layer of Meringue. Immediately place under broiler of oven
and brown the meringue. Watch
carefully to prevent burning.
Freeze until firm.

● To serve, pour hot fudge sauce
on individual plates. Place a slice
of ice cream cake on each plate.
(The chef personally likes a little
amaretto drizzled over the fudge
sauce.)

(continued)

Graham Cracker Crust

2 cups graham cracker
crumbs
½ cup melted butter
dash ground cinnamon

● Combine ingredients, mixing
well.

Meringue

1 cup egg whites, room
temperature
1 cup sugar
½ teaspoon vanilla
1 drop lemon juice
1 cup sugar

● Using clean bowl and beaters,
whip egg whites, 1 cup sugar,
vanilla and lemon juice until stiff
peaks form when beater is lifted.
Fold in additional 1 cup sugar.
Use immediately.

FRESH PEACH ICE CREAM   Yields 2 quarts

A summer favorite in the Northwest. Let everyone have a turn at
cranking the freezer.

1 cup sugar
2 tablespoons flour
1 cup milk
2 cups mashed peach pulp
2 tablespoons lemon juice
1 cup heavy cream, whipped

● Combine sugar and flour; add
milk and cook until thick,
stirring occasionally. Cool. Add
peach pulp and lemon juice. Fold
in whipped cream. Freeze, using
ice cream freezer directions.

Note: Double this recipe for standard 1-gallon freezer.

FROZEN DELIGHT

Serves 16

A dessert to keep on hand for busy entertaining days.

2 oz. unsweetened chocolate
½ cup butter
2 cups powdered sugar
3 egg yolks
pinch salt
1 teaspoon vanilla
3 egg whites
¾ cup sliced almonds,
   toasted
2 quarts ice cream, softened

● Prepare Crumb Crust and reserve.

● Melt chocolate and butter in top of a double boiler. Add powdered sugar and mix well. Add egg yolks, one at a time, beating well after each. Beat in the salt and vanilla. Remove from heat.

● Beat egg whites until stiff peaks form and fold into chocolate mixture.

● Sprinkle sliced almonds over crust. Spread chocolate mixture over nuts and then softened ice cream over all. Freeze well before serving.

Crumb Crust

3 cups crushed vanilla
   wafers
½ cup butter, melted
¼ cup sugar

● Combine ingredients and press into a 9x13-inch baking pan. Bake at 350 degrees for 15 minutes. Cool.

307

FRESH LEMON FREEZE

Serves 6

Especially refreshing after a heavy meal.

6 large lemons
2 cups half & half
1 cup sugar
1½ tablespoons grated
lemon peel

● Cut off the top third of lemons. Scoop out and reserve all pulp and juice. Strain the pulp, pressing to obtain ½ cup juice.

● Stir together half & half and sugar until sugar is dissolved. Mix in lemon peel and the ½ cup reserved lemon juice. Freeze mixture in loaf pan 2 to 3 hours.

● Remove pan from freezer, break frozen mixture into bowl and beat until fluffy. Mound sherbet into hollowed lemon shells. Place filled shells in freezer in upright position and freeze until firm. Serve with lemon caps on top.

POPCORN CAKE

Serves 12 to 15

A fun treat to serve by the fire after a hard day of skiing.

20 to 30 cups popped corn
(white hull-less)
½ cup butter
21 oz. miniature marsh-
mallows
4 teaspoons vanilla
2 cups chocolate M&M's
1 cup salted peanuts

● Remove any unpopped kernels of corn from measured popped corn. Make a syrup from butter, marshmallows and vanilla and pour over popped corn. Stir in candy and nuts.

● With greased hands, firmly press mixture into a well-greased large tube pan. Allow to stand 10 minutes; then loosen and turn out onto cake plate. If not using immediately, cool thoroughly and wrap in plastic to store or freeze.

INDEX

311

317

Assistance League of Corvallis
534 NW Fourth Street
Corvallis, OR 97330
(503) 753-0408

Oregon Sampler

Name _____

Address _____

City _____ State _____ Zip _____

Please send _____ copies of *Oregon Sampler* at $14.95 per copy plus $2.05 per copy to cover shipping and handling. Make check payable to Assistance League of Corvallis.

☐ Visa
☐ MasterCard

Signature _____ Exp. Date _____

Assistance League of Corvallis
534 NW Fourth Street
Corvallis, OR 97330
(503) 753-0408

Oregon Sampler

Name _____

Address _____

City _____ State _____ Zip _____

Please send _____ copies of *Oregon Sampler* at $14.95 per copy plus $2.05 per copy to cover shipping and handling. Make check payable to Assistance League of Corvallis.

☐ Visa
☐ MasterCard

Signature _____ Exp. Date _____

Assistance League of Corvallis
534 NW Fourth Street
Corvallis, OR 97330
(503) 753-0408

Oregon Sampler

Name _____

Address _____

City _____ State _____ Zip _____

Please send _____ copies of *Oregon Sampler* at $14.95 per copy plus $2.05 per copy to cover shipping and handling. Make check payable to Assistance League of Corvallis.

☐ Visa
☐ MasterCard

Signature _____ Exp. Date _____

We are always looking for additional stores in which to market *Oregon Sampler.* Will you please help us by listing the names of stores you think would be appropriate for our unique cookbook? Consider bookstores, gift shops, cooking and kitchen stores, department stores, boutiques. Thank you!

- Store Name _____
  Store Address _____
  City _____ State _____ Zip _____
- Store Name _____
  Store Address _____
  City _____ State _____ Zip _____
- Store Name _____
  Store Address _____
  City _____ State _____ Zip _____

We are always looking for additional stores in which to market *Oregon Sampler.* Will you please help us by listing the names of stores you think would be appropriate for our unique cookbook? Consider bookstores, gift shops, cooking and kitchen stores, department stores, boutiques. Thank you!

- Store Name _____
  Store Address _____
  City _____ State _____ Zip _____
- Store Name _____
  Store Address _____
  City _____ State _____ Zip _____
- Store Name _____
  Store Address _____
  City _____ State _____ Zip _____

We are always looking for additional stores in which to market *Oregon Sampler.* Will you please help us by listing the names of stores you think would be appropriate for our unique cookbook? Consider bookstores, gift shops, cooking and kitchen stores, department stores, boutiques. Thank you!

- Store Name _____
  Store Address _____
  City _____ State _____ Zip _____
- Store Name _____
  Store Address _____
  City _____ State _____ Zip _____
- Store Name _____
  Store Address _____
  City _____ State _____ Zip _____